Reconsidering the Moveab Psychoanalysis

Reconsidering the Moveable Frame in Psychoanalysis explores the idea of 'the frame' at a time when this concept is undergoing both systematic revival and widespread transformation. It has always been tempting to see the frame as a relatively static, finite and definable feature of psychoanalytic work. At its most basic, the frame establishes agreed upon conditions of undertaking psychoanalytic work. But as this book shows, the frame has taken on a protean quality. It is sometimes a source of stability and sometimes a site of ethical regulation or discipline. It can be a place of imaginative mobility, and in certain analytic hands, a device for psychic work on projections and disavowals.

Beginning with a seminal essay on the frame by José Bleger, this book includes commentary on that work and proceeds to explorations of the frame across different psychoanalytic theories. The frame is perhaps one of the spots in psychoanalysis where psyche and world come into contact, a place where the psychoanalytic project is both protected and challenged. Inevitably, extra-transferential forces intrude onto the psychoanalytic frame, rendering it flexible and fluid. Psychoanalysts and analysands, supervisors and candidates are relying increasingly on virtual communication, a development that has effected significant revisions of the classical psychoanalytic frame. This book presents a dialogue among distinct and different voices. It re-examines the state and status of the frame, searching for its limits and sifting through its unexpected contents whilst expanding upon the meaning, purview and state of the frame.

Reconsidering the Moveable Frame in Psychoanalysis will appeal to all psychoanalysts and psychoanalytic psychotherapists interested in how best to understand the frame and to use it most effectively in their clinical practice.

Isaac Tylim, Psy.D., ABPP, FIPA, is a Training and Supervising analyst at the Institute for Psychoanalytic Training and Research (IPTAR). He is a clinical professor, training analyst and consultant for the New York University Postdoctoral Program in Psychotherapy and Psychoanalysis.

Adrienne Harris, Ph.D., is a Faculty member and Supervisor for the New York University Postdoctoral Program in Psychotherapy and Psychoanalysis and at the Psychoanalytic Institute of Northern California. She is an Associate Editor of *Psychoanalytic Dialogues* and of *Studies in Gender and Sexuality* and she is on the Editorial Boards of *Psychoanalytic Inquiry* and *American Imago*. She publishes in the areas of gender and development.

Relational Perspectives Book Series
Lewis Aron and Adrienne Harris
Series Co-Editors
Steven Kuchuck and Eyal Rozmarin
Associate Editors

The Relational Perspectives Book Series (RPBS) publishes books that grow out of or contribute to the relational tradition in contemporary psychoanalysis. The term *relational psychoanalysis* was first used by Greenberg and Mitchell[1] to bridge the traditions of interpersonal relations, as developed within interpersonal psychoanalysis and object relations, as developed within contemporary British theory. But, under the seminal work of the late Stephen A. Mitchell, the term *relational psychoanalysis* grew and began to accrue to itself many other influences and developments. Various tributaries—interpersonal psychoanalysis, object relations theory, self psychology, empirical infancy research and elements of contemporary Freudian and Kleinian thought—flow into this tradition, which understands relational configurations between self and others, both real and fantasied, as the primary subject of psychoanalytic investigation.

We refer to the relational tradition, rather than to a relational school, to highlight that we are identifying a trend, a tendency within contemporary psychoanalysis, not a more formally organized or coherent school or system of beliefs. Our use of the term *relational* signifies a dimension of theory and practice that has become salient across the wide spectrum of contemporary psychoanalysis. Now under the editorial supervision of Lewis Aron and Adrienne Harris, with the assistance of Associate Editors Steven Kuchuck and Eyal Rozmarin, the Relational Perspectives Book Series originated in 1990 under the editorial eye of the late Stephen A. Mitchell. Mitchell was the most prolific and influential of the originators of the relational tradition. Committed to dialogue among psychoanalysts, he abhorred the authoritarianism that dictated adherence to a rigid set of beliefs or technical restrictions. He championed open discussion, comparative and integrative approaches, and promoted new voices across the generations.

Included in the Relational Perspectives Book Series are authors and works that come from within the relational tradition, extend and develop that tradition, as well as works that critique relational approaches or compare and contrast it with alternative points of view. The series includes our most distinguished senior psychoanalysts, along with younger contributors who bring fresh vision. A full list of titles in this series is available at https://www.routledge.com/series/LEARPBS.

1   Greenberg, J. & Mitchell, S. (1983). *Object relations in psychoanalytic theory.* Cambridge, MA: Harvard University Press.

Reconsidering the Moveable Frame in Psychoanalysis

Its Function and Structure in Contemporary Psychoanalytic Theory

Edited by
Isaac Tylim and Adrienne Harris

Routledge
Taylor & Francis Group

LONDON AND NEW YORK

First published 2018
by Routledge
2 Park Square, Milton Park, Abingdon, Oxon OX14 4RN

and by Routledge
711 Third Avenue, New York, NY 10017

Routledge is an imprint of the Taylor & Francis Group, an informa business

British Library Cataloguing in Publication Data
A catalogue record for this book is available from the British Library

Library of Congress Cataloging in Publication Data
Names: Tylim, Isaac, editor. | Harris, Adrienne, editor. Title: Reconsidering the moveable frame in psychoanalysis : its function and structure in contemporary psychoanalytic theory / edited by Isaac Tylim and Adrienne Harris. Description: New York : Routledge, 2018. | Includes bibliographical references and index. Identifiers: LCCN 2017013317| ISBN 9781138943438 (hardback : alk. paper) | ISBN 9781138943469 (pbk. : alk. paper) | ISBN 9781315672434 (master electronic) | ISBN 9781317373148 (epub) | ISBN 9781317373155 (web pdf) | ISBN 9781317373131 (mobi/kindle) Subjects: LCSH: Psychoanalysis. | Cyberspace--Psychological aspects. Classification: LCC BF173 .R3667 2018 | DDC 150.19/5--dc23LC record available at https://lccn.loc.gov/2017013317

ISBN: 978-1-138-94343-8 (hbk)
ISBN: 978-1-138-94346-9 (pbk)
ISBN: 978-1-315-67243-4 (ebk)

Typeset in Times New Roman
by FiSH Books Ltd, Enfield
Printed and bound by CPI Group (UK) Ltd, Croydon, CR0 4YY

This book is dedicated to the seminal work of
Latin American psychoanalysts who have contributed
so much to the theoretical and clinical development
of our discipline.

Contents

Contributors

Anthony Bass, Ph.D., is a supervising analyst and on the teaching faculty of several institutes and training programs, including the NYU Postdoctoral Program for Relational Psychoanalysis and Psychotherapy, the Columbia University Center for Psychoanalytic Training and Research, the National Institute for the Psychotherapies National Training Program, the Institute for Relational Psychoanalysis of Philadelphia, and the Stephen Mitchell Relational Study Center, where he is also President. He is Editor in Chief of *Psychoanalytic Dialogues: The International Journal of Relational Perspectives*.

José Bleger was born in Argentina in 1922. An active member of the Asociación Psicoanalítica Argentina, he was also a highly regarded Professor of Psychology and a well-known intellectual. Author of many books and papers, his reputation grew steadily after his early death in 1972. He is now considered a major figure of Argentinian psychoanalysis. His 1967 book *Symbiosis and Ambiguity: A psychoanalytic study* was published in English in 2013.

Leopoldo Bleger has lived and worked in Paris since leaving Argentina in 1976. A member of the French Psychoanalytical Association (APF), he is currently its President, and was General Secretary of the European Psychoanalytical Federation (EPF) from 2012 to 2016. He works in private practice. With John Churcher he edited the first English edition of José Bleger's *Symbiosis and Ambiguity: A psychoanalytic study*.

Luca Caldironi, M.D., is a Psychiatrist-Psychoanalyst and member of the Italian Society of Psychoanalysis (SPI) and American Psychoanalytic Association (APsaA). He is also an IPA member.

Velleda C. Ceccoli is a psychoanalyst/psychologist in private practice in New York City. She is on the faculties of the NYU Postdoctoral Program in Psychotherapy and Psychoanalysis, The Stephen Mitchell Center, and the American Academy of Psychoanalysis, where she is also a training and supervising analyst. Dr. Ceccoli is on the editorial boards of *Psychoanalytic Dialogues* and *Studies in Gender and Sexuality*. She writes the ongoing psychoanalytic blog called *Out of My Mind* and is the dance critic for the online magazine *Psychology Tomorrow*.

John Churcher is a psychoanalyst based in Manchester, England, a member of the British Psychoanalytical Society, and former Book Review Editor of the *International Journal of Psychoanalysis*. He retired from clinical practice in 2013. From 1979 to 2002 he was a lecturer in Psychology at the University of Manchester. With Leopoldo Bleger he edited the first English edition of José Bleger's *Symbiosis and Ambiguity: A psychoanalytic study*.

Cláudio Laks Eizirik is a Training and Supervising analyst, Porto Alegre Psychoanalytical Society, and Professor of Psychiatry, Federal University of Rio Grande do Sul. He is a former President of IPA and FEPAL and winner of the Sigourney Award in 2011. He has authored books, chapters, and papers on analytic theory, practice and training, the process of ageing, and the relation of psychoanalysis and culture.

Haydée Faimberg, M.D., is a Training and Supervising analyst (SPP, APA) and recipient of the Haskell Norman Award (2005) and the Mary Sigourney Award (Europe, 2013). She is in a private practice in Paris. One of her main interests is the way that one culture understands how another culture addresses essential psychoanalytic problems. Using a concept she initially coined for listening in the session, she created what came to be called the '*Haydée Faimberg "listening to listening" method*' aimed at recognizing in clinical discussion groups the basic assumptions of presenter and participants. She coined the concept of the 'as yet situation.' In her study on the Freudian concept of psychic temporality (*Nachträglichkeit*) she proposed a broader concept and established a link with the Winnicottian concept of 'Fear of Breakdown' (Faimberg [1998] 1912); proposed a new reading of Winnicott's *Fragment of Analysis* including *Nachträglichkeit* and the

paternal function (Faimberg, 2013, 2014). She has studies on transmission of the narcissistic mode of solving conflicts between three (or
more) generations; on psychic consequences of Nazism and on Italo
Calvino and Lewis Carroll. She is the contributing author to 15 books
(18 chapters). She authored *The Telescoping of Generations: Listening
to the Narcissistic Links between Generations* (Routledge, 2005).

Yolanda Gampel, Ph.D., is a Professor at Tel-Aviv University; a training
analyst, and past president (1989–1991) of the Israel Psychoanalytic
Society; vice-president, European Federation of Psychoanalysis
(2001–2005); a representative for Europe on the board of the IPA
(2007–2011); and won the Hayman International Prize for Published
Work to Traumatized Children and Adults, 2001 and the Mary S.
Sigourney Award, 2006. She has published papers in various psychoanalytic journals and several books on the effects of social and political
violence in children, the analyst, and the psychoanalytic process. She
has written the book *Ces Parents qui vivent a travers moi. Les enfants
de guerres* (Fayard, Paris, 2005), which has been translated into four
languages.

Peter Goldberg, Ph.D., is a Personal and Supervising analyst at the
Psychoanalytic Institute of Northern California, is Chair of Faculty at
the San Francisco Center for Psychoanalysis, and on the faculty of the
Wright Institute in Berkeley. He has written on a range of clinical and
theoretical topics, including evolution of clinical theory in psychoanalysis; sensory experience in analysis; the concept of the analytic
frame; the theory and treatment of dissociative states; non-representational states; and the impact of social trauma on individual psychology.

Adrienne Harris, Ph.D., is a Faculty member and Supervisor for the New
York University Postdoctoral Program in Psychotherapy and
Psychoanalysis and at the Psychoanalytic Institute of Northern
California. She is Associate Editor of *Psychoanalytic Dialogues* and of
Studies in Gender and Sexuality and she is on the Editorial Boards of
Psychoanalytic Inquiry and *American Imago*. She publishes in the
areas of gender and development. She coedited *The Legacy of Sandor
Ferenczi* with Lewis Aron. They also edited *Relational Tradition* Vol.
2 and the upcoming *Relational Tradition* Vol. 3, New Voices (with
Melanie Suchet). Adrienne and Muriel Dimen edited *Storms in Her*

Head, a volume of essays on the Centenniel of Studies on Hysteria. Her book *Gender as Soft Assembly* was published in 2005 by TAP. She is in private practice in New York City.

Stephen Hartman, Ph.D., is a co-editor of *Studies in Gender and Sexuality* and Associate Editor *of Psychoanalytic Dialogues* as well as an editor of the Psychoanalytic Dialogues Blog. A faculty member of the Psychoanalytic Institute of Northern California and in the relational track of the NYU Postdoctoral Program in Psychoanalysis and Psychotherapy, he teaches and practices in San Francisco and New York City. His writing addresses the interface of digital culture and psychoanalysis as well as the recursive engagement of psychic life with social and political experience. Currently, he is at work editing a posthumous volume of essays by Muriel Dimen, *Relating, Symbolization and Intersubjectivity: Psychosocial landscapes from the work of Muriel Dimen*.

Monica Horovitz, born in Buenos Aires, M.D., Ph.D. of Letters, DESS in clinical psychopathology, is a full member of the Paris Psychoanalytic Society (SPP) and of the Italian Psychoanalytical Society (SPI) and Full Member of the IPA, and works in private practice with adolescents and adults in Paris. She has run a seminar for the last 13 years on Bion. Monica conceived of the idea of an international seminar on Bion. It was then initiated with Lawrence Brown and became 'Bion in Marrakech' in 2013, of which she is now the Chair. She has published a number of articles in national and international journals and has also contributed to several books published in French, English, and Spanish on the works of Wilfred R. Bion.

Janine Puget, M.D., is Full Member and Training analyst of the Asociación Psicoanalítica de Buenos Aires (APdeBA), the IPA, and the Federación Psicoanalítica de América Latina (FEPAL), and Founding Member and Honorary Member of the Asociación Argentina de Psicología y Psicoterapia de Grupo (Argentine Group Psychology and Psychotherapy Association). She directed the Master's Program in Family and Couple Psychoanalysis at IUSAM (ApdeBa's University Institute) between 2006 and 2013, and is Emeritus Professor in this program. Dr Puget received the Sigourney Award in 2011 and was named Leading Authority in Psychoanalysis by FEPAL in 2014.

Harvey L. Rich, M.D., is a retired Training and Supervising analyst, Washington Psychoanalytic Institute and Society. He is a member of the American Psychoanalytic Association; Corresponding Member of the Parisian Psychoanalytic Society; Founder of the American Psychoanalytic Foundation; author of the book *In The Moment: Celebrating the Everyday*. He resides and still practices in Washington, DC and Paris, France.

Kim Rosenfield is a poet and psychotherapist. She is the author of several books of poetry and is a recipient of a *Fund For Poetry* grant. Rosenfield is a founding member of the international artist/writers collective, *Collective Task*. Her clinical writing can be found in *Psychoanalytic Dialogues* and *Studies in Gender and Sexuality.* Rosenfield lives and practices in New York City.

Jon Tabakin is a Training and Supervising analyst at the Psychoanalytic Center of California, in Los Angeles. His interest in psychoanalysis stems from his education at UCLA in Music Composition, English, and Comparative Literature, and the history of ideas. This background found fruit in the psychoanalysis of Freud, Klein, Bion, and the philosophy of Paul Ricoeur. It is the capacity to engage one's emotional experience (music), to see the way that experience achieves representation (literature), and to understand how these representations create an organization (philosophy) that determines how one's mind works.

Isaac Tylim, PsyD, ABPP, FIPA, is a Training and Supervising analyst at the Institute for Psychoanalytic Training and Research (IPTAR). He is a clinical professor, training analyst and consultant for the New York University Postdoctoral Program in Psychotherapy and Psychoanalysis. He is a member of the Argentina Psychoanalytic Association. Since 1997 he has served as Secretary of the International Psychoanalytic Association Committee on the United Nations. He is the former Vice-chair of the UN Committee on Mental Health, and a member of the IPA Cultural Committee. Dr Tylim is the co-founder of the Trauma and Disaster Specialization Program at NYU Postdoctoral Program, and former Chair of the Art, Psychoanalysis, and Society Project at IPTAR. For many years he was a member of the editorial board of the *Journal of the American Psychoanalytic Association*, and a regular contributor to *The*

Buenos Aires Herald cultural section. Multilingual, he lectures domestically and internationally, having published numerous papers and book chapters on clinical issues, and on a dialogue between psychoanalysis and other disciplines. Publications include *Terrorism and the Psychoanalytic Space* (co-editor); *The Power of Forgiveness in Transforming Resentment into Forgiveness*; *Memorials to Dead Objects in the Culture of Desire*; *Multilingualism and Countertransference*; *Technology and the Future of Psychoanalysis*; *Machismo and the Limits of Male Heterosexuality*, and numerous papers on psychosomatics. For the last two years he has been involved in the dramatization of the Freud and Ferenczi 30 years' correspondence that has been presented in the USA, Buenos Aires, and at the Freud Museum in London.

Lynne Zeavin is a clinical psychologist and psychoanalyst practicing in New York City. On the faculties of the New York Psychoanalytic Institute and IPTAR, she teaches and supervises widely on Kleinian theory and technique. The author of several papers on 'The countertransference, beauty, womens' sexuality', and 'Psychoanalysis and the environment', Dr Zeavin serves on the editorial boards of *JAPA* and *The Psychoanalytic Quarterly*.

Acknowledgements

We thank our authors for their thoughtful and attentive work on this project. Adrienne thanks her colleagues in the Relational Perspectives Book Series, Lewis Aron, Steven Kuchuck and Eyal Rozmaran. Isaac thanks all international colleagues with whom over decades he forged a global frame of stimulating and thought-provoking exchange. We thank the hardworking and extremely supportive publishers at Taylor and Francis, Kate Hawes and with this book Charles Bath. We thank our research assistant and copy editor Samuel Bodian for all his efforts and care with the manuscript.

Chapter 1 first appeared as 'Psychoanalysis of the psychoanalytic setting' in *Symbiosis and Ambiguity: A Psychoanalytic Study* by José Bleger and edited by John Churcher and Leopoldo Bleger (Routledge, 2012). Reprinted by permission of Taylor & Francis, LLC.

Chapter 2 was first published in Spanish as 'José Bleger y su encuadre dialéctico: vigencia actual', *Calibán*, Vol. 10, No. 1, 2012, pp. 194–203, ISSN: 2304-5531. It was translated with permission of *Calibán* from the original with some modifications.

Chapter 6 was first published as 'When the frame doesn't fit the picture', *Psychoanalytic Dialogues*, Vol. 17, No. 1, 2007, pp. 1–27. Reprinted by permission of Taylor & Francis, LLC.

Introduction
The frame

Adrienne Harris and Isaac Tylim

Definition of the frame

The Random House *Dictionary of the English Language* offers 35 definitions of *frame*. Among them:

an open border or case for enclosing a picture, mirror, etc.

a rigid structure formed of relatively slender pieces, joined as to surround sizeable empty spaces and non structural panels, and usually used as a major support in building or engineering work.

to contrive or prearrange fraudulently or falsely.

In this volume of essays, we take up a wide comparative examination of the idea of 'the frame' at a time when this concept is undergoing both systematic revival and widespread transformation. It has always been tempting to see the frame as a relatively static, finite and definable feature of psychoanalytic work. But as this collection of papers shows, the frame has taken on a protean quality. It is sometimes a source of stability and at others a site of ethical regulation or discipline. It can be a place of imaginative mobility, and in certain analytic hands, a device for psychic work on projections and disavowals.

Our aim, in this collection, is to examine the history and longstanding theorizing of the concept of the frame, to be alert to changes and evolutions in the concept and to observe the powerful impact of social, cultural and technological forces upon this and other aspects of analytic work. The frame is perhaps one of the spots in psychoanalysis where psyche and world come into contact, a place where the psychoanalytic project is both protected and challenged.

Inevitably, extra-transferential forces intrude onto the psychoanalytic frame, rendering it flexible and fluid. Psychoanalysts and analysands, supervisors and candidates are relying increasingly on virtual communication, a development that has effected significant revisions of the classical psychoanalytic frame. In this collection of essays, we present a dialogue among distinct and different voices. We re-examine the state and status of the frame, we search for its limits, we sift through its unexpected contents and we expand upon the meaning, purview and state of the frame.

New translations of traditional (Bion, Racker, Lewin, Barangers, Bleger) and contemporary (Ferro, Civitarese, Lombardi) field theories have provided North American and English speaking analysts with a broad and significantly new approach to thinking about the frame. However, the origin and defining influences on these works from Europe and Latin America have a long and distinguished history of their own, going back to the 1920s, to field theory (Lewin) and, in the middle of the 20th century, to the seminal ideas of Bion. These theories have been deeply inscribed in Latin American analytic understandings and writings on technique and, in one way or another, influence all the essays contained in this volume to varying degrees.

Whether employing terms like 'frame' or 'setting', or as Puget suggests, 'device', these papers and their authors ask new questions of what has often seemed a relatively unremarkable element in the psychoanalytic experience. In addition to longstanding and renewed ways of thinking about the material context and frame of analytic work, a number of these authors introduce and discuss quite radically transformed ideas of the social and ideological elements that have become imbued and implicated in the frame. Additionally, these papers build an understanding of the ways in which careful attention to the unique uses of the frame is of paramount importance in the analyses of particularly difficult, primitively organized and traumatized patients.

So we approach this topic and offer these papers, each of which, in its own special way, contributes fascinating, useful and even provocative tools. To use José Bleger's wonderful phrase, we want to see that the frame and setting, initially imagined as so fixed and prosaic, will, on occasion, 'cry'. The frame comes to carry disavowed aspects of both analyst and patient, elements outside of or liminal to the internal process, elements that are largely institutional and social – in Puget and Gampel's terms, psychic materials that are *radioactive*.

We would like to refer to the work of Mark Kingwell, the self-styled philosopher of furniture, who argues for the organic and living material character of many elements we like to think of as rigid and fixed. Thinking along these lines, if we change the frame or the materiality of the analytic room we are likely to find that the therapeutic process is changed as well.

Consider the case of a colleague of ours who had been having weekly sessions with a five-year-old boy who had been part of the foster care system. One Monday, she brings him to her office after a weekend during which the walls were painted and the furniture changed. The boy walks with her into the room, looks around and faints. Shifts in the frame can, under certain contexts, have catastrophic consequences. But the attention to materiality, the quality of light and sound in the consulting room, the placement of chairs or decorations all may contribute to the positive mutative effects of shifts in frame.

Whether we wish to radicalize the frame or reinvigorate it, as analysts we need to use all our creativity and strength to understand what is happening and take responsibility for the work on, around and against frame. Once we have liberated the concept of the frame from its prosaic, static structure and function, as all of these papers attest to, something crucial and potentially mutative is necessarily destabilized and unleashed. Often it is in the work of restabilizing the frame that allows powerful change to occur in the treatment.

We wish to assert one of Bleger's crucial points here. While the tumbling, shaking and weeping of the setting will inevitably befall any and all analyses, it is uniquely the responsibility of the analyst to reconfigure and reset the frame. While it is not always within the analyst's power to keep the frame distinct from the process it surrounds, it is nonetheless his or her responsibility to adjust and, if necessary, reset the system. This brings ethics into the picture and reveals an aspect of the analytic situation that is inherently asymmetrical regardless of how 'mutual' the analysis is. This insight emerges from both field and relational theories, though these two lines of thought articulate it in their own distinct ways.

The present volume appears at a moment in history when it has become impossible to ignore the potency and complexity of technological and social forces. As stated earlier, the increasing reliance upon virtual communication in psychoanalysis and psychoanalytic training has forever changed the analytic frame, though exactly how the frame has been altered by new communication technologies has yet to be articulated. Rather than seeking to provide definitive answers to the question of how new informational technologies, chief among them virtual communication, have altered the frame, this volume seeks to keep these questions and their potential answers in play.

Here are some thoughts that we, as editors, have had on the subject. These novel modes of communication, or 'devices', to take up Puget's term, are newly emergent and it seems likely that whatever their limitations, advantages and character, they will function differently for individuals who have grown up with these forms of linking than they will for individuals who developed prior to such devices.

In discussing 'virtual' and therefore implicitly immaterial forms of communication, it might be useful to keep open the question of what counts as materiality in the session and what 'materiality', in this context, really means. We must recognize that whatever constitutes the device or frame can and will be both bastion and portal. We want to focus as well on what is unique, what may be lost, altered or enhanced by the use of screens. While we may question the depth or quality of regression in analyses conducted through screens rather than in person, this way of working clearly still allows for the expression and interpretation of unconscious phenomena, regardless of its potential limitations. Even in this virtual format, the physical and aesthetic aspects of the setting and frame must be considered. For instance we may ask: does the size of screen make a difference?

Psychoanalytic theory has been extensively deployed to consider our responses to images, moving and still. The camera, as seen in film theory, has been regarded as a mechanism of control, a form of patriarchy, a directive force largely outside of the filmgoer's conscious awareness that nonetheless shapes the viewer's experience of the film – in essence a framing device. What unexpected experiences of visual pleasure fear or disgust will emerge when the filmic and psychoanalytic frames are merged? The room in vivo and the screen are different of course, but the screen is not devoid of unconscious stimulation, or of *joussance* for that matter.

What is added or altered by conducting treatment within the same medium through which we watch pornography, pay our bills, engage with social media and, more often than not, aimlessly surf through the endless informational sea of the web? The authors featured in this volume land on different spots in this discussion, however there is a shared determination to deploy ethics and responsibility for the construction and maintenance of the frame through our usual means of analytic work: inquiry, interpretation and curiosity in a context of ambiguity. It should be noted that regardless of how their material forms are established, the setting and the frame are crucial to any given analysis, and as always are susceptible to being hijacked by unconscious forces and enactments, to eclipsing and inadequately containing dangerous parts of the patient, the analyst and the scene.

The internet in particular, and the cultural force it exerts, is prone to intrude into the analyst's privacy. This form of communication harbours the potential for exposing once-private aspects of analytic work into public spaces, as well as providing or even provoking patients' ability to puncture the frame with varieties of instruments and technological gadgets.

Another consequence of the shift from anonymity to transparency is a change in how, if it all, we are able to write about patients. Writing is part of the frame, and writing about patients, now that what we write is more readily accessible via the internet, may have a great impact upon the frame and the analytic relationship. Writing, presenting and publication have always been entangled in transference and countertransference forces, but now that these once relatively private professional and scholarly discussions can be readily viewed by patients, the dynamic has radically changed. While the authors in this volume and the larger analytic community have not reached a broad agreement regarding how to best manage these new realities, we cannot ignore these matters and must search for answers and solutions while acknowledging that any such answers are potential and provisional responses to complex and continually unfolding issues. It is in this spirit that we feel compelled to respond to these new dilemmas by crafting this book – a collection of distinct voices that speak of the frame – its past, present and future.

Is cyberspace fated to become the new space or dwelling of individuals' inner thoughts, fantasies and dreams? Is the analytic transitional space being challenged by electronic/virtual archives that by-pass the presence/absence paradigm of the transference and countertransference domain? Our authors are divided on these matters. Many analysts have attempted to adapt to modern cultural and technological changes by suggesting the adoption of a more flexible frame. Does a 'flexible' frame delineate a no-man's land that both analyst and analysand have the right to alter? Indeed, one important idea here is that the cast of characters in psychoanalysis is no longer limited to analyst and analysand. Insurance companies, cyberculture and technological devices all alter, to follow Bleger's organization, who is visible, audible, interactive within the frame and the process.

The effects of these changes have reached beyond the enactments of analysands or shifts in the organization of the frame. The current techno-culture modifies the public presence of psychoanalytic work, exposing its most private elements – among them the intimate written and spoken thoughts of analysts regarding their work with their patients. In the current technical state of affairs, in which papers once published in professional journals viewed by a select few are now a Google Scholar search away, there is no sure guarantee of privacy.

Perhaps ironically, this dilemma predates the internet. The discipline of psychoanalysis owes a big part of its development to snail mail, as Freud's avid, perhaps obsessive penchant for written correspondence helped the field to spread beyond his small inner circle. Has email contributed to a significant shift in the content and form of what analysts and analysand alike record of their psychic life? Some may argue that the spontaneous mnemic association may be on its way out. Are psychoanalysts beginning to witness the death of psychic representations? Derrida (1994) poses the question of whether computers or machines in general may destroy spon-taneity, going so far as to question whether they may render obsolete the existence and necessity of the psyche.

Consider the following clinical incident. Last spring a colleague alerted one of us (Tylim) that someone was commenting on his therapeu-tic skills over the internet. It was one of his analysands who did not feel the need to conceal his identity on the web, choosing instead to write under his given name. The analysand had created a blog and was posting comments after each of his four weekly sessions. Was the analysand stretching the frame like some patients do by coming early to the analyst's waiting room with a cup of soup in hand? Fortunately, holding back his own countertransference, Tylim caught an enactment at its early stages. The analysand appeared to have concealed and then broadcast a wish to increase the frequency of his sessions. Thus, in this instance, cyberspace became an expansion of the analytic setting.

It is relevant to note that the intrusion of extra-transferential forces onto the psychoanalytic frame existed long before the present revolutions in technology and communication. For instance, George Makari (2009) has explored the role that trauma and racialization among those emigrating from Europe to America may have had upon the formation of ego psychology and its retreat from the social dimension. Maria Torok et al. in 1998 considered that Klein minimized the trauma in her own family and in the surrounding European scenes of the 1930s and the role it played in the creation of her theories regarding persecutory anxiety, fantasy and aggression in the infant. Every theory is no doubt marked by the unspeakable, the unbearable dread which bastions protect us from. The relational world struggles with the dangers and possibilities of its ties to Ferenczi, and the intersubjective can surely be the bastion for fears of the unconscious.

Organization of the book

In the first section of the book, we revisit and refresh our understanding of one of Bleger's classic papers on the frame, the content and message of which is still potent. Anchored in field theory, indebted to the Barangers' views of the materiality and bipersonal unconscious stream of experience, Bleger is sensitive to the vulnerability, uncertainty and simultaneous responsibility of the analyst in relation to the frame. Leopoldo Bleger updates and orients us to his father's seminal work.

We are also very fortunate to have, newly translated into English, Haydee Faimberg's paper on Bleger. Deeply rooted in the educational and clinical forums that Bleger, the Barangers and in particular Etienne Pichon-Rivière created to shape psychoanalysis in Latin America, Faimberg is a unique voice in the discourse around these figures. Her own highly original work on narcissistic alienations and identifications, the telescoping of generations and the presence of a dialectic in the actions and transmissions of clinical process informs her reading of Bleger. She shows us how his commitment and imaginative use of the dialectic and the spiral in clinical transactions and interactions was integrated with another crucial concept – that of the double frame.

The paper continues to explore the idea of the double frame, consisting firstly of the frame established by the analyst and, secondly, of the aspects of the frame that are ritualized and often secretly added to the clinical process by the analysand, effecting and potentially corrupting the clinical process. In the case of this often-surprising occurrence in analytic work, the analyst must take the responsibility of analysing what has happened and restore the original frame.

The second section of the book explores four views of the frame emerging from distinct psychoanalytic orientations. Kleinian (Zeavin), Winnicottian (Tabakin), Bionian (Goldberg) and relational (Bass) considerations of the frame are offered to ground the reader in key arguments and issues that analysts working in different traditions can offer. Each of these analysts, thinking from within but also beyond their respective disciplines and sets of theoretical convictions, approaches the concept of the frame with a high degree of care and personal ethics.

The third section of the book takes up the question of the frame in the context of conditions and phenomena that challenge conventional presentations and uses of the frame. This section explores psychoanalytic work taking place in conditions of socio-political violence, or social disruption, as well as in the context of complex new technologies of surveillance and communication that challenge every psychoanalyst to consider the frame not as a fetish but as a condition.

Papers by Gampel, Puget and Hartman challenge us to a mix of flexibility, courage and responsibility. Gampel poses a crucial question: just what kind of device is psychoanalysis, where a device, in the Lacanian sense, is some apparatus made for a special purpose?

In Puget and Gampel's work we confront the intrusion, surround and effect of social forces upon the analytic frame. Puget sets out some interesting groundwork. She sees within analytic work both the process of identity formation and the process of linking. The inalienable presence of alterity is alongside, not orthogonal with, but intertwined with linking. Thinking of how to frame these processes, Puget asks us to attend to the social frame, including frameworks that are corrupt, dangerous, emergent and traumatic. Gampel also draws on these ideas, arguing that there is a double layer of traumatic impact on analysis in contexts where there is both historical and ongoing trauma (for instance in Israel and Palestine).

The frame carries this doubled burden, an idea Andrea Ritter has explored in her thinking about intergenerational transmission of trauma, following the work of Ferenczi in Hungary and Martin Mahler and Michael Sebek who looked at psychoanalysis in totalitarian regimes. The layers of political and social life surrounding treatment alter, infect and corrupt the frame in ways that too often escape our attention and consciousness.

Hartman examines the frame from the perspective that is both outside the frame looking in and inside conducting treatments. He is sensitive to the frame simultaneously as a bastion (real and illusory) that protects the analytic work and as a registration of terror and violence and state tyrannies that infuse treatment. He argues for a need to see the frame as discursive, as mobile and as porous. His paper seems particularly cogent in our current post-Trump election world.

The final section of the book takes up particular experiences of the variation and multiplicity of the definitions and uses of the psychoanalytic frame. The materiality of the spaces for analytic work, the demands for inventiveness, the complex, still contentious element of technology and the frame are taken up by an international group of authors. Unsurprisingly, the frame is shaped by theoretical approach, cultural context and socio-political realities. Horovitz focuses on the particular transformation of the frame that has come with the increasing use of the internet, Skype, the phone and other communication technologies in treatment. She makes a number of insightful, relevant and challenging observations about the use of new media in conducting psychoanalytic treatment. Any thorough discussion of the frame and contemporary technosocial life must visit these critiques and be consistently willing to consider what conditions corrupt or intrude upon psychoanalysis and what conditions constitute a variation that nonetheless can be compatible with psychoanalytic aims. One of the most interesting questions explored in this section is the discussion of how changes to the classical frame are both a matter of technique and a matter of ethics.

While other authors consider the possible dangers of changes imposed upon the frame by new developments in technology and communication, Rich presents a radically alternative view in which the permanent but also shifting arrangements of a bi-continental life shape his practice for the better.

Is treatment with a radically modified frame better than no treatment? Are untraditionally framed analyses psychoanalytic? Aron and Starr draw linkages between psychotherapy and psychoanalysis. Winnicott centres on transference and countertransference. Everyone makes some room for unconscious phantasy. Are these forces precluded by these technologies even as these technologies impact these elements profoundly?

Horovitz is concerned for what is denuded and minimized in work over the internet. For example, she wonders how the analyst conducting analysis through virtual communication can track the bodily state of the patient and make use of his or her own body to track.

Caldironi asserts that it is fundamental that psychoanalysts, in facing current technological advances, maintain their critical function. In the analytical room, it's not only the complex emotional history of the patient that is actualized – analysis also brings to life a vivid representation of the complexity of the human mind itself. This includes the complexities related to the risks introduced by cybernetics. Among the risks he considers are the loss of 'physical' individual encounters, the confusion between internal and external worlds, and the addicted aspects of 'constant connection'. In line with Bion, Caldironi believes that the best psychoanalysts can do is try to 'contain' these risks while exploring and embracing them as they would any other experience.

Ceccoli asks the pertinent question of whether technology facilitates or interferes with the relationship between the intrapsychic and the intersubjective. She embraces the idea that psychoanalysis, in order to maintain its relevance across generations, has to evolve and be open to the complexities of human experience and interaction. Technology has made it possible for people to choose the mode and tool of communication, and this is relevant to how the frame must adapt.

Eizirik highlights changes in analytic practices, reminding us that 'the method and structure developed by Freud as ideal for analysis would invariably undergo changes, adaptations and modernization'. His paper encourages analytic institutes to consider new scenarios in analytic training and education. Eizirik examines aspects of personal analysis, supervision and psychoanalytic institutional practices, raising interesting questions regarding psychoanalysis' contemporary challenges to the classical frame.

Finally, Rosenfield brings us back to the magic and unconscious power of the frame for analyst and analysand. The focus on materiality in some of these papers, and surely in hers, speaks from a phenomenological perspective. To borrow from Merleau Ponty, the frame is an organ of perception.

References

Derrida, J. (1994) *Specters of Marx, the State of the Debt, the Work of Mourning, and the New International*, translated by Peggy Kamuf. London: Routledge.

Makari, G. (2009) *Revolution in Mind: Freud, the Freudians and the Making of Psychoanalysis*. New York: Harper Collins.

Torok, M., Sylvan, B. and Covello, A. (1998) Melanie Mell by herself. In J. Phillips and L. Stonebridge (eds), *Reading Melanie Klein*. London: Routledge, pp. 51–80.

Introduction to Chapter I
José Bleger and the psychoanalytic setting[1]

John Churcher and Leopoldo Bleger

The setting is the subject of one of José Bleger's best-known papers. Published in 1967 in the *International Journal of Psychoanalysis* under the title 'Psycho-analysis of the psycho-analytic frame', it was originally published earlier that year in Spanish as an integral chapter in his book *Simbiosis y ambigüedad* (Bleger, 1967a, 1967b), where it was titled 'Psicoanálisis del encuadre psicoanalítico'. The book is now available in English as *Symbiosis and Ambiguity* (Bleger, 2013 [1967]) and the version of the paper that is reproduced here is taken from this edition, where we have translated the title as 'Psychoanalysis of the psychoanalytic setting'.[2] It is a paper towards which many lines in his own work lead and from which many others stem. Its contents are rather condensed, however, and at first sight they can seem unnecessarily complicated. We hope to show that it is not a matter of unnecessary complication, but rather that an unavoidable complexity lies behind an apparently simple situation.

The context: Argentinian psychoanalysis in the 1950s and 1960s

Bleger's paper provides a good example of a thread that runs throughout Argentinian psychoanalysis, which is its strong interest in 'concrete', or situational, aspects of clinical work. The founders of the Argentinian psychoanalytic group were interested not only in the 'classical' clinical practice of psychoanalysis but also in its application to problems such as psychosis, psychosomatic illness and childhood difficulties, as well as in group work and work with institutions. In the years between the fall of Perón in 1955 and the military coup of 1976, there was a remarkable burgeoning of intellectual and artistic life in Argentina, in which the development of psychoanalysis was not an isolated phenomenon.

A crucial influence in the mainstream of psychoanalysis in Argentina and Uruguay between the 1950s and 1970s was the work of Melanie Klein and her followers. The commitment of the first Argentinian psychoanalysts to all aspects of the clinical practice of psychoanalysis was one of the main reasons for their rapid adoption of Melanie Klein's ideas and those of her followers, and in particular of the concept of projective identification which became such a powerful clinical tool for enabling the analyst to make interpretations which could set the treatment on the path of symbolisation and psychic work. This led naturally to important exchanges with the British Psychoanalytical Society, despite the difficulties of geographical distance that were much greater in those days.

No less important to the development of psychoanalysis in South America during this period was the role played by Enrique Pichon-Rivière, a psychiatrist of French-Swiss origin, a man of wide interests and a gifted teacher, who was a formative influence on José Bleger and all of his contemporaries. Pichon-Rivière and his colleagues developed group and institutional methods for the treatment of psychotic patients, and for thinking about the group and the institution (see: Bleger, 1966; Tubert-Oklander & de Tubert, 2004). Some of Pichon-Rivière's concepts are exemplified and developed by José Bleger in *Symbiosis and Ambiguity*, including: the 'link' (*vinculo*); the distinction between 'depositor', 'depository' and 'deposited' in the process of projection; and the three 'areas' of mind, body and external world.

Meanwhile, the concept of the countertransference was also growing strongly in importance with Enrique Racker in Buenos Aires and with Paula Heimann in London. It may be that the way in which countertransference came to be so important for the Argentinian psychoanalytic movement is connected with the everyday reality of Argentina, where politics touches all aspects of life, from the most public to the most intimate. As in other countries in which democracy is not firmly rooted historically, politics is felt to be omnipresent: you cannot get away from it. In such an environment you are forced to try to understand what someone else is trying to make of you, what the current political reality is in the process of turning you into at each moment, in order to be able to distinguish among the various elements that are in play, and thereby to be able to discriminate something of your own position.

This is also the predicament in the consulting room. In an earlier chapter of *Symbiosis and Ambiguity* José Bleger (2013 [1967], p. 91) wrote:

'The transference interpretation must refer to what the patient does with us at each precise moment, what the patient rejects, accepts, expects, etc., including determination of the affect that is present'.

From the session to the setting

The combination of a clinical orientation with an omnipresent political awareness perhaps explains the strong interest, mentioned earlier, in 'concrete' aspects of clinical work. We mean, for example, such aspects as the 'analytic situation', the session, the contract, the setting. In 1957 Bleger wrote a paper on 'The psychoanalytic session', which can be seen as a precursor of his paper on the setting a decade later (Bleger, 1958, Ch. 6). The 1957 paper builds in particular on Pichon-Rivière's notion of the psychoanalytic process as a 'spiral', in which interpretations serve to break open the closed circle of repetition compulsion, as well as on Racker's work on the countertransference and on a critique of the notion of instinct by the French philosopher George Politzer (1994 [1928]; 1965–66).

Briefly we could say that the 1957 paper examines the psychoanalytic situation from a 'dialectical' perspective, which emphasises its openness to development and change, whereas the 1967 paper on the setting approaches the same situation more from the perspective of repetition compulsion, the operation of which can be seen more clearly by exploring the functioning of the setting.

The paper on the setting

Until recently, knowledge of José Bleger's work in the English-speaking world was based almost exclusively on his paper on the psychoanalytic setting. Although it has been for some time a classic among writings on the setting, its isolation from the clinical and theoretical context in which it originally appeared in Spanish, as well as some serious deficiencies in the 1967 translation, meant that English readers were for a long time denied an opportunity to make a proper assessment of his distinctive contribution to psychoanalysis. The English edition of *Symbiosis and Ambiguity* (Bleger, 2013 [1967]) seeks to remedy this situation by restoring the paper to its original context. As the sixth and final substantive chapter of the book, it represents not only an approach to the particular problem of psychoanalytic technique that is presented by the analysis of the setting, but also a culmination and synthesis of work described in the preceding five chapters which enable this problem to be seen in its wider psychological and institutional context.

Bleger considers the psychoanalytic setting from a number of different viewpoints at the same time. He begins by defining the psychoanalytic situation as comprised of an analytic process and what he calls a 'non-process'. This 'non-process' is the setting, which as far as possible is held constant and within which the analytic process occurs. The relation between the process and the setting is also described in *Gestalt* terms as a figure-ground relation, the process being the figure and the setting being the background.

Sometimes the setting changes from being the background to being the figure, from being a non-process to being a process, but only when something happens to make us aware of its existence. Such changes are usually temporary, because as clinicians we seek to maintain or restore the setting, to return it to the background, so that we can continue to observe and analyse the process that is occurring within it. However, Bleger indicates that he is interested specifically in the function of the setting when it is *not* being noticed, when it remains as background. As he succinctly puts it, 'The problem that I wish to examine is the problem of those analyses in which the setting is not a problem. And I want to do this precisely to show that it is a problem' (2013 [1967], p. 229).

The 'problem' that he believes can go unrecognised is that something has been deposited in the setting and remains hidden there as long as the setting itself is not analysed. To understand what this something is, we need to consider a cluster of interdependent ideas in his account which derive from his work on the psychology of social institutions, building on work by Pichon-Rivière and by Elliot Jaques.

The setting as institution and as part of the body schema

First, the psychoanalytic setting can be regarded as a certain kind of institution. He writes: 'A relationship that lasts for years with the maintenance of a set of norms and attitudes is precisely the definition of an *institution*' (2013 [1967], p. 230). Second, the various institutions in which someone participates form parts of his or her individual personality, so that personal identity always has a group or institutional aspect. Third, institutions also enter into the determination of the body-schema, and the setting is no

exception. This last idea, which is perhaps the least obvious one, is introduced initially by way of an analogy: just as in neurology the body schema
reveals itself in the phenomenon of the 'phantom limb' following an
amputation, so the psychoanalytic setting makes its presence known only
when it is broken or disrupted. However, for Bleger this is more than an
analogy. He writes:

> The setting forms part of the patient's body schema. It *is* the body
> schema in the part where this has not yet been structured and
> discriminated. This means that it is something different from the body
> schema in the narrow sense of the term: it is the undifferentiation of
> body and space, and of body and environment.
>
> (2013 [1967], pp. 238–239)

Now this statement is somewhat obscure, even in the original Spanish, but
its meaning becomes clearer when the chapter on the setting is read in the
context of the book as a whole. The normal, silent, continuous presence of
the setting offers the patient an opportunity for a relationship at a bodily
level that reproduces an early symbiosis of the infant with the mother, in
which there is as yet neither an object nor even a part-object, and no
differentiation between good and bad, internal and external, ego and non-
ego. Instead of a real object-relation there are only various 'ego-nuclei'
together with the objects to which they correspond. These nuclei and their
objects exist psychologically but they are not yet differentiated, because
the splitting that will later characterise the paranoid-schizoid position has
not yet occurred.

Symbiosis, undifferentiation and the glischro-caric position

In the early chapters of *Symbiosis and Ambiguity*, the emphasis is on
symbiosis, whereby part of the mind is projected into a 'depositary' in the
external world, who thereby comes under pressure to play a role; in other
words, it is described as operating by means of projective identification.
In the infant's case, the depositary is primarily the mother; in a fully
symbiotic relationship between adults, such as the one he analyses in a
novel,[3] 'the projections are crossed, and each person acts according to the
compensatory roles of the other' (2013 [1967], p. 14).

Symbiotic relationships thus involve an unconscious phantasy of total dependence. The first chapter of the book is a detailed study of dependence and independence in a young woman suffering acute difficulties in separating from her family. The clinical material brings out the coexistence in the transference of symbiosis and autism: in symbiosis the receiver of the projection, the depositary, belongs to the external world, whereas in autism it belongs to a zone of the patient's own mind or body.

It is important to note that for Bleger, 'undifferentiation' is not simply the absence of differentiation; it implies a certain structure and organisation. Prior to the paranoid-schizoid position as described by Melanie Klein, he argues, there is a more primitive position, whose characteristic defences are immobilisation and fragmentation,[4] and which symptomatically gives rise to confusional rather than persecutory anxiety. He calls this the 'glischro-caric position', from the Greek words for viscosity, or adhesiveness, and for nucleus. The hypothesis is grounded in observations by both Klein and Rosenfeld of confusional states as normal phenomena of early development, but he attributes these to an original fusion or lack of discrimination.

The relational structure of the glischro-caric position persists into adulthood in what he calls the 'agglutinated nucleus', and he explicitly equates this with what Bion had called 'the psychotic part of the personality'. Throughout life, this nucleus remains ready to form new symbiotic relationships characterised by massive projective identifications. It is this nucleus, Bleger argues, that is silently deposited in the setting, where it remains hidden and unanalysed, until a disruption of some kind causes it to become manifest.

As long as the setting is *not* disrupted, it remains unnoticed. The psychotic part of the patient's personality, the undifferentiated and unresolved infantile symbiotic relationship, remains deposited in the setting. Like a phantom limb that has not yet been experienced because the body is still intact, it silently persists in the setting as a 'phantom world', undetected but nonetheless psychically real. The setting thus forms a tenacious and invisible 'bastion' (Baranger & Baranger, 1961–62), a refuge or retreat for the psychotic part of the personality, which demands that nothing shall change. José Bleger observes that precisely because the setting is so much respected and preserved in psychoanalysis, much of this area of the mind may never be analysed.

Analysing the setting: the 'two settings'

The implications for psychoanalytic technique, then, are that at some point the setting itself has to be analysed, and the analyst–patient relationship has to be 'de-symbiotised', but he observes that this will meet strong resistance because the symbiosis is something which has never before been recognised by the patient. For this reason, he argues, we need to distinguish carefully between the setting that the analyst provides and the setting that the patient 'brings' to the analysis. As an example, he describes a patient who continues to address the analyst in a familiar way even when the analyst's own setting implies an expectation of formality.

The analyst, he writes, needs to 'accept' the setting brought by the patient because within it will be found, in summary form, all of the primitive unresolved symbiosis. At the same time, the analyst must hold firmly to his own setting in order to be able analyse both the process and the patient's setting when this has been transformed into process. In other words, he accepts the patient's setting in order to interpret it. José Bleger concludes:

> In sum, we may say that the patient's setting is his most primitive fusion with the mother's body and that the psychoanalyst's setting must serve to re-establish the original symbiosis, but only in order to change it. Both the disruption of the setting and its ideal or normal maintenance are technical and theoretical problems, but what fundamentally disturbs the possibility of thoroughgoing treatment is the disruption introduced or accepted by the psychoanalyst in the setting. *The setting can only be analysed within the setting*; in other words, the patient's dependence and most primitive psychological organisation can only be analysed within the analyst's setting, which should be neither ambiguous nor changing, nor altered.
>
> (2013 [1967], p. 241)

Ambiguity, syncretic participation and the risk of an 'adapted ego'

Up to this point we have discussed the context of José Bleger's ideas about the setting primarily in terms of the early *symbiosis* that it reproduces. But what about *ambiguity*, that other key term in the title of the book? In the course of his argument there is a shift of emphasis, away from the study of the agglutinated nucleus as it persists alongside, and split-off from a more mature ego, and towards the manifestations by the ego of the inherently ambiguous nature of this nucleus, in different personality types or traits.

It needs to be stressed that in José Bleger's view, the agglutinated nucleus is present in everyone. It is normally split off from the more mature ego, but if this split is absent or reduced, we find instead a characterological expression of the nucleus, in the form of an 'ambiguous personality'. He distinguishes a number of ways in which this typically happens, of which we will here mention only two. In one of these, the ambiguous personality simply persists into adulthood as a '*syncretic ego*', lacking firm attachments and characterised by a constantly shifting identity, shallowness and inconsistency, giving rise to an impression of 'fictitiousness' or falseness. In another, the personality becomes partly organised as a '*factic ego*': attached to an institution, group or person from which it has not yet distinguished itself, the factic ego exists only in the action, the job, etc., and lacks an autonomous interior life.

In distinguishing various forms of ambiguous personality he remarks that he is only 'describing a typology and not necessarily a pathology' (2013 [1967], p. 176, n. 128). He points out that although ambiguity may involve contradiction for the observer, 'there is no contradiction for the subject, since this has not yet come into play' (2013 [1967], p. 175). He wants to avoid thinking solely in pathological terms with a normative notion of 'deficit', and to allow instead for other kinds of identity and other senses of reality.

The 'syncretic ego', for example, is understood as an ensemble of personal relations in which the individual knows himself only by virtue of his various relationships with others, for example the members of his family, and not as someone with a separate and constant identity. Before projection and introjection come into play with the paranoid-schizoid position, it operates by simple 'participation' in the undifferentiated inter-action, or what Fairbairn had called 'primary identification'.[5] Among the clinical examples that Bleger describes is a patient who frequently makes appointments with different persons for the same hour on the same day, and then if both of them turn up he lets 'chance' resolve it and takes no responsibility for the situation.

In this way of thinking about syncretic participation as occurring without the use of defences characteristic of the paranoid-schizoid position, we can see that he has moved away from his earlier emphasis on symbiosis as involving massive projection into a depositary, and towards an emphasis instead on the ambiguous nature of the agglutinated nucleus.

The characterological aspect of ambiguity is an important element in his discussion of a risk that is inherent in the psychoanalytic setting. He writes:

> The setting may thus be considered an 'addiction'. If it is not analysed systematically it may become a stabilised organisation, the basis of the organisation of the personality, and the subject may obtain an 'adapted' ego as a function of an external moulding by institutions.
>
> (2013 [1967], p. 237)

This process of 'moulding by institutions' is the basis of the factic ego, of which he writes:

> [It] is an 'ego of belonging': it is constituted and maintained by the subject's inclusion in an institution (which may be the therapeutic relationship, the Psychoanalytical Society, a study group or any other institution): there is no 'interiorised ego' to provide the subject with internal stability. We could say, in other words, that the entire personality is made up of 'characters', that is, of roles, or else that the whole personality is a façade.
>
> (2013 [1967], p. 237)

It is in the context of this risk that we can understand why José Bleger insists that the analyst's setting must be *un*ambiguous, while accepting and tolerating the different setting brought by the patient, in order to analyse it. The setting is both what makes a psychoanalysis possible at all and, at the same time, it constantly threatens to compromise or destroy it.

Notes

1   An earlier version of this paper was read to the British Psychoanalytical Society on 15 October 2014.
2   In translating *Symbiosis and Ambiguity* we decided to translate *encuadre* as 'setting'. For discussion of this decision, and of the translation of other key

concepts in the book, see our Editorial Introduction (Bleger, 2013 [1967]), pp. xl–xliv.
3 *Le repos du guerrier* by Christiane Rochefort (1958).
4 'Fragmentation' in the sense of *Zerspaltung* (Bleuler) or 'abnormal splitting' (Rosenfeld).
5 Fairbairn (1952), p. 145; see Bleger (2013 [1967]), 185, n. 141. The term 'participation' is taken from Lévy-Bruhl; see Bleger (2013 [1967]), p. 234, n. 184.

References

Baranger, M. and Baranger, W. (1961–62). 'La situación analítica como campo dinámico'. *Revista Uruguaya de Psicoanálisis*, 4(1): 3–54; S. Rogers and J. Churcher, translators (2008) 'The analytic situation as a dynamic field', *International Journal of Psychoanalysis*, 89(4): 795–826.

Bleger, J. (1958). *Psicoanálisis y dialéctica materialista: Estudio sobre la estructura de psicoanalisis*. Buenos Aires: Paidós.

Bleger, J. (1966). *Psicohigiene y psicología institucional*. Buenos Aires: Paidós.

Bleger, J. (1967a). *Simbiosis y ambigüedad: Estudio psicoanalítico*. Buenos Aires: Paidós.

Bleger, J. (1967b). 'Psycho-analysis of the psycho-analytic frame', *International Journal of Psychoanalysis*, 48: 511–519.

Bleger, J. (2013 [1967]). *Symbiosis and ambiguity: A psychoanalytic study.* [(1967) Simbiosis y ambigüedad: Estudio psicoanalítico]. S. Rogers, L. Bleger and J. Churcher, translators; J. Churcher and L. Bleger, editors. New Library of Psychoanalysis. London: Routledge.

Fairbairn, W.R. (1952). *Psychoanalytic studies of the personality*. London: Tavistock Publications.

Politzer, G. (1994 [1928]). *Critique of the foundations of psychology*, M. Apprey, translator, Pittsburgh, PA: Duquesne University Press. [1928. *Critique des fondements de la psychologie*. I. La psychologie et la psychanalyse. Paris: Les Editions Rieder].

Politzer, G. (1965–66). *Escritos psicológicos de Georges Politzer*. E. Ramos, translator. J. Bleger, editor. 3 vols. Buenos Aires: Jorge Alvarez.

Rochefort, C. (1958). *Le repos du guerrier*. Paris: Éditions Bernard Grasset, L. Bair, translator (1962 [1960]), *Warrior's rest*. London: The New English Library Limited.

Tubert-Oklander, J. and de Tubert, R.H. (2004) *Operative groups: The Latin-American approach to group analysis*. London & New York: Jessica Kingsley.

Chapter 1

Psychoanalysis of the psychoanalytic setting[1]

José Bleger

Winnicott defines the '*setting*' as 'the summation of all the details of management' (Winnicott, 1956, p. 297).[2] For reasons that will be discussed as we develop this theme, I propose that we adopt the term *psychoanalytic situation* for the totality of the phenomena included *in the therapeutic relationship* between analyst and patient. This situation encompasses phenomena that constitute a *process*, which is what we study, analyse and interpret. However, it also includes a *setting*,[3] in other words a 'non-process' in the sense that these are the constants within the framework of which the process takes place.[4]

The analytic situation may thus be studied from the perspective of the methodology that it represents, the setting corresponding to the *constants* of a phenomenon, a method or a technique, and the process to the set of *variables*. However, we shall here put to one side this methodological aspect and mention it only for the purpose of making clear that a process can only be investigated while these constants (the setting) are maintained. Thus, within the psychoanalytic setting we include the role of the analyst, the combination of spatial factors (the surroundings), temporal factors and part of the technique[5] (including the establishment and maintenance of session times, fees, regular breaks, etc.).

For now, my concern is with the psychoanalysis of the psychoanalytic setting and there is a considerable literature on the need to maintain it and on the disruptions and distortions that the patient provokes in it in the course of any analysis (of various kinds and degrees, from exaggerated obsessional compliance to repression, acting out or psychotic disintegration). My work with the psychoanalysis of psychotics has taught me clearly the importance of maintaining and defending those fragments or elements of the setting that may have survived, which is sometimes achieved only with hospitalisation. However, I will not focus just now on the problem of 'disruption' or 'attacks' on the setting. I wish to examine what is involved in the maintenance of an *ideally normal setting*.[6]

Stated in these terms, such a study would seem to be impossible, since this ideal analysis does not exist. I agree with this opinion. The fact is that, sometimes permanently and at other times sporadically, the setting is transformed from the background of a *Gestalt* into a figure, that is, into a process. However, even in these cases, it is not the same as the process of the analytic situation itself, because in relation to the 'failures' of the setting, our interpretation *always tends* to maintain or re-establish it: which is an important difference from our attitude in the analysis of the process itself. In this sense, I am interested in examining the psychoanalytic meaning of the setting *when it is not a problem*, in an 'ideal' analysis (or in the moments or periods when it is being that). I mean that I am proposing the psychoanalysis of the setting when it is being maintained and not when it is broken; when it continues being a set of constants and not when it has turned into variables. The problem that I wish to examine is the problem of those analyses in which the setting is not a problem. And I want to do this precisely to show that it is a problem. This will necessarily take up a good part of my available time, since it is not possible to analyse a problem that has not been clearly stated and is not yet recognised as a problem.

ψ

A relationship that lasts for years with the maintenance of a set of norms and attitudes is precisely the definition of an *institution*. The setting is therefore an institution within whose framework, or in the midst of which, phenomena occur that we call behaviour.[7]

What became evident to me is that each institution is a part of the individual's personality, and this is of such importance that identity is always – wholly or partially – group or institutional, in the sense that always at least a part of one's identity is configured by belonging to a group, an institution, an ideology, a party, etc. Fenichel wrote: 'Unquestionably, the individual structures created by institutions help to preserve these institutions' (Fenichel, 1946, p. 447). However, in addition to this interaction between individuals and institutions, institutions always function (in varying degrees) as boundaries of the body schema and as the fundamental nucleus of identity.

The setting is maintained and tends to be maintained (actively by the psychoanalyst) as invariable. As long as it exists in this way, it seem to be nonexistent or not to count, like institutions or relationships that we only take notice of precisely when they are missing or obstructed or come to an end. (Someone said about love and children that you only know they exist when they cry.) What is the meaning of the setting while it is being maintained (when it 'doesn't cry')? In every instance this is the problem of symbiosis, which is 'silent' and which only manifests itself when it is broken or on the point of being broken. It is the same as what happens with the body schema, the study of which began with pathology, which is what revealed its existence in the first place. Just as we speak of the 'phantom limb' we need to recognise that institutions and the setting are *always* constituted in a 'phantom world': the world of the most primitive and undifferentiated organisation. What is always there remains unperceived unless it is missing. We could apply to the setting Wallon's term 'ultra-things': that is, everything that is experienced as vague, undetermined, without any conception or knowledge of what it is. What organises the ego are not just stable relationships with objects and institutions but also the ulterior frustrations and gratifications that are due to them. There is no perception of what is always there. The perception of the missing object and of the gratifying object comes later; at first there is only the perception of an 'incompleteness'. What exists in the *subject's perception* is whatever experience has shown him might be missing. By contrast, stable or immobilised relationships (non-absences) organise and maintain the non-ego and form the *basis* for structuring the ego as a function of frustrating and gratifying experiences. The fact that the non-ego is not perceived does not mean that it does not exist psychologically for the organisation of the personality. The knowledge of something arises only in the absence of that something, until it is organised as an internal object. But that which we do not perceive also exists. This 'phantom world' exists deposited in the setting even though the setting has not been broken, or precisely because of that.

ψ

I want to digress again briefly and thereby, I hope, provide more elements for the investigation that I am undertaking. Until quite recently, we were very comfortable working in science, language, logic, etc., without realising that all these phenomena or behaviours (I am interested in all of them

as behaviours, that is, as human phenomena) occur in a context of assumptions that we ignored or treated as nonexistent or invariable. However, we
now know that communication includes a meta-communication, science a
meta-science, theory a meta-theory, language a meta-language, logic a
meta-logic, etc. If the 'meta...' varies the content varies radically.[8] Thus
the setting, being constant, is decisive for the phenomena of the *process*
of behaviour. In other words, the setting is a *meta-behaviour* and the
phenomena that we will identify as behaviour depend on it. It is what is
implicit, but what is explicit depends on it.

The *meta-behaviour* functions as what M. and W. Baranger call 'the
bastion': an aspect that the patient, by avoiding the fundamental rule, tries
not to put at risk (Baranger and Baranger, 1961–1962). But in the meta-
behaviour that I am interested in analysing *the fundamental rule is being
observed*,[9] and what interests me is precisely the examination of this
observance. I agree with these authors in considering the analytic relation
as a symbiotic relation. But in cases where the setting is being respected,
the problem is that the setting itself is the depositary of the symbiosis and
the latter is not present in the analytic *process* proper. Symbiosis with the
mother (the immobilisation of the non-ego) allows the child to develop his
ego. The function of the setting is the same: it is a support and a framework, but it can only be seen – for now – when it changes or is broken.
The most persistent, tenacious and unnoticeable 'bastion' is the one
deposited in the setting.

ψ

I now wish to illustrate this description of the setting with the brief example of a patient (A.A.) who has a phobic character and intense dependence
concealed beneath a reactive independence. For a long time he vacillated,
wishing and fearing to buy an apartment, a purchase that never materi-
alised. At a certain moment, he accidentally learned that I had bought an
apartment some time previously in a building that was still under
construction, and at that point a period of anxiety and of various kinds of
acting began.

One day he told me what he had learned and I interpreted his attitude:
the way he told me about it included a reproach that I had not told him
about my purchase, even though I knew that this was a fundamental problem for him. He tried to ignore or forget the episode, offering strong

resistance every time I insisted on connecting this fact with his acting, until strong feelings of hate, envy and frustration began to appear, with violent verbal attacks, followed by an atmosphere of withdrawal and despair. As we continued the analysis of these situations, the 'background' of his infantile experience gradually began to emerge, which I was able to reconstruct through his narration of different memories: at home his parents would do nothing, absolutely nothing, without informing and consulting him so that he knew every detail of the course of family life. After the appearance and reiterated interpretation of these memories (which had to overcome strong resistance), he started on the accusation that everything between us had been broken and he could no longer trust me. Frequent fantasies of suicide, disorientation and confusion and hypochondriacal symptoms appeared.[10]

For the patient, 'something' was broken which *was so* and which *had to be* as it had always been, and he could not conceive of it being otherwise. He demanded the repetition of what he had experienced, of what was 'always that way' for him. It was a demand or condition that he was able to maintain throughout his life by means of a restriction or limitation of his ego in social relationships and by always keeping hold of the management of those relationships, and by demanding a strong dependence from his objects.

In this example I wish to point out how the 'non-repetition', by respecting the setting, brought to light a very important part of his personality: the most fixed and stable part of his personality, his 'phantom world', the delusional transference (Little, 1958) or the psychotic part of his personality: a non-ego that formed the framework of his ego and identity. Only with the 'non-observance' of his 'phantom world' could he see that 'my' setting was not the same as his, and that his was already present as a 'phantom world' before the 'non-observance'. But I want to emphasise that the maintenance of the setting is what allowed the analysis of the psychotic part of the personality. What I am trying to bring out is not how many of these phenomena appear because of frustration or a collision with reality (the setting) but – more importantly – the question: how much of it does *not* appear and may therefore possibly never be analysable? I have no answer to this question. What concerns me at present is to make clear (to discriminate) what the problem is. It is similar to what happens with the character trait that has to be transformed into symptoms in order to be analysed; that is, it has to cease to be ego-syntonic. And should we not do

with the setting as we do in character-analysis? The problem is different
and even more difficult, since not only is the setting not ego-syntonic but
it is the framework on which the subject's ego and identity are constructed, and it gets strongly split off from the analytic process, and from
the ego that configures the neurotic transference. Although we assume that
in the case of A.A. this material would somehow have come up anyway,
since it was already present, the problem remains unsolved in terms of the
psychoanalytic meaning of the setting.

ψ

Summarising, we could say that the setting (thus defined as a problem)
constitutes the most perfect repetition compulsion[11] and that there are actually *two settings*: one which is proposed and maintained by the
psychoanalyst, and accepted consciously by the patient, and another, that
of the 'phantom world', into which the patient projects.[12] The latter is such
a perfect repetition compulsion, because it is the most complete, the least
recognised and the most unnoticed.[13] Something that has always surprised
and fascinated me, in the analysis of psychotics, is the co-existence of
total denial of the analyst with an exaggerated sensitivity concerning the
infringement of any detail of what the patient is 'used to' (in the setting),
and how the patient may become disorganised or violent, for example, if
there is a difference of a few minutes at the start or end of the session.
Now I understand this better: what becomes disorganised is the 'meta-
ego', which to a large extent is *all the patient has*.[14] In the psychotic
transference, it is not affect that is transferred but instead 'a total situation,
the totality of a development' (Lagache, 1952);[15] it would be better to say
the totality of a 'non-development'. For Melanie Klein, the transference
repeats the primitive object relations, but I believe that something even
more primitive (the undifferentiation) is repeated in the setting.[16]

E. Jacques says that institutions are unconsciously used as defence
mechanisms against psychotic anxieties, but I think it would be better to
say that they are depositaries of the psychotic part of the personality, that
is, of the undifferentiated and unresolved part of primitive symbiotic relationships. Psychotic anxieties are played out within the institution and, in
the case of the psychoanalytic situation, within what we have characterised as the *process* (that which is 'in motion', as opposed to that which
isn't: the setting).[17]

The development of the ego (in analysis, in the family, or in any institution) depends on the immobilisation of the non-ego. This term 'non-ego'
induces us to think of it as something non-existent, but its existence is real:
so much so that it is this 'meta-ego' on which the possibility of the formation and maintenance of the ego itself, and thus the ego's very existence,
depends. On this basis we were able to say that identity depends on the way
in which the non-ego is maintained or handled. If the meta-behaviour
varies, the entire ego is modified (possibly to equivalent degrees in terms
of quantity and quality).[18] The non-ego is the background or framework of
the organised ego: they are the 'ground' and 'figure' of a single *Gestalt*.
Between ego and non-ego (or between the neurotic and the psychotic parts
of the personality) there is no dissociation but instead a splitting, in the
sense that I have used this term in a previous text.[19]

N.N. was a very rigid and limited patient who always lived with her
parents in hotels in different countries. The only thing that she always took
with her was a small picture. Her poor relationship with her parents and
the incessant moves made this picture her 'surroundings', her non-ego:
her meta-behaviour, which gave her 'non-change' for her identity.

The setting '*is*' the most primitive part of the personality, the ego-
body-world fusion on whose *immobilisation* depend the formation,
existence and discrimination (of the ego, the object, the body schema, the
body, the mind, etc.). Patients with 'acting in' or psychotics also bring
'their own setting': *the institution of their primitive symbiotic relation*. But
all patients also bring this.

Thus, we are better able now to acknowledge the catastrophic situation
that the analyst's disruption of the setting (holidays, or cancelled, missed
or incomplete sessions, etc.) *always* entails to a variable degree, since in
these disruptions (disruptions that are part of the setting) a 'crack' is
created through which reality is introduced, which is catastrophic for the
patient. 'His' setting and his 'phantom world' lose their depositary and it
becomes evident that 'his' setting is not the psychoanalytic setting, as
occurred with A.A. Now I want to offer an example of a 'crack' that the
patient tolerated until he felt the need to recover his omnipotence and 'his'
setting.

Z., the only son in a family that in his childhood was very wealthy,
socially quite prominent and very close-knit, lived in an enormous and
luxurious mansion with his parents and grandparents, for whom he was
the centre of attention and lavish care.

For political reasons many of their possessions were expropriated, which resulted in a considerable economic decline. For a time, the entire family made an effort to keep up appearances as rich people, hiding the disaster and poverty, but his parents ultimately moved into a small apartment and accepted employment (his grandparents had died in the meantime). While the family faced and accepted the change, he continued to 'keep up appearances'. He separated from his parents and earned a living from his profession as an architect, while covering up his great insecurity and economic instability. So much so that everyone believed he was wealthy, while he lived and kept alive his phantasy that 'nothing had happened', thus preserving the secure and idealised world of his childhood (his 'phantom world'). This was also the impression that he produced in me in the treatment: a 'person of good standing', from a superior social and economic class, who without any '*nouveau riche*' ostentation preserved an air of security, dignity and superiority, of being outside and above the 'penuries' and 'pettiness' of life, which included money.

The setting was well maintained, he paid regularly and punctually. When his attitude and his duality (the split in his personality), his way of moving in two worlds, of maintaining a fiction, were analysed more and more closely, he began to owe me money and to be late, as well as to speak (with great difficulty) about his lack of money, which made him feel 'humiliated'.

Here, the disruption of the setting meant a certain disruption in his omnipotent organisation: the emergence of a 'breach' that became the route for penetration 'against' his omnipotence (the stable and secure world of his childhood).

His respecting the setting was here the deposition of his magical omnipotent world, infantile dependence and psychotic transference: his deepest phantasy was that the analysis would consolidate this omnipotence and give completely back to him 'his' 'phantom world'. The disruption of the setting meant the disruption of a splitting and the emergence of a 'breach' where reality broke through.

'Living' in the past was not his unconscious phantasy; it was the immediate, basic organisation of his existence. I shall transcribe parts of a session at a moment when his parents suddenly had an accident and were gravely ill. In the previous session he paid part of his debt and began that session by telling me that today he brought me this many pesos, that this many remain and that this debt feels 'like a breach', like something that's missing'. (Pause) He goes on: 'Yesterday I had sexual relations with my wife and at the beginning I was impotent and this frightened me very much'. (He had been impotent at the beginning of his marriage.)

I interpret that now that he is going through a difficult situation because of his parents' accident, he wishes to return to the security he had in his childhood, to the parents and grandparents inside him, and that the relationship with his wife, with me and with today's reality leaves him impotent in relation to that; that he needs to close the breach by paying me everything, so that the money will disappear from between us, so that I will disappear along with everything that now makes him suffer.

He answers that yesterday he had the thought that he only needs his wife in order not to be alone, and that she was a mere add-on to his life.

I interpret that he also wishes that I would satisfy his needs in reality so that they might disappear and thus allow him to return to the security of his childhood and his fantasy of reunion with his grandparents, father and mother, just as everything was in childhood.

(Silence) After this he says that when he heard the word fantasy, it seemed strange that I would talk about fantasies and that he was afraid of going mad.

I tell him that he needs me to give him back all the security of his child-hood that he tries to hold inside himself in order to confront the difficult situation, and that he also feels that I, and reality with its requirements and pains, get into the breach that money, his debt, puts between us.

He ends the session by talking about a transvestite. I interpret that he feels like a transvestite: sometimes like a rich and only child, sometimes like the father, sometimes like the mother, at times like the grandfather, and as each of them, he feels both rich and poor.

ψ

Any variation of the setting throws the non-ego into crisis, 'disavows' the fusion, renders 'problematic' the ego and forces re-introjection, a fresh working-through of the ego or activation of the defences in order to immo-bilise or re-project the psychotic part of the personality. This patient (Z.) was able to accept the analysis of 'his' setting until he needed to recover it defen-sively, and what is interesting to emphasise is that his 'phantom world' appears and is put in question by 'faults' in the setting (his debt) and that the recovery of his 'phantom world' was connected with 'respecting' 'my' setting, precisely in order to ignore me or cancel me out. The phenomenon of the reactivation of symptoms described at the end of psychoanalytic treatment is also due to the mobilisation and regression of the ego through mobilisation of the meta-ego. The background of the *Gestalt* becomes the figure.[20]

The setting may thus be considered an 'addiction'. If it is not analysed systematically it may become a stabilised organisation, the basis of the organisation of the personality, and the subject may obtain an 'adapted' ego as a function of an external moulding by institutions. This is the basis, I believe, for what Álvarez de Toledo, Grinberg and Langer (1964) have called the 'psychoanalytic personality', which the Existentialists call a 'factic' existence, and which we could identify as a truly 'factic ego'.

This 'factic ego' is an 'ego of belonging': it is constituted and maintained by the subject's inclusion in an institution (which may be the therapeutic relationship, the Psychoanalytical Society, a study group or any other institution): there is no 'interiorised ego' to provide the subject with internal stability. We could say, in other words, that the entire personality is made up of 'characters', that is, of roles, or else that the whole personality is a façade. I am now describing the 'extreme case', but we need to take the quantitative variation into account, since there is no way in which this 'factic ego' can stop existing entirely (nor do I consider it necessary that it should).

The negative therapeutic reaction or 'pact' is the perfect installation of the patient's non-ego in the setting and its non-recognition and acceptance by the psychoanalyst. We could also say that the negative therapeutic reaction is a real perversion of the transference-countertransference relation. The 'therapeutic alliance' is, by contrast, an alliance with the patient's healthiest part (Greenacre, 1959). This is true for the process but not for the setting. In the latter, the alliance is with the psychotic (or symbiotic) part of the patient's personality (with the corresponding part in the analyst? I do not know yet).[21]

Winnicott says that:

> For the neurotic the couch and warmth and comfort can be *symbolical* of the mother's love; for the psychotic it would be more true to say that these things *are* the analyst's physical expression of love. The couch *is* the analyst's lap or womb, and the warmth *is* the live warmth of the analyst's body.
>
> (Winnicott, 1949, p. 72)

With regard to the setting, this is always the most regressive, psychotic part of the patient (for every type of patient).

The setting is what is most present, as the parents are for the child. Without them there is no development of the ego, but its maintenance beyond what is necessary or the lack of any modification of the relationship (either with the setting or with the parents) may indicate a negative factor, a paralysis of development.[22] In every analysis, even with an ideally maintained setting, the setting anyway needs to become an object of analysis. This does not mean that this is not being done in practice, but I wish to emphasise the interpretation or the meaning of what is being done or not being done, and its importance. The de-symbiotisation of the analyst–patient relation is attained only by the systematic analysis of the setting at the right moment. With this, we meet with the most tenacious resistance, because it is not something repressed but something split off which has never been discriminated. Its analysis is an upheaval for the ego and for the more mature identity reached by the patient. We do not interpret the repressed, but instead we create the secondary process. We are not interpreting gaps in memory but something that was never a part of memory. Nor is it a projective identification, but the manifestation of the patient's syncretism or 'participation'.

The setting forms part of the patient's body schema. It *is* the body schema in the part where this has not yet been structured and discriminated. This means that it is something different from the body schema in the narrow sense of the term: it is the undifferentiation of body and space, and of body and environment. For this reason, the interpretation of gestures or physical positions is often quite persecutory, because we are not 'moving' the patient's ego but his 'meta-ego'.

ψ

I now wish to give another example that also has the peculiarity which is precisely that I cannot describe the 'muteness' of the setting but only the moment at which it is revealed, when it ceases to be mute. I have already compared this to the body schema, which we began to study precisely because of its disturbances. But in this case, the psychoanalyst's setting itself was also vitiated.

A colleague brings to supervision the analysis of a patient whose transference neurosis he has been interpreting for several years, but chronicity and therapeutic inefficacy have set in, for which reason he decides to bring the case to supervision. The patient 'respected' the requirements of the setting and in this sense 'there were no problems': the patient associated well, there was no acting out and the analyst interpreted well (concerning the part he worked on). But the *patient and the therapist spoke to each other using the familiar form of address*[23] because the patient had proposed this at the beginning of his analysis (and this had been accepted by the therapist). It took many months to analyse the therapist's countertransference until he 'found the courage' to rectify the familiar form of address by interpreting to the patient what was happening, and what was hidden inside it. The cancelling of the familiar form, through its systematic analysis, made manifest the narcissistic relation and omnipotent control and the annihilation of the person and role of the therapist, which had become immobilised in the familiar form of address.

In using the familiar form of address, the patient superimposed his 'own setting' on that of the analyst, but in reality he was annihilating the latter. The colleague was faced with work that demanded very great effort in the session with his patient (and in his countertransference) and this led to an intense change in the analytic process and to disruption of the patient's ego, which was being maintained in precarious conditions, with a very limited 'spectrum' of interests and with intense and widespread inhibitions. The change in the form of address through analysis led the analyst to see that it was a question not of phobic character but of a simple schizophrenia with a phobic-obsessional 'façade'.

I do not believe that it would have been feasible to modify the familiar form of address from the outset, since the candidate was not technically equipped to handle a patient with a highly narcissistic organisation.

I do know that the analyst should not use the familiar form of address to the patient, although he may accept it from the patient and analyse it at the appropriate moment (which I cannot identify retrospectively). The analyst needs to accept the setting brought by the patient (which is the patient's 'meta-ego'), because within it will be found in summary form the primitive unresolved symbiosis. However, we need to state at the same time that accepting the patient's meta-ego (his setting) does not mean giving up the therapist's own, as a function of which it is possible to analyse the process and the setting itself when this has been transformed into process. Any interpretation of the (unaltered) setting mobilises the psychotic part of the personality. It constitutes what I have called a split interpretation.[24] But the analyst–patient relation outside the rigorous setting (as in this example), as well as in 'extra-analytic' relations, make possible a covering up of the psychotic transference and allows a 'cultivation' of the 'psychoanalytic character'.

ψ

Another patient (B.C.) always kept to the setting, but as her pregnancy advanced, she stopped greeting me as she entered and left (from the beginning of the treatment she had never shaken hands with me). My inclusion of her interrupted greeting in an interpretation was hugely resisted, but in that one could see the mobilisation of her symbiotic relationship with her mother, with some very persecutory characteristics, which had been brought about by her pregnancy.

She still does not shake my hand as she enters or leaves, and this is where a large part of 'her setting' resides, which is different from mine. I believe that the situation is even more complex, because not shaking hands is not a *detail* that is missing to complete the setting. It is an indicator that she has a *different* setting, a different *Gestalt* that is not mine (that of the psychoanalytic treatment), in which she keeps her idealised relationship with her mother split off.

The more we deal with the psychotic part of the personality, the more we need to bear in mind that a detail is not a detail, but instead the sign of a *Gestalt*, that is, of the entirety of a particular organisation or structure.

ψ

In sum, we may say that the patient's setting is his most primitive fusion with the mother's body and that the psychoanalyst's setting must serve to re-establish the original symbiosis, but only in order to change it. Both the disruption of the setting and its ideal or normal maintenance are technical and theoretical problems, but what fundamentally disturbs the possibility of thoroughgoing treatment is the disruption introduced or accepted by the psychoanalyst in the setting. *The setting can only be analysed within the setting*; in other words, the patient's dependence and most primitive psychological organisation can only be analysed within the analyst's setting, which should be neither ambiguous nor changing, nor altered.

Summary

It is proposed to consider the *analytic situation* as the totality of the phenomena included in the therapeutic relationship between the analyst and the patient. This situation encompasses phenomena that constitute a *process*, which is what we study, analyse and interpret; but it also includes a *setting*, which is a 'non-process' in the sense that it provides the constants within whose framework the process takes place.

The relations between the two are studied and the setting is defined as the set of constants within which the process (the variables) occurs. The basic aim is to study, not the disruption of the setting, but its psychoanalytic meaning when it is being maintained under 'ideally normal' conditions.

Thus, the setting is studied as an *institution* within whose framework phenomena occur that we call behaviour. In this sense, the setting is 'mute' yet not non-existent; it forms the patient's non-ego on the basis of which the ego is configured. This non-ego is the patient's 'phantom world', which is deposited precisely in the setting, and represents a 'meta-behaviour'.

The role of the setting is illustrated with several clinical examples showing the deposition of the patient's most primitive 'family institution' into the setting. This is a most perfect repetition compulsion, which actualises the primitive undifferentiation of the initial stages of personality organisation.

The setting as an institution is the depositary of the psychotic part of the personality, which is the undifferentiated and unresolved part of the primitive symbiotic links.

The psychoanalytic meaning of the setting thus defined is studied, as well as the repercussions of these considerations for clinical work and psychoanalytic technique.

Notes

1   Reproduced by kind permission of Taylor & Francis, LLC, from Chapter 6 of Bleger (2013 [1967]) *Symbiosis and Ambiguity*, pp. 228–241. [Footnotes in square brackets contain added editorial material; footnotes not in square brackets are by the author. This is the chapter previously published in English in the *International Journal of Psychoanalysis* as 'Psycho-analysis of the psycho-analytic frame' (Bleger, 1967b). See Bleger (2013 [1967]), p. xvii, and concerning the translation of *encuadre* as 'setting' instead of 'frame' see *ibid.* pp. xli–xlii).]

2   [In this instance Bleger has translated 'management' into Spanish as *técnica* instead of *manejo*.]

3   [When quoting Winnicott at the start of this paragraph, Bleger uses the English word 'setting' in quotation marks; here he uses the Spanish *encuadre*.]

4   We could compare this terminology with that used respectively by D. Liberman and E. Rodrigué.

5   The setting corresponds more to a strategy than to a technique. Part of the setting includes 'the analytic contract', which 'is an agreement between two persons, with two formal elements of reciprocal exchange: time and money' (Liberman *et al.*, 1961, p. 86).

6   The problem as I present it is similar to what physicists call a thought experiment: a problem that does not occur totally or precisely in the form in which it is defined or presented, but which is of great usefulness (theoretical and practical). Perhaps this ideal analysis or problem was what E. Rodrigué once referred to as the case history of the patient that nobody wrote or could ever write. [The reference is to what in German is called a *Gedankenexperiment*, the Spanish for which is *experiencia ideal*, literally 'ideal experiment', which then gives rise by analogy to the notion of 'ideal analysis', the ideally normally maintained setting, etc.]

7   I have arrived at this study, in part, precisely as a result of a series of seminars on institutional psychology and of my experience in this field (although this is still rather limited).

8   This variation of the 'meta...', or variation of fixed or constant assumptions, is the starting-point of non-Euclidean geometry and of Boolean algebra (Lieber, 1960). In psychotherapy, each technique has its assumptions (its setting) and therefore also its specific 'contents' or processes.

9   [The Spanish is *se cumple con la regla fundamental*, and later in the same sentence we render *cumplimiento* as 'observance', while in the next sentence but one we translate *en que se cumple con el encuadre* by 'where the setting is being respected'. In each case something more voluntary than mere compliance is implied.]

10 As Little (1958) describes in regard to delusional transference, there appeared associations referring to his body, from very early experiences: that he felt immobilised, and he associated that when he was a baby he was wrapped in a swaddling cloth that kept him completely immobile. The non-ego of the setting includes the body, and if the setting is broken the boundaries of the ego formed by the non-ego have to be recovered at the bodily level.

11 This repetition compulsion is not only 'a way of remembering' (Freud) but a way of living or the *condition for living*.

12 Wender (1965) wrote in his paper that there are two patients and two analysts, to which I now add that there are also two settings. [A handwritten note by the author, in his copy of the Spanish original, elaborates the phrase 'into which the patient projects', so that it reads 'into which the patient projects his own phantom world'.]

13 Rodrigué (1965) describes a 'suspended transference' and writes that the 'difficulty stems from speaking about a phenomenon that, if it existed in a pure form, would have to be silent by definition'. [See Rodrigué, E and Rodrigué, G.T., 1966, p. 225.]

14 I believe that it is rash to speak always in terms of an 'attack' on the setting when the patient does not comply with it. The patient brings 'what he has' and this is not always an 'attack' but the patient's own organisation (even though it is disorganised).

15 [The phrase 'total situation' was a quotation by Lagache of M. Klein's paper given at the Amsterdam Congress of 1951 and published the following year (Klein, 1952, p. 55).]

16 The ambiguity of the 'as if' of the analytic situation, studied by W. and M. Baranger, does not cover 'all aspects of the analytic field', as these authors say (Baranger and Baranger, 1961–1962, p. 800), but only the process. The setting does not admit ambiguity: either in the psychoanalyst's technique or in the patient. Each setting is what it is and does not admit ambiguity. Equally, I consider that the phenomenon of participation (Lévy Bruhl) or syncretism, which they accept for the analytic situation, applies only to the setting.

17 Reider describes different types of transference to the institution instead of to the therapist: psychoanalysis as an institution seems to be a way to recover lost omnipotence by participating in the prestige of a great institution. I believe that what is important here is to consider the psychoanalytic situation as an institution in itself, especially the setting.

18 G. Reinoso has remarked that although, as Freud pointed out, the ego is a body ego, *the non-ego is too* (García Reinoso, 1956a, 1956b). We could add something more: the non-ego is a different ego, with different qualities. This also means that there is not *one* sense of reality or lack of it: there are different structures of the ego and of the sense of reality. [In the previously published translation of this chapter in the *International Journal of Psychoanalysis*, this footnote was incorporated into the text, and the following clause appended to the second sentence: 'and I suggest (Bleger, 1967a) calling it a *syncretic ego*' (Bleger, 1967a, p. 514). The reference was to Chapter 5 of the present book.]

19 [This probably refers to Chapter 5.]

20 This must be what has led some authors (Christoffel, 1952) to use the disruption of the setting as a technique (abandoning the use of the couch and interviewing face to face); I do not agree with this opinion.

21 I do not believe that this psychotic split transference deposited in the setting is a consequence of repression or infantile amnesia.

22 E. Rodrigué, in 'The context of the transference' (1965), compares the analytic process with evolution.

It has been emphasised that the child's ego is organised according to the mobility of the environment that creates and satisfies the child's needs. The

rest of the environment that does not promote needs is not discriminated and
remains as such (as background) in the structure of personality. The significance of this fact has not yet been fully recognised.
23 [… *paciente y terapeuta se tuteaban* … that is, they addressed each other as
tu (familiar) instead of *usted* (formal).]
24 [See Bleger (2013 [1967]), p. 91.]

References

Note: Items marked with an asterisk have been added by the Editors. *Revista de
Psicoanálisis* refers to the journal of that name published by the *Asociación
Psicoanalítica Argentina.*

Álvarez de Toledo, L., Grinberg, L. and Langer, M. (1964). 'Terminación de análi-
sis'. Relato oficial al *Primer Congreso Psicoanalítico Panamericano*, Mexico.
Baranger, M. and Baranger, W. (1961–1962). 'La situación analítica como campo
dinámico'. *Revista Uruguaya de Psicoanálisis*, 4(1): 3–54; trans. S. Rogers
and J. Churcher (2008) 'The analytic situation as a dynamic field', *Inter-
national Journal of Psychoanalysis*, 89(4): 795–826.
Bleger, J. (1967a) *Simbiosis y ambigüedad: estudio psicoanalítico*. Buenos Aires:
Paidós.
*Bleger, J. (1967b). 'Psycho-analysis of the psycho-analytic frame'. *Inter-
national Journal of Psychoanalysis*, 48: 511–519.
*Bleger, J. (2013 [1967]) *Symbiosis and ambiguity: a psychoanalytic study.*
[1967. *Simbiosis y ambigüedad: estudio psicoanalítico*. Buenos Aires:
Paidós.] trans. S. Rogers and J. Churcher (eds J. Churcher and L. Bleger. *New
Library of Psychoanalysis*.) London: Routledge.
Christoffel, H. (1952). 'Le problème du transfert'. *Revue Francaise de
Psychanalyse*, 16(1–2): 178–203.
Fenichel, O. (1946). *The psychoanalytic theory of neurosis*. London: Kegan Paul,
Trench, Trubner & Co.
García Reinoso, D. (1956a). 'Cuerpo y mente'. *Revista de Psicoanálisis*, 13:
312–319.
García Reinoso, D. (1956b). 'Sobre el esquema corporal'. *Revista de
Psicoanálisis*, 13: 536–539.
Greenacre, P. (1959). 'Certain technical problems in the transference relation-
ship'. *Journal of the American Psychoanalytic Association*, 7: 484–502.
*Klein, M. (1952). 'The origins of transference'. In (1975) *Envy and gratitude
and other works 1946–1963* (pp. 48–56). London: The Hogarth Press.
Lagache, D. (1952). 'Le problème du transfert'. *Revue Française de
Psychanalyse*, 16(1–2): 5–122.
Liberman, D., Ferschtut, G. and Sor, D. (1961). 'El contrato analítico'. *Revista de
Psicoanálisis*, 18: 85–98.
Lieber, L.R. (1960). 'THE great discovery of modern mathematics'. *General
Semantics Bulletin*, 26–27.

Little, M. (1958). 'On delusional transference'. *International Journal of Psychoanalysis*, 39: 134–138.

Rodrigué, E. (1965). 'El contexto de la transferencia'. Buenos Aires: Asociación Psicoanalitica Argentina. Also in Rodrigué, E. and Rodrigué, G.T. (1966) *El contexto del proceso analítico* (pp. 202–232). Buenos Aires: Paidós.

Rodrigué, E. and Rodrigué, G.T. (1966). *El contexto del proceso analítico*. Buenos Aires: Paidós.

Wender, L. (1965). 'Reparación patológica y perversión'. Buenos Aires: Asociación Psicoanalitica Argentina.

Winnicott, D.W. (1949). 'Hate in the countertransference'. *International Journal of Psychoanalysis*, 30: 69–74; also in (1958) *Collected Papers* (pp. 194–203). London: Tavistock Publications Ltd.

Winnicott, D.W. (1956). 'On transference'. *International Journal of Psychoanalysis*, 37: 386–388; also in (1958) *Collected Papers* (pp. 295–299). London: Tavistock Publications Ltd.

Chapter 2

José Bleger and the relevance today of his dialectical frame[1]

Haydée Faimberg

Thinking is always a dialogue and its tool is dialectics, or rather, the very process of thinking is dialectical, whether consciously or not.[2]

(José Bleger)

Thinking about what makes a classic

Italo Calvino wrote that a classic is *a book that has never finished saying what it has to say*; and also that *every re-reading of a classic is as much a voyage of discovery as the first reading*. (I have proposed putting this definition to the test in order to distinguish true classics from idealized works.)

I have felt tempted by the 'possibility' suggested by Borges in one of his stories of making a map of the work of José Bleger on a scale of 1:1. In the new readings that will be made of Bleger's work, we need to confirm that the creative potential of his dialectical thinking goes on saying what it has to say.

Personally, my own mind is made up: José Bleger *is* a classic. This is the context in which I propose to consider the relevance today of this author's dialectical thinking. (As an ironic aside on my function as commentator, Calvino urges us to always read the original text itself and not the commentaries, since a classic is a work that constantly generates a pulviscular cloud of critical discourse around it, but always shakes the particles off.)

Were I to attempt to summarize Bleger's thinking, I might well defeat my own aims and deprive the reader of the means of gaining access unaided to the specific dialectics of the author's thinking. I have chosen to focus on the Blegerian concept of the dialectical frame. Even at the risk of yielding to a rather impressionistic style, I shall also mention some of the many problems raised by Bleger in his writings – his classes, courses, research groups, study groups, supervisions – in order to show how far ahead of his time he was and emphasize his *relevance to the present time*, on the condition that the reader thinks to re-contextualize them in the time when they were written.

José Bleger explored the implicit basic assumptions of psychoanalysis in order to frame problems, seek appropriate answers and contextualize a particular issue; he sought to compare in what ways different authors use the same terms. He would say, quoting Freud, that 'if you start by compromising with regard to words, you end up by falsifying ideas'. He was particularly careful to acknowledge his sources, always giving the names of authors. The position of not knowing (of which Marion Milner and W.R. Bion spoke, as did Lacan), we saw in action in his way of thinking, of teaching us a dialectic, of *teaching us to think*.

The quotation at the opening of this chapter continues as follows:

> Being able to think … means being able to tolerate the unknown, being able to accept a quantum of anxiety, being able to set problems; and being able to accept the eventuality of having to start again, because systematic (dialectical) thinking is like Kronos: it eats its own children.

Co-thinking (thinking with someone else) is what Enrique Pichon-Rivière called this function, brilliantly embodied by Bleger, the function of finding in ourselves a way of thinking that *concerns us*. A central concern that José Bleger was addressing throughout his work is the following: we should not be asking how man becomes social but about the process of his individuation.

It could be said that José Bleger wrote his first book on psychoanalysis, published in 1958 (at the age of 34), as an ethical act in order to create a theoretical context that would support him in his decision to be trained as an analyst (earlier in the 1950s) in the Argentine Psychoanalytical Association. The book received negative reviews, one of which Bleger answered by referring to 'Freud, my teacher' (*mi maestro Freud*). (While handing me the offprint in which he demonstrated the false reasoning of a critic, Bleger said mischievously that he did not want the gentleman in question to make a name for himself through having engaged in a polemic with him. And that he was therefore closing the discussion with that article.)

In the term 'psychoanalytical praxis', Bleger (1969, p. 993) includes the complex relationship between psychoanalytical theory, technique and psychoanalytical institutions. He criticizes an investigation conducted from a naturalistic standpoint and encourages what he calls phenomenal research (which he also often refers to as phenomenological research); he analyses the assumptions implicit in meta-psychological theorization and in the theorization of clinical experience, pointing out the *contradictions* with which they are approached. He likewise explores the *contradictions implicit in the theory of clinical experience*. Thus, for example:

> *Postulating the existence of projective-introjective identification for all cases implies the assumption that each subject is a 'closed system'* and that each one communicates through other channels with other human beings, while conceiving the participation of an original phenomenon implies that … human beings start from an 'open system' of organization and that … they become individualized.
>   (Bleger, 1967, p. 189 [pp. 186–187], italics added)

Together with Enrique Pichon-Rivière, José Bleger bases his psychoanalytical thinking on praxis. In his dialectical approach, he includes *contradiction* as an object of study. He considers that when the object of study is de-dialecticized, its exploration should be framed by dialectical logic. He thereby establishes a difference between the problem and how the problem is thought about (Bleger, 1969, pp. 997–999). This became the basic assumption of his epistemological project.

Bleger considered it an error to conduct research according to the rules of formal logic, which is the same logic that governs the process studied; because in this case, he writes, there is no longer any differentiation between the problem and the method of its investigation.

It might have been imagined in view of my training with José Bleger, but I was surprised to realize (when recently reading for the first time his 1969 study) that in a way I had been unknowingly endorsing *his epistemological project* in wondering whether 'in order to listen to narcissism I could propose a "non-narcissistic theory" *that would study narcissism without espousing the ego's narcissistic beliefs*' (Faimberg, 2005a, p. 3).

The theory I proposed is based on a dialectical logic to study (among other issues) the *dilemmatic* problems posed by narcissistic discourse and the narcissistic links between generations. (Almost all chapters of my book develop, from different angles and through clinical examples, this problematic.)

In this context I proposed the concept of the Oedipal Configuration and its narcissistic dimension:

> In the working through of the Oedipal conflict *in each and every analysis* we reach a moment of struggle against narcissistic figures. In this situation the subject feels that he totally possesses the object or he is totally excluded by the object: the patient functions with the logic of 'either–or'. I have called the product of this kind of logic a 'narcissistic dilemma'.
>
> (Faimberg, 1993a, p. 50)

I coined a particular expression to designate the narcissistic dilemma of the Oedipus myth: *Laïus is the filicide of a parricide*. This dilemma is the resultant of a narcissistic logic by which Laïus *interprets* that a son shall be necessarily parricidal and incestuous (Faimberg 1993b, pp. 69–71).

I had been studying narcissism as an *open model*. My approach is based on the Freudian idea that 'parental love, which is so moving and at bottom so childish, is nothing but the *parents' narcissism born again, which, transformed into object-love*, unmistakably reveals its former nature' (Freud, 1914, p. 91, italics added).

From his side, Bleger persistently criticized Freud's model of narcissism because he considered it to be a meta-psychological theory based on a *closed model*. In fact, I consider that I chose one of the two models that Freud follows in his 1914 essay 'On narcissism: an introduction'.

This example leads to the conclusion that Bleger's dialectical thinking gave me the means to study narcissism from my *own* perspective. *While my reading of Freud differs from Bleger's on this point,* I could, *on the basis of Bleger's own conceptualization*, think about the *dialectical pair* (open model/closed model) by which my hypothesis was framed. Indeed I think that narcissistic *discourse* is based on a closed model with a formal logic, and the approach to its study I propose is based on an open model and a dialectical logic (also based on *one* of Freud's models of narcissism).

The relevance of José Bleger's thinking is shown in the very way of going *in search of the contradiction*, since the formulation of contradictions *changes as new problems arise.*

We may thus see that in this precise example my debt to Bleger is that he suggested to me a possible approach, notwithstanding that I have a different object of study, the narcissistic link between generations (as well a different interpretation of Freud's point of view).

Such an example of disagreement brings us face to face with problems of misunderstanding through anachronism that stem unavoidably from Bleger's early death at the age of 49, on 20 June 1972.

Misunderstandings by anachronism

We do not know what José Bleger's re-reading of Freud would have been; this was a project he was planning (personal communication) in the year of his unexpected death.

We have already noted his position with regard to narcissism.

Bleger's repeated criticism of the 'biological' conception of the theory of the instincts *contains an error that paradoxically legitimizes his own criticism*: he understood Freud to be giving the name of 'instinct' to what Freud himself named *Trieb* (drive). In this sense, in its very wrongness, *his criticism anticipated* what was later recognized to be a mistranslation (in the light, I believe, of the writings of Lacan and of the *Vocabulaire* by Laplanche and Pontalis).

Furthermore, José Bleger maintained, in his classes and writings, *that the modes of psychic functioning defined by Freud anticipate the use of dialectical logic to study the psyche* in the place of formal logic. He also introduced us to Lacan's mirror stage (connecting it with Henri Wallon) at a time when it was not yet usual for that classic study to be cited.

To a question of mine (when he published his book [Bleger 1963]) about how it serves to think in terms of behaviour, Bleger replied with an example: tears *do not represent* sadness, they *are* sadness. I understood that he implicitly criticized the position of those who would take interpretation to be a work of 'simultaneous translation' (so to speak).

Jean-Luc Donnet (in a seminar held in the 1980s in the Paris Psychoanalytical Society) presented as an example of an excellent interpretation 'his sadness are his tears' formulated by Joyce McDougall.[3]

José Bleger anticipated as well *a way of thinking about psychotic functioning and psychosis* that has the potential for generating new ideas. The fact of viewing the formation of the psyche in accordance with an open model underpins one of José Bleger's most original contributions: the postulation of *[handwritten annotations in top margin:]* contradiction — Dialectic — evolution but no logical fit — Being — Nothing — Loa discourse between two or more people with different views

what he called a 'glischrocaric position'[4] (*posición glischo-cárica*), logically and chronologically[5,6] preceding the Kleinian paranoid-schizoid position.

In so far as he considers along with Bion *that in all patients there is a psychotic functioning that coexists with the neurotic functioning*, Bleger writes that there is a *dialectical* movement between the two.

Let me repeat that for our author the question is not how the patient became a social being but rather how he became an individual. For José Bleger, *the first categories for introducing order into the original state of un-differentiation* (conceptualized by the 'glischrocaric position'[7]) *are created in the paranoid-schizoid position*.

On the basis of praxis, José Bleger establishes the dialectical pair 'neurotic Oedipus' (conflictualizable) and 'psychotic Oedipus' (dilemmatic). The symbolic places that point to the unconscious family structure (father, mother, sons and daughters, brothers and sisters) are not differentiated in these cases and *cannot form conflictualizable dialectical pairs* (unless they are analysed). An example could be the paradigmatic case of Ana Maria described in his writings. This broadening of the psychoanalytical listening to psychotic functioning also enables Bleger to make psychotic patients analysable through the differentiation of what was previously un-differentiated. *He thereby avoids the error of applying the same Oedipal model to neurosis and to psychosis, as well as any 'orthopedic' attempt* (as Lacan would say) *to adapt the patient to a single, univocal reality*. Bleger thus questions, in order to criticize it, a basic assumption that could inform some psychoanalysis that there is *only one possible key to reality*, held by the analyst who would have then a normative role; and that the analysand must adapt to that one reality (a remarkable coincidence with Loewald's 1951 paper 'Ego and reality').

Could the reader see in what I have said any possible link with Lacan's 'the real' (*le réel*)?

José Bleger's dialectical frame

In his 1967 essay 'Psychoanalysis of the psychoanalytic frame', our author examines the psychoanalytical significance of the frame, not when it raises a problem (usual object of study) but indeed when the said frame does not constitute a problem. Bleger used to say that certain infinite 'pseudoscientific' precautions applied in psychoanalytical investigations or discussions were obsessional rituals reflecting a resistance against thinking.

[handwritten annotation at bottom:] Dialectical thinking → ability to view issues from multiple perspectives & arrives at most economical & reasonable reconciliation of contradictory information.

In the same context of resistance, Bleger studied the analytical frame as an institution in which an obsessional ritual can be established whose sole purpose is *to ensure the psychic survival of the analysand* – and, I would add, also perhaps of the analyst.[8]

Bleger would say that in order to investigate the frame and decide whether it has been turned into a ritual, we must employ dialectical logic to 'diagnose' whether the object of study (the frame itself) only ensures its survival *instead of facilitating psychic transformation.* (The difficulty in conceiving of a ritualization of the frame, before being noted by Bleger, might be due to the fact that a frame is by definition repetitive and consti-tutes the logical frame in which the analytical method is deployed to disclose the unconscious dimension.)

I shall now go on to introduce an additional key to facilitate our read-ing of Bleger. José Bleger implicitly draws on the Hegelian concept of *Aufhebung.*[9] This concept designates simultaneously the negation, aboli-tion *and* preservation of a term, a term that has been transformed and stands at a higher level (in the sense given to it by Kojève in his teachings; I understand in the same way the dialectical spiral proposed by Pichon-Rivière). As we know, in the Hegelian tradition, the *Aufhebung* constitutes an operation in relation to a dialectical pair. From the Blegerian text I shall select two dialectical pairs.

Bleger starts implicitly from a dialectical pair 'me/not-me' when refer-ring from the outset to the 'not-me'. He states that the 'not-me' has an *existence*, that it is not possible to consider that the 'not-me' is 'nothing' (p. 243 [p. 234]). Once he has affirmed the existence of the 'not-me', the author can postulate, as he does, that the patient's 'not-me' is lodged in the frame. In the Hegelian tradition, the 'not-me' constitutes the 'determined negation of me' (the 'not-me' defines something that is determined by the negation of me).

What I call the second dialectical pair constitutes the most original central thesis of José Bleger: there are *two frames* (and not only one) to be *differentiated each from the other.* One frame, proposed and maintained by the psychoanalyst, is consciously accepted by the patient; the other *is brought by the patient* and long remains mute.

Jacques Lacan and José Bleger were the only ones to raise the crucial problem of the ritualization of the frame, but their positions differ on this specific point. *Lacan, on the basis of his theory of the signifier, seeks to address the ritualization of the frame by investing it with movement* (scansion). *For Bleger, the ritualization of the frame is a symptom of resistance that can only be analysed by the psychoanalytical method itself, within a fixed frame. The analyst must guarantee the preservation of the frame since a process can only be investigated when the same constants are maintained – those, precisely, are what constitute the fixed frame.*

As paradoxical as may seem at first sight, the strict maintenance of the frame by the analyst is a *necessary and absolute condition* for going beyond its ritualized functioning. But Bleger goes on to add that its strict maintenance is *not a sufficient* condition. Since the frame is an institution, like every institution it follows the law of *transforming into a goal of survival the original goal* for which it was created. *And also the frame runs the risk of being ritualized in order to guarantee only its survival, and not the vitality of the psychoanalytical process with its capacity to produce psychic transformation.*

By preserving the psychoanalytical frame, the analyst preserves the 'not-me' of the analysand (his alienated aspects) until the second frame, which has long remained mute, begins to 'speak'. This is possible provided that the analyst is capable of listening to it and interpreting it so that the analysand can *hear in what way he is concerned* by what he brought with his second frame. Thus, without closing problems prematurely, he can leave questions open for as long as is necessary until the moment when a key is found.

> *What is always surprising and fascinating to me*, in analysing psychotics, is the fact that a total negation of the analyst coexists with an exaggerated susceptibility to any small deviation from 'what is usual' (the frame) and how the patient can become disorganized or turn violent, for example, because of a few minutes' difference at the beginning or end of the session. *I understand better now*: it is his meta-ego that becomes disorganized and that is to a large extent *all that he has*.
>
> (Bleger, 1967, p. 238 [p. 238], italics added)

I shall now refer to one of Bleger's cases and to one of my own. For both, the following comment by José Bleger is particularly relevant:

> I think that it does not make sense to always speak of an 'attack' on the frame when it is not respected by the patient. The patient 'brings

what he has' and it is not always an 'attack' but his own psychic organization (even though it is disorganized).

(Belger, 1967, p. 233, n. 10 [p. 233, n. 182])

The example of Bleger's patient will help us to understand how we *detect what condition of the patient's very existence comes into play when 'his' frame begins to speak.*

Bleger writes about this patient who had always paid punctually. A moment came when he contracted a debt with his analyst, and the second, mute, frame began to 'speak'. Bleger interprets that, up to that moment, the analysis had the role of preserving the patient's fantasy world (*his condition of existence*) in which he did not recognize any loss; in this case, the loss of the family fortune many years before. Up to that moment, paying on time meant to disavow that loss: 'I pay, therefore I am rich as my father and grandfather have *always been*'. If only one frame was conceived of, it would have been possible to speak of the debt as an 'attack' on the frame, and the aim would be to rapidly cancel it.

With the dialectic of the two frames, the patient's mute frame (masked by the ritualization of the frame) begins to 'speak'. When the patient subsequently wants to rush to settle the debt, Bleger *affirms the differentiation of the two frames through his interpretation*: he interprets that paying rapidly means bringing about the disappearance of the analyst in his *otherness and putting a stop to the painful process of transformation of his central fantasy.*

My hypothesis is that Bleger's interpretation is a moment of *Aufhebung* of the dialectic between the two frames: in this case it marks the moment of *recognition of otherness* (the analyst's and the patient's). I am referring not to the actual person of the analyst but to a recognition of the analytical function and also to the recognition of the analyst in his otherness.

We now see *in what way* José Bleger was the first to address *simultaneously* the problem of the ritualization of the frame and the need to keep it stable. Raising the problem of the ritualization of the frame without having at hand the two-frame solution would have created an insurmountable dilemma.

Now to a patient who had been for seven years in analysis with me.

I shall be talking about a session that led me to wonder, retroactively, why I had chosen to interpret as I did, given that evidently another way of listening was possible. On the basis of a segment of that session, I shall speak of the current relevance of José Bleger's thinking, there where I could most clearly hear its truth: on the basis of the experience of the session and *where I least expected it*. (I have italicized what caught my evenly suspended attention and the points I wish to bring to the attention of the reader.)

Jean had consulted me because he did not recognize his own desire regarding a life project (he had brilliantly completed his studies and was now trying to find his calling). In the months preceding the session he was weighing up the possibility of saying that perhaps he might consider that … he might end his analysis. His reluctance to say so made me think that *saying it* would be dangerous.

That day he rang 30 minutes before his time. (It had never happened before.)

I answered, and on the interphone asked him to return at the agreed time of the session.

Half an hour later, now on the couch, he said:

Jean: I don't know what came over me. I was sure it was the time of my session … (Silence). Yesterday afternoon, my father called on the phone. He was a bit confused. He asked if my mother was at my place … She should have been half an hour before at an appointment they had, and she still had not arrived. Father didn't tell me that he was at the entrance of my building. When I came here this morning I was wondering *whether I would recount* what happened, whether I would relate to you that he came up to my apartment, whether I would tell you what we spoke about. (Silence).

(In French, '*sonnette*' can designate the ring of the intercom; '*sonnette d'alarme*' is the term used for the alarm siren of ambulances or the fact of drawing attention to a danger … .)

Analyst: You rang my '*sonnette d'alarme*' (alarm bell) to tell me that *something that you were not going to say had to be heard by me at any price*.

Jean: Yes … I didn't want to say why was I feeling bad; I was telling myself that I should already have done something for my father, should have got him looked at by a doctor. And I imagined that *you would say to me* something like 'non-assistance to a person in danger'.

Analyst: As you are the one accusing yourself of that, we might think that *what I do not know does not exist, even if these are your own thoughts*.

Jean: Yesterday I asked my father some clear questions and discovered that he speaks easily if I ask him. Imagine my surprise when he told me that since he was small *he had always known* that his father had a double life. (Short silence.) *But of that he had never spoken,* neither with his father nor with his mother. Nor with us. *My father told me that when I was born he left me with his mother, my grandmother, who was feeling so abandoned by her own husband, as though dead, and never went anywhere. As soon as I was in her arms she revived and I became her source of life.* My sister didn't want to visit her *and I found it normal to revive her, visiting her often as a child.* She was so happy!! ...

Analyst: I heard another *'sonnette d'alarme'* in the last sessions, when you said that you did not know how some day you might be able to consider ending your analysis. Now we can hear that you are wondering if you would leave in me a *grandmother deprived of her 'therapeutic grandson'. An analyst who would only be able to keep on living through her patient.* (In that regard I thought that he was looking to see whether I had other patients in 'his session' [his second frame] half an hour before).

Jean: Yes ... (Thoughtful silence).

The rest of the session he talked *about what in his family (maternal and paternal) 'was known', and also about what it was known that 'it should not be mentioned'*: the disavowed aspects of family history.

Thinking about it retroactively, I was able to recognize the implicit position from which I had been listening and interpreting. Bleger's original concept of the *double frame* became the backdrop against which my listening and interpretation were organized. *A posteriori*, at that particular moment of crisis in the frame, I discovered (with Bleger) that *the frame that had never presented any problem had been gradually ritualized.*

The condition for this discovery to occur was that the analyst maintained the same frame, thereby highlighting the existence of a second frame that in the session began to 'speak'.

The analyst heard *'something that should not have been listened to, and interpreted that she had effectively listened to'* ... what?: *'to something that both should and should not be considered to be existing'* ('something that I do not know does not exist, even if these are your thoughts').

I realized that Jean is bringing here his second frame that had up to then been mute: we can reconstruct with the analysand for the first time *one* of Jean's versions of how *he interpreted ... the interpretation his father gave to his birth* as a therapeutic grandson offered to save the paternal mother from dying.

Conclusion/opening

In meeting the Argentine writer Vicente Zito Lema, Enrique Pichon-Rivière was able to maintain an unforgettable dialogue and recount his history as part of history with a capital H. Because of his early death, José Bleger could not meet 'his' Zito Lema so as to be able to tell us how to situate his history.

I wondered how Bleger's dialectical approach to problems will be taken up by the new generations who did not know him personally. The fact that his approach concerns *a different problem area*, in a new dialectical spiral, is wholly in keeping with Bleger's thinking. Recognizing this legacy does not endanger our otherness since he respected, in his dialogue, the personal path chosen by each one of us and helped us *to think what we did not even know we were thinking*. For him, disciples did not mean followers: I would say that it meant learning to question what remains hidden by so-called 'common sense', by the 'naturalistic approach'. Bleger led us to question what appears as a natural given that does not need to be examined.

José Bleger was the first to address simultaneously the problem of the ritualization of the frame and the need to keep it stable. The solution he brings is the dialectic of the two frames: this is his original concept that allows for the Aufhebung *of the problem.*

Should Italo Calvino's criterion allow us to think that José Bleger is a classic, it would still be up to his readers to make his writings say what they never finish saying ...

Notes

1   Translated from the original (published in *Calibán*) with some modifications. In contradistinction to a previous paper of mine where I use the word setting and also as is translated in the recent publication of Bleger, J. *Symbiosis and ambigüity* (Routledge 2013 [1967]), I prefer now to translate *'encuadre'* as *frame*, to better develop my idea of a dialectical pair of frames. Consequently, the quotations from Bleger are translated by me from the original edition in Spanish. The page numbers in parentheses refer to that edition and the page numbers between square brackets refer to the English edition of Bleger's book.

2   *Acta Neuropsiquiátrica Argentina* 1959, 5, 478.
3   In relation to behaviour, Pichon-Rivière would have said along with Bleger –
in order to criticize them – that behaviourists (like Watson and William
McDougall) focused on areas of the body and the external world, while disre-
garding the functioning of the mind. In addition, both Pichon-Rivière and
Bleger criticized those analysts who saw the study of the body and the external world as being dependent *exclusively* on the mind. Bleger's approach to
behaviour was related to the writings of Georges Politzer (which he managed
to have translated in full, writing a preface and numerous notes), of Daniel
Lagache, Merleau-Ponty and Sartre.
    To partially contextualize in a nutshell Bleger's thinking when saying
'tears *do not represent* sadness, they *are* sadness', reference may be made to
Enrique Pichon-Rivière's theory on the *three areas* (mind, body, world). We
do not have room here to develop this point or look at the close relationship
between the ideas of Pichon-Rivière (who was his teacher) and those of
Bleger (who was his most brilliant disciple). Let us just say that Pichon-
Rivière's theory of the '*vínculo*' (word that may be approximately translated
as 'link') provided an essential dialectical matrix for the thinking of José
Bleger. And it was because of this theory of the '*vínculo*' that the ideas of
Melanie Klein and of Fairbairn were *already reinterpreted* by those authors.
The paranoid-schizoid and depressive positions of Melanie Klein were used
by Pichon-Rivière and Bleger in their thinking, but the object relation theory
underwent a change: those positions were already subjected to a *reinterpre-
tation*. In Latin America, the highly appreciated studies of Isidoro Berenstein
and Janine Puget developed the theory of '*vínculo*'. As regards my own
thinking, both the theory of the '*vínculo*' (I became so familiarized with in the
seminars of Pichon-Rivière and José Bleger) along with the *unconscious
inclusion of the analysand in a family structure*, brought about a *radical
decentring* of my way of conceiving the theory of object relations, the
construction of the different spaces we study in psychoanalysis and the function of recognizing otherness as well as the difference between generations.
When my book was studied in Argentina, its way of approaching problems
was associated by some readers with the thinking of Piera Aulagnier.
Curiously enough, when I told Piera in what way I was in agreement with her
ideas … we could not manage to agree! Probably this was due in part to the
fact that she did not accept the ideas of Winnicott or Bion even when I linked
them to Freud's thinking. Piera Aulagnier preferred to speak of what she
called her theoretical 'options' and disregarded some authors. Did she occupy
a function in Argentina in particular in the 1980s, representing aspects of
French psychoanalytical culture that could be compared to that occupied in
Latin America in the 1960s by Enrique Pichon-Rivière and José Bleger? Let
us close this short parenthesis.
4   For the concept of 'glischrocaric position' see Chapter 2 of Bleger, J. (2013
[1967]) *Symbiosis and ambiguity: a psychoanalytic study*. Rogers, S., Bleger,

L. & Churcher, J., translators; Churcher, J. & Bleger L., editors. New Library of Psychoanalysis. London (Routledge).
5   In relation to psychic temporality, see Faimberg 1998, 2007, 2012, 2013.
6   Thomas Ogden referred to a position preceding the paranoid-schizoid position, probably without knowing that Bleger had proposed and developed it from his perspective during the 1960s ('glischrocaric position').
7   Studied in particular in Chapter 3 of *Simbiosis and ambigüity*.
8   I am thinking here of the concept of 'bastion' (Baranger & Baranager, 1961).
9   This term could be roughly translated as 'overcome'. I suggest that it should not be translated by 'synthesis' if we wish to respect the meaning given by Kojève (as I do, and I believe as Bleger does).

Bibliography

Baranger, M. & Baranger, W. (1961). La situación analítica como campo dinámico, in W. Baranger, M. Baranger (1969), *Problemas del campo psicoanalítico*, pp. 129–164. Buenos Aires, Kargieman.

Bleger, J. (1958). *Psicoanálisis y dialéctica materialista*, Buenos Aires, Paidós.

Bleger, J. (1959). *Acta neuropsiquiátrica Argentina*, 5, p. 478.

Bleger, J. (1963). *Psicología de la conducta*, Buenos Aires, eUDeBA.

Bleger, J. (1967). Psicoanálisis del encuadre psicoanalítico, in J. Bleger, *Simbiosis y ambigüedad*, pp. 237–250. Buenos Aires, Paidós..

Bleger, J. (1969). Teoría y práctica en psicoanálisis. la praxis psicoanalítica, *Revista Uruguaya de Psicoanálisis*, T. XI, pp. 287–303. Montevideo, APU. Also in: *Rev. de Psicoanálisis* (2003), T. IX, 4, pp. 1191–1204. Buenos Aires, APA.

Calvino, I. (1981 [1991]). *Perché leggere i classici*, Milán, Palomar.

Faimberg, H. (1993a). The narcississtic dimension of the Oedipal Configuration, in H. Faimberg (2005), *The telescoping of generations: listening to the narcissistic links between generations*. London and New York, Routledge.

Faimberg, H. (1993b). The Oedipus myth revisited, in H. Faimberg (2005), *The telescoping of generations: listening to the narcissistic links between generations*, pp. 63–75. London and New York, Routledge.

Faimberg, H. (2005a). Introducción, in H. Faimberg (2007), *El telescopaje de generaciones: a la escucha de los lazos narcisistas entre generaciones*, pp. 19–22. Buenos Aires, Amorrortu.

Faimberg, H. (2005b [2007]). *El telescopaje de generaciones: a la escucha de los lazos narcisistas entre generaciones*, Buenos Aires, Amorrortu.

Faimberg, H. (2006). José Bleger y su encuadre dialéctico, *La Jornada de Homenaje al Dr. José Bleger*, la Facultad de Psicología de la Universidad de Buenos Aires (UBA), inédito.

Faimberg, H. ([1998] 2012). *Nachträglichkeit* and Winnicott's 'Fear of Breakdown', in J. Abram (ed.), *Donald Winnicott Today*. Chap. 8, pp. 205–212, London.

Faimberg, H. (2007). Plea for a broader concept of *Nachträglichkeit*. *Psychoanalytic Quarterly*, 76:4, pp. 1221–1240.

Faimberg, H. (2012). Listening to the Psychic Consequences of Nazism in Psychoanalytic Patients. *Psychoanalytic Quarterly*, 81:1, pp. 157–169.

Faimberg, H. (2013). The as yet situation in Winnicott's *Fragment of an Analysis* (1955). « You Father did no make you the honour of ... yet », *The Psychoanalytic Quarterly*, LXXXII:4, 849–875.

Freud, S. (1914). On narcissism: an introduction. *S.E. vol XIV*, pp. 67–104. London, Hogarth Press.

Loewald, H. (1951). Ego and reality, in H. Loewald (1989), *Papers on psychoanalysis*, pp. 3–20. New Haven and London, Yale University Press.

Pichon-Rivière, E. (1957 [1980]). *Teoría del vínculo*, Buenos Aires, Nueva Vision.

Politzer, G. (1928 [1951]). *Critique des fondements de la psychologie*, París, Rieder.

Politzer, G. (1947 [1954]). *La crise de la psychologie contemporaine*, París, éditions Sociales.

Zito Lema, V. (1976). *Conversaciones con Enrique Pichon-Rivière: Sobre el arte y la locura*, Buenos Aires, Timerman editores.

Supplementary bibliography

Aragonés, R. J. (1975). Narcisismo y sincretismo, dos teorías complementarias, *Rev. Psicoanálisis*, Vol. 32, 3, pp. 429–462. Buenos Aires, APA.

Aragonés, R. J. (1977). Estudio del vínculo narcisista: algunas consecuencias de su revisión, *Rev. Psicoanálisis*, Vol. 34, 2, pp. 213–267. Buenos Aires, APA.

Lagache, D. (1949). De la psychanalyse à la analyse de la conduite, *Rev. Franç. de Psychan*, Vol. 1.

Lagache, D. (1953). Conduite et communications en psychanalyse, *Bull. Psychol.*, Vol. 6, 7.

Lorenz, K. (1935). Companionship in bird life, in C. H. Schiller (ed.) (1957), *Instinctive behaviour. The development of a modern concept*, pp. 83–128. Nueva York, Int. Univ. Press.

Lorenz, K. (1937). The nature of instinct, in C. H. Schiller (ed.) (1957), *Instinctive behaviour. The development of a modern concept*, pp. 129–175. Nueva York, Int. Univ. Press.

Merleau-Ponty, M. (1945). *Phénoménologie de la perception*, París, Gallimard.

Merleau-Ponty, M. (1957). *La estructura del comportamiento*, Buenos Aires, Hachette.

Sartre, J.-P. (1940). *L'imaginaire*, París, N.r.F.

Part I

Comparative models of the function of the frame

Chapter 3

Frame matters

Lynne Zeavin

Fred Sandback's minimalist works are colorful structures made of yarn or string, often in the shape of rectangles or squares configuring the image of a frame. These frames constructed from string are suspended in space and bracket an area, giving it a designation. The effect is that of a picture the content of which is not so much missing as pending. These are fragile structures, nearly virtual, marking an area, an opening. It would seem that they reference what is not there, namely a painting or a work of art, but they refer more actively and broadly to perception itself, a testament to the fact that our minds contribute to what is being seen, to that which is made or undone, imagined, and engaged through the workings of our wishes and our phantasies. Sandback once said that he wanted to make sculpture that didn't have an inside, but given that his sculptures occur in space, they are always being given an inside through the active engagement of the viewer. The figure of the string designates a ground that only comes alive through seeing it, seeing into and through and around it for what is and what isn't there. I am reminded of a quote from Ellsworth Kelley (1992) who said that what we want from art is "a sense of fixity, a sense of opposing the chaos of daily living. This is an illusion, of course. What I've tried to capture is the reality of flux, to keep art an open, incomplete situation, to get at the rapture of seeing."

Something similar might be said of Sandback—though Sandback is interested in exposing the wishes involved in looking and perceiving alongside whatever might be presumed to be rapturous. Both artists emphasize perception and seeing, each is occupied with form in a way that parallels the psychoanalytic situation, where we also have a frame, a frame that really only becomes meaningful when infused with the work-ings of imagination and phantasy of both analyst and patient. Superimpose the frame—for example by saying to the patient "you must be feeling deserted by me," and you lose the possibility of using the frame for generating an unexpected psychoanalytic understanding. However, if you see the frame as providing an opening that is not prematurely filled with assumption it becomes the space for psychoanalytic meaning-making, the structural ground upon which psychoanalytic conversations rest, and without which they lose their orienting vector. I would argue that illusion and phantasy can only be recognized fully against the backdrop of the frame. Furthermore, I want to suggest that the frame, inflected from the start with the analyst's presence (the analyst sets the hours, fee, etc.) fuses the structure and function of analysis—form and content. The analyst is always part of the frame, the frame is inextricable from transference meanings ascribed to the analyst. The frame is imbued with the analyst's function and in no small way, when referred to meaningfully, simultaneously conjures the analyst's role as witness in analysis.

Like the string hung at varying lengths, achieving different proportions, the psychoanalytic frame varies in form and structure depending on the practitioner. Still, it is felt as a delimiting presence. What exactly constitutes this presence is certainly different for different analysts coming from diverse theoretical orientations, philosophical traditions, and bodies of technique. I imagine that some of what I take to be a vital function of the frame—the fixed hour, adhering to time, the fee, the schedule—might to some seem unnecessary impositions of analytic order.

For an analysis to proceed something must act as a frame—something that implicitly and explicitly binds the setting. The frame is both an arena of safety, where the most private dimensions of human experience can be expressed and addressed, and an area of meaning, a designation, an available referent for analytic work. It seems to me that the frame draws a boundary around an area that both participants can view, can think and talk about, a bounded arena that becomes the site of psychoanalytic conversation and inquiry. Such boundaries are important—they designate areas that one does not cross.

What allows for therapeutic dialogue, what gives particular forms of saying their meaning is the fact of the frame in its place. Take for example the patient who arrives on a Monday feeling dejected after a weekend away. This experience—however commonplace—will be understood differently in different treatments depending on one's understanding of the frame. Here, when I speak of "the frame," I am adding something in addition to the schedule, the time of the session and the fee—I am adding not

only these structural perimeters, but what they point to, what they necessarily derive from and stand in relation to. For me what is potentiated by
the frame, and what is inextricably bound to it, is the transference and
countertransference of the analyst and patient in the sessions.

I would suggest that the weekend only has meaning if it arises in the
context of a clearly defined and sustained schedule that itself acquires
meaning through its very repetitiveness. The patient experiences the
analyst's explicit requirement to attend regularly and on time (a frame
issue) and in this way a relationship to the time (and by extension the
analyst) is established. Being late or prompt, missing sessions, taking time
away, the analyst's holidays, are all imbued with phantasy and meaning.
The frame is both integral to the analytic work and inextricable from the
analytic relationship, by which I mean the transference relationship. The
aforementioned weekend couldn't be a weekend were the analyst's expectation of (and the patient's reactions to) the daily ritual of analysis not in
place. In addition, the weekend becomes a weekend not only in its prox-
imity to the analytic week, but also in relation to the host of ideas and
feelings set in motion by the analyst setting up the schedule, offering the
hours, billing for the time, being available and then not, etc.

Along these lines, John Steiner (personal communication) often gives
the advice that the analyst should write the word holiday or weekend in
big bold letters above the couch as a reminder that schedule adjustments
have distinct and far-reaching meaning for the patient that—at least in
America—might go unnoticed or unmentioned by analyst and patient
alike. His advice refers to the belief that the frame—and here I mean the
time and frequency of the session, the fee, and the analyst's analytic attitude (a specific form of very intense attention, which I will describe
shortly) all undergird the work of analysis and give it its particular meaning. It is in this context that breaks, separations, and holidays acquire
meanings that inform how the patient views the analytic set up, and how
the patient experiences the analytic process. I suppose one of the very
fundamental developmental aspects of how the frame matters refers to the
presence or absence of the analyst. O'Shaughnessy, writing about the
development of the internal object world, notes (following Bion) that the
absent object—the breast or mother absent, is at first experienced as a bad
breast present, and that initially the real good external object is required to
keep terrible anxieties at bay. Specifically, because of the child's own
attacks on the object, the internal object can be felt to be damaged, and the

real external object is a reassuring proof that the object is all right. Over the course of development and in analysis this feature of object relations is relived.

O'Shaughnessy (2015) describes a progression by which the absent object can cease to be a bad object present. Psychoanalysis can work to achieve this, particularly when the work is sensitized to absences, phantasized or real. O'Shaughnessy remarks that developmental progress demands that the child require that his object be absent some of the time: "Indeed the continuous presence of the object would be persecuting; the child would feel the object was intruding into his identity and he would also be burdened by guilt for claiming the object for himself" (2015, p. 31). It is the depressive position and concern for the object that eventually allows the child to give the object some freedom, to realize that the mother is not his sole possession. Eventually, if all goes well, the child can come to feel that the absence is "reasonable and desirable even while it is missed. This means that the object that the child internalizes is not in decline, but is alive, and can sustain him from within in the absence of his external object" (p. 31).

The comings and goings of the analyst therefore have a crucial place in the inner life of our patients, recalling formative absences and proximities that when attended to can potentiate psychic change. Absences in analysis, the analyst's or the patient's, are both quotidian and rife with meaning. In no small way absences and separations refer to a crucial, necessarily idiosyncratic, aspect of early life, one that fundamentally structures for the mind and the individual in relation with his objects. It is essential to pick these things up and address them, but essentially impossible without a working frame.

The analyst's attention

The frame activates experiences on the part of the patient and the analyst—and here we encounter an additional dimension of the work, the setting itself, something we could think of as that which is framed. Frames are everywhere in analysis. The analyst's attention and interpretation affords a kind of framing, an underscoring, a demarcation. In addition to the hours and the fee, the setting is made up of the analyst's bearing, how she attends, what she orients herself by, how she organizes her analytic listening, and her modes of understanding. The frame has several functions and manifests broadly even while having specificities: it marks off the area that is analytic, it is imbued with the analyst's own subjective force, it stands for the analyst, it allows the analysis to proceed. However, it requires the analyst's own labor, what Sodre (2015, p. 158) has called a very specific form of analytic listening:

> What is unique and uniquely effective in the capacity to provide mutative interpretations of unconscious communications is a very particular quality of attention (if you don't have the capacity for it, you can't be an analyst, no matter how loving, clever, or knowledgeable you may be). It is this particular kind of very intense attention which holds the patient, it consists of a very un-natural way of hearing communications, backed by a very complex picture of how the mind works, and a very specialized technique of imparting the information, the new knowledge achieved by the combination of observations and theory. What is being carefully observed takes place within an artificially created situation … the situation is unique, emphasized by its very strict boundaries and fostering of as much freedom in thinking and verbalizing as is possible.

The contemporary Kleinian notion of the here and now places an emphasis on the patient's internal object world and phantasy as it finds expression in the moment to moment unfolding of the analytic session. As such, the concept of the here and now is orienting to the analyst—both to the here of the session—(the frame as it pertains to setting), and the now—(the frame as it pertains to time). For Klein the mind is constructed from the very first by the presence of an archaic ego and object (along with the drive). The early ego (capable of archaic defense) in conjunction with the presence of the object form the basis for all of development and lay down the foundations of an internal object world. This internal object world contains the history of one's object relationships. History therefore for the Kleinians doesn't involve a retelling or a discussion about one's object relations. Rather, object relations are lived/relived in the transference and countertransference, are vivified in the present: hence the here and now. The here and now designates a frame within the session—deriving from the idea that a patient will communicate, via projection, projective identifications, and other means, internalized object relationships that are alive in the moment even while representing the patient's past. These object relations are activated by the analytic space and are expressed within the frame of the here and now.

In her paper, "Where is here, when is now," O'Shaughnessy (2015) makes the point that analysis occurs in a specific space and a time—the here and the now of the analytic setting. Like Sandback's string paintings, the analytic setting, and specifically the frame, designates a point, a here, and a time, the now. The analytic frame however, is also a container and awaits the patient's fantasy material (the contained) to give it its actual shape. Until this material is contained, the now of the patient might be anywhere but now, and the here other than here. Like the String sculpture, nothing might occupy the space, we might assume the patient's presence when he is anything but here with us. O'Shaughnessy understands this beautifully when she writes (2015, p. 262):

> But where is here? In material reality X is in analysis – he comes for sessions, and in a corner of my room I sit in my chair and he lies on my couch. However, in psychic reality I think he is in a corner outside the house of analysis.

She then describes the way her patient attempts to get her to meet him "outside the ordinary frame of analysis." The here where he wants to meet is a place of special treatment, special engagement—and were there not a frame this aspect of the patient's inner world of object relationships might go overlooked. The "here" of the frame illuminates the "there" that the patient actually may be occupying.

The frame in practice

I would like to turn now to a few clinical examples that explore different aspects of the frame. The following three vignettes illustrate a broad variety of ways in which the frame can be experienced and worked with in day-to-day clinical practice.

Ms. A.

Ms. A., a patient who is reluctant to discuss transference, brings up her anxieties about an upcoming holiday. She will be going to a country that is a favorite holiday destination and this holiday means that she will miss two weeks of analysis. Ordinarily she won't discuss anything about breaks, often giving me the impression that she doesn't register her being away or my own. It seems that acknowledging anything about the interruption might stir up some uneasiness about my thinking she is somehow "too much"—itself a familiar theme. It is important to this patient that she not need something from me, and she avoids recognizing herself as at all vulnerable within the analytic process. However, before this trip (and we have been talking about her way of negating any response to breaks for some time) she becomes stricken with the fear that she will contract a terrible disease and worries about getting the proper "shots" before going. As the analytic week unfolds Ms. A. discusses with great intensity her fears about disease and a variety of somatic anxieties for which she has sought the proper inoculations. As she talks, it becomes clear that having been able to acquire these inoculations is important to my patient, a testament to her abilities, her control, and her self-sufficiency.

It occurs to me that we can view this as her way of inoculating herself against the break from analysis and her analyst—that is she inoculates herself against depending on her analyst and her treatment through a regressive return to the somatic anxieties of her childhood, which she is able to master through enlisting the care of another doctor who she feels in charge of. Her somatic anxieties, though they are troubling to her and reflect anxiety about herself at a deeper level, remain an area that she feels she can and must solve by herself, whereas transference feelings and fears are profoundly unsettling to her and feel beyond her control. She is reluctant to acknowledge her concerns about her analyst's investment in her, her worries about the realness of the analyst's feelings. These concerns come up in passing but are difficult to sustain an interest in. Nonetheless, they find their way into discussions of her schedule, the fee, and other aspects of the frame where she absolutely feels the analyst's presence and exertion of control. The inoculation that she is so concerned with acquiring refers directly to her need to be immune to the effects of the analyst's bearing, separateness, and private life—all of which contribute to the frame.

Ms. B.

Here is another moment taken from my work with a different patient, Ms. B. In this particular session I had decided to refrain from going along with the patient's request to use the outlet in my office to charge her phone. Though it is common for patients to ask to charge their phones, to me the request always raises an issue regarding the frame—i.e. what part of the analyst's office is available and what is off limits. At this moment, with this patient, it felt important to ask her to see if she could wait. In any other context outside the frame of analysis, to refuse such a request would be ludicrous, but in the logic of analytic work, it seemed the correct thing to do.

The session in question occurred after a devastating hurricane when my office had been closed for a week. During the previous session she had described how she and her family had gone uptown and had stayed in a very expensive and luxurious hotel in order to be near a friend about whom she feels very ambivalent. In the session she said that she resented how expensive the hotel was and that she wished she could feel more grateful. There was something very uncomfortable about this session; it felt as if the patient had no awareness of anything beyond her own comfort but also some awareness of a "lack of gratitude" that I thought might refer to her experience of being a bit cut off and removed from other people and also from her analysis. In this context she arrived for the following session, phone in hand, and asked if she could charge it using my charger. I asked her to "hang on" and to see if it might be possible to hold off so that we could talk about it.

She was aghast and visibly angered and unsettled by my analytic/ frame-oriented stance.

"My phone is *dead*," she exclaimed. She explained that her son and his babysitter were coming to meet her after her session and that they wouldn't be able to get in touch with her. She was almost immediately upset and slightly tearful. She said, "You will have to contend with knowing that you have denied me something." I know that it is unusual to do in analysis but also so culturally ordinary to charge a phone. She found it outrageous that I would withhold something from her after all we had discussed about her difficulty feeling need and her uncertainty about whether anyone really cares or not. Here, she has asked for something she needs and I have dared to withhold it. What kind of analyst does that make me? "I really think this is a mistake," she says. "You are making a mistake. I just want my telephone charged. Nothing else matters. Nothing else can matter. I suppose you want to have a meaningful conversation. That's not going to happen."

I commented that she seemed to be experiencing my suggestion that we talk about this as purposely withholding and that she felt I was doing something to her about which I should feel bad. I said that I thought she sensed my interest in trying to understand and in having a useful conversation and observed that she seemed intent on frustrating my wish. She smiled when I said this, then repeated that a meaningful conversation was not going to happen.

I reflected that she felt I had made a mistake—I then suggested the mistake might be in thinking we could have a conversation, and that now we were in a struggle about that. She sensed that I wanted to have a conversation but she wouldn't have that conversation. It seemed to me to be very much about power—who has power, who withholds from whom. Being without power was an important theme during the hurricane and also an important theme in our work together. Ms. B. was mute as a child and there was a muteness in the analysis which was especially active underneath a current of apparent compliance and attentiveness. Here, in this session something felt less mute to me and more alive.

She became tearful and asked, "How can you do this? There is nothing to learn, what is there to learn? I just want my phone charged. It's such a culturally normal thing to do."

"Yes" I said, "you can go into Starbucks or anywhere and charge your phone, but there is something about analysis not being like everywhere else, and perhaps that rankles or unsettles you. Can we think about what that is?"

"I suppose I would be taking something I am not supposed to take" she responded, "getting something—wanting you to give to me special treatment. When I said you have to contend with knowing you have deprived me you have to contend with my anger. Maybe that's it, maybe that's relevant."

"Yes" I said, "I have to be able to contend with your feeling of anger and your feelings of disappointment, criticism and frustration in a moment where you are taken aback—you feel you should have a different kind of treatment and this kind of treatment makes you call everything into question. I guess I also have to deal with my anger and frustration. Maybe it's right that I feel myself holding out, I won't give you what you want if you won't give me what I need."

I am aware that my not 'allowing' my patient to charge her phone was a rather old-fashioned psychoanalytic maneuver. Regardless, I would suggest that by holding a frame around the hour, around the boundaries of what I do and do not provide as a psychoanalyst, I was able to allow something to be expressed that otherwise would be avoided, or simply comfortably kept out of view. What emerged in later sessions was Ms. B.'s appreciation of my ability to say no to her, that 'no' is something she fears saying, for example to her children, because of its communicative force—i.e. she worries that 'no' signals not so much the lack of love, but the presence of hatred. She eventually told me that my saying no to her suggested that I am not too afraid of my hatred.

Framing the here and now

Dr. T., a patient in her mid-forties came to analysis after a melancholic reaction to the death of her mother. Dr. T. was a thoughtful, successful married mother of two young children who worked as an internist in a busy New York City medical practice. She often felt gripped by a feeling of insufficiency despite her obvious success in her professional and family life. This initial feeling would lead to an internal onslaught of self-berating thoughts that left her feeling that everything in her life really amounted to nothing. At the same time she was driven to give to others in a most generous way, though she rarely felt she was doing or giving enough.

In the treatment I felt from Dr. T. a need to see me as capable, very engaged, extremely thoughtful and caring in order to keep at bay a picture of me as more demanding, needy, fragile, or preoccupied. As long as she could conjure an image of me in this way analysis proceeded well—but when she sensed, however slightly, a wavering of my attention or a shift in my mood—and she was highly tuned in and sensitive to such shifts—she reacted with great upset and with a powerful shift of her own.

One such moment occurred in the second year of treatment. I had asked Dr. T. if she could move her time from the afternoon to the early morning to accommodate a change in my own schedule that I needed to make. Dr. T., as usual, was accommodating. She then had two dreams one night apart.

The first dream was that she and her daughter were laughing. It was a very pleasurable laughter, not too manic, she said, just a very full-hearted pleasurable laughter, the way they would laugh at times when things were going well and they were happy. She loved the feeling of this in the dream. Then she said to the daughter "we have to stop" and woke up.

As she told me the dream I was thinking of the ways that she and I have to be engaged in a kind of laughter, not laughter precisely, but a kind of good feeling, even an excessively good feeling that protects against what manic feelings protect against in general: a sense of something coming between us of a more persecutory valence. The laughter present in the dream, and in our work together, was more than simple mania though—for laughter can be very positive, generative, even. As long as there is laughter, everything is felt to be good—good until there is, inevitably, an ending. The dream contains the ending—not only of laughter, but of the dream itself, and more specifically, the session itself, which had also ended, and ended with more of a troubled feeling than either my patient or I could recognize at the time.

In the session I got caught up somehow in this very good feeling, and I was unable at the time to see the ways in which it shielded her feelings about the change of hour. We did discuss her need to feel very good with me and about me, how the "we have to stop" might be a reference to me in the analysis keeping a lid on things, not letting things get too out of control or too "manic". The crucial thing though—the dream as a response to my asking for a change of session—didn't come up sufficiently. The point I mean to illustrate here is how a simple issue of the frame gave rise to an enormously important set of reactions in the patient that were of great use to the analysis—in part because we both had a role in it, and the ground was unambiguously clear.

After this session Dr. T. had a second, much more frightening dream that disturbed her sleep and left her acutely anxious. The dream featured the band, Pussy Riot, a performance group from Russia who participated in various protests against the Russian government, acts of defiance for which they were harshly punished with imprisonment. In the dream Dr. T. was a member of Pussy Riot and she was going to help to stage a revolt. She was up all night in a state of acute turbulence and anxiety and the next day came to her session very upset.

What emerged was a progression. She had consoled herself with the laughter dream—a dream in which everything really was good and more than all right between us—where there was nothing to worry about, nothing to fear. I had in effect bought into it, missing her underlying feelings about changing her hour. During the night of the Pussy Riot dream she felt besieged, filled with feelings of hatred that were felt to be a source of persecutory attack.

She kept wondering, why had I asked her to change her afternoon hour for a morning one. *Didn't I know* that the mornings were important to her, a time with her children before work, a rare space in which she had time for herself? Why did I want to take that from her? Why didn't I care that I was taking it from her?

And furthermore, what was I doing with that time—a Friday afternoon—she imagined I had asked her to change because I was going off with my family or my husband, maybe to my country house, or maybe just selfishly wanting to rearrange for other reasons of convenience. This caused a riot. *Riot.* I'm drawn to another association of the word—when two people laugh together they can say, "what a riot." Somehow in missing her important underlying experience and expression in the dream, I missed the other dimension—her fury, her hurt, her rivalry—but most important of all, I think, her need for me to see, to know, not to leave her alone with a most terrible experience which then becomes a torture.

In the laughter dream there is a recapitulation of an early idealized relationship between mother and daughter, a pleasurable union that admits of no one else. This state of mind screens out fears of various sorts—fears of rivalry with others, with the unpleasant states of feeling which arise in the context of rivalry—in particular fear of confronting the analyst, fear of her own anger and disappointment, fear of the states of mind that idealization shields, in other words. It also at least pretends to a certain kind of knowing together, being together, which is very different from the isolation and attack present in Dr. T.'s awful night and her terrifying dream.

Two people together, laughing in sync, in harmony, no otherness, no divide—and no problem with the frame. The frame and my disregard of the frame generates a powerful anxiety that I am not adequately tuned in to my patient's needs. This riot of feeling protects against a much more disturbing riot—starting perhaps with a sexual rivalry—a pussy riot—that has to do with my patient feeling me as not only not with her, but against her. Having dropped her, a riot ensues as she lets me know (possibly for the first time) how dreadful it is to have an object who can be so thoughtless and so misattuned.

About six months later, on a Friday the patient reported the following dream:

"I am in the car with Robin Williams, and he is in a bad way. He is self-absorbed and recalcitrant, but then I realize that in my presence he cheers up. I can make him laugh." (This was before the suicide of Williams, but his addictions were well known and his diagnosis of bipolar illness already in the press.)

Dr. T. explained how, "It is such a wonderful feeling to be able to make him laugh—to be the one who can cheer him up." She discussed her sense of having that capacity, as well as the pressure, the imperative to persue it. If she doesn't do it she will feel the onslaught of guilt. She feels that with me—the need to keep me buoyant and alive in the transference, and she feels it with all of her objects—the imperative to keep them alive and happy.

I said it must be very unsettling to think of me as not-buoyant. She worries about my real feelings toward her, my irritation or self-absorption, and this is a weekend—she worries about me on the weekend, what happens to me when I am not in her sight.

Agreeing with my interpretation, she then described how she worries that I may be glad to see her go. Returning to the dream, Dr. T. said she didn't really believe I was depressed, even though she could see she has conjured a very worrisome figure in her dream—someone who makes people laugh, gives a great deal to others, but secretly is in bad shape, maybe terrible shape. She then associated with the name in the dream, Robin Williams, which is an amalgam of two of her brothers—Robin and William, one of whom is often in a state of significant psychological torment, near breakdown.

Dr. T.'s effort to keep things nice between us, very close and sympathetic, came into full expression in relation to the frame and the issues that arose in her reactions to the schedule. For Dr. T., working with the transference meant working with the frame and visa versa. Working with the frame allowed us to hone in on the various meanings of the internalized object relationships that arose in response to our work at the intersection of structure and content. It was also a Friday session (before a weekend), so feelings of exclusion were incipiently present, as was the fear that she can't know exactly where I will be over the weekend.

On the Monday after the weekend Dr. T. brought a very different dream into our session:

"I am on the street with my daughter. We are walking on this street and everything seems fine until a taxi goes by. The driver catches my eye, and then he turns his car, and I know I am in for it. I know he is going to kill me. I scream to my daughter, 'RUN!'"

Upon waking from this dream the overwhelming persecutory dimension is clear to her. She has been caught and she will be turned against, turned on, stamped out, killed. It is a terrifying dream. When analyzing the dream in session, Dr. T.'s associations included the weekend, feeling far away from me, and feeling cut off from feelings of love and of goodness inside herself. What was harder to acknowledge was her anger at me for leaving her in this state, alone with an anger that still feels too dangerous to acknowledge as it seems to summon an internal attack, a vengeful attack like the one represented in her dream.

Here again I have the sense that the frame is a mode of containment, or put another way, offers the opportunity for a kind of witnessing, an acknowledgment that time in analysis matters, that sessions and continuity matter, that the patient's personal sense of what matters does not have to be borne entirely alone. The effort to keep things warm and close on one level, covers over another more frightening and anxiety-ridden level. In Kleinian terms, depressive anxieties give way to a much more paranoid state. Tracking these various levels is part of the framing work of analysis. My guess is that for Dr. T. there is a deep experience of being dropped early in her life, and a premature need to be a "big girl" and manage too much on her own. Analyzing the frame brought us together in some important ways. She revolted against having to be so nice in the Pussy Riot dream. Another way of thinking of this is to inquire, as Edna O'Shaughnessy (2015) does, "what is a clinical fact." For O'Shaughnessy, a clinical fact is a shared emotional understanding that can only be derived in the shared setting of the here and now of analytic work. A shared view is only possible if there is an agreed upon area, an area both parties sign on to, even if the meanings are only incipient and as yet to be derived.

When the frame is in place, i.e. we meet on a Friday at 10 a.m., then the question of moving that hour or missing the hour becomes potentially relevant in a way that is not merely logistical but is infused with phantasy and meaning. Like Sandback's string sculptures, the frame of the hour and the fee merely designate a border, suspended in space. It is what comes through this border that is of interest—the unconscious phantasies concerning the analyst's actions, state of mind, intentions, concerns, alongside and mingled in with the patient's concerns about her own state of mind, her own life. It is the same with our theories, whatever the conceptualizations, they provide a frame for our listening and interpretative activities. Having a way to frame the understandings gleaned in any hour, having a way to track them, is what allows for that understanding to accrue, for meaning to develop, for containment to begin.

Bibliography

Feldman, M. (2009) *Doubt, Conviction and the Analytic Process*, London: Routledge.
Joseph, B. (1989) *Psychic Equilibrium and Psychic Change*, edited by M. Feldman and E Spillius, London: Routledge.
Kelly, E. (1992) *Plant Drawings*, New York: Matthew Marks Gallery.
O'Shaughnessy, E. (2015) *Inquiries in Psychoanalysis: The Collected Papers of Edna O'Shaughnessy*, London: Routledge/The New Library of Psychoanalysis.
Sodre, I. (2015) *Imaginary Existences: A Psychoanalytic Exploration of Phantasies, Fiction, Dreams and Daydreams,* London: Routledge.

Chapter 4

The setting and the frame

Subjectivity and objectivity in the psychoanalytic relationship

Jon Tabakin

The psychoanalytic conception of how to organize the therapeutic relationship has toggled between two different nominations—the "setting" and the "frame," which are usually taken to be fundamentally the same. In this paper I want to explore the idea that these two concepts might actually refer to different aspects of the establishment and maintenance of the analytic relationship.

Let us start by providing a preliminary distinction between the two. I suggest that the "frame" conceptualization connotes structure, while the "setting" idea implicates relationship. The idea of the frame-as-structure serves as a guide to gauging and interpreting acting-out against that structure. The frame tracks the patient's struggles with accepting external and, by reflection, internal reality; the idea being that reality frames our existence. Attacks on the frame reveal the patient's ability to accept, or to fight against, the limitations and frustrations of dependent needs focused on a relationship with a representative of a specific object – which, in the transference, is recapitulated in the figure of the analyst. In this structure, which implies the rules of reality, the frame is implicitly linked to the superego, in both of its visages – guiding and punishing. Thus, reactions to the frame simulate reactions to the superego. The frame serves as a measure for grasping the degree to which the patient functions under phantasies of omnipotence, in that omnipotence tends to hate the restrictions of external reality – essentially space and time – as well as the stubborn emotional facts of internal reality.

The setting, as distinguished from the frame, implies the atmosphere that defines the potential transformative effect of the treatment. The idea of the setting narrates the shared space between the analyst and the analysand. This space involves a dynamic process, as it requires a factor of development to occur between the two participants. Whereas the frame is generally set down in the first session or so and then watched to see how the patient relates to it – tracking levels of frustration and acceptance – the setting is the ongoing result of the establishment of a therapeutic space between both participants. The frame is imposed externally at the beginning of the treatment, while the setting is constructed internally during the course of treatment. The setting is the tacit or implicit agreement that governs the why and how two people engage to work together.

This distinction between the setting and the frame helps to account for what many analysts would refer to as necessary breaks in the frame. One hears analysts say, "I broke the frame with this patient because of these or those factors ..." This places one's theory into a negative valence that suggests, "I am changing the rules because of this patient, but I don't want my analytic superego to look badly on me." By differentiating the setting from the frame one is enabled to avoid self-apology by creating a category in which the analyst can modify his or her approach to a specific patient. Thus the analyst is protected from making an excuse "this one time with this patient." There should not have to be an excuse for what we soberly adjudicate as necessary for the treatment. This idea also prevents the therapist from thinking that all patients are to be treated the same, which ignores patient individuality as well as the individuality of each analytic couple.

So we have distinguished two aspects of the analytic relationship – the structure of the frame and what we might call the "atmosphere" of the setting. Structure is relatively unchangeable, while atmosphere is both enduring and constantly shifting, perpetually in the process of formation. The atmosphere of the setting reflects the enduring aliveness of the interaction between the patient and the analyst. Setting keeps us in the present because we must constantly re-evaluate the nature of this ever-evolving relationship.

The kind of psychoanalytic atmosphere that is created in any given treatment seems on the surface to originate as a function of personalities – something one can think of as the chemistry between two people. Upon reflection, though, one can see that the concept of the creation of a psychoanalytic atmosphere is inseparable from the analyst's theoretical orientation, which in turn informs his or her technique.

This being the case, I would like to trace here the differing conceptualizations of psychoanalytic atmospheres that have emanated from the British object relations school. Object relations theory was founded on

Freud, expanded by Melanie Klein, challenged by Winnicott, deepened by Meltzer and has recently bifurcated into early and late versions of Bion – an early version that is an extension of Klein, and a late version that is currently decoupled from Klein and linked back with Winnicott (the last of which is an interesting story in itself).

Freud

Freud (1912) initiated several ideas that established the concept of the psychoanalytic setting, which he referred to as "technical rules" (p. 111). Though familiar to many, I think they bear revisiting. The reading I propose involves considering these rules in the spirit of the atmosphere they intend to create. The guiding principle that generates Freud's analytic setting concerns the state of mind of both the analyst and the analysand – what he refers to as "the fundamental rule of psychoanalysis." Freud (1912) writes:

> The rule of giving equal notice to everything is the necessary counter-part to the demand made on the patient that he should communicate everything that occurs to him without criticism or selection ... [so that] The rule for the doctor may be expressed: 'He should withhold all conscious influences from his capacity to attend, and give himself over completely to his "unconscious memory".
>
> (Freud, 1912, p. 114)

For Freud this "technique ... consists simply in not directing one's notice to anything in particular and in maintaining the same 'evenly-suspended attention'" (p. 111). The goal, then, is the creation of an atmosphere of radical openness to both the patient's unconscious as well as the analyst's – a remarkably contemporary idea. Like Bion after him, Freud suggests that: "the most successful cases are those in which one proceeds, as it were, without any purpose in view, allows oneself to be taken by surprise by any new turn in them, and always meets them with an open mind, free from any presuppositions" (Freud, 1912, p. 114). This leads Freud to describe the analytic setting as a space where two unconscious minds are in communication. He tells us that the analyst:

> must turn his own unconscious like a receptive organ towards the transmitting unconscious of the patient. He must adjust himself to the

patient as a telephone receiver is adjusted to the transmitting microphone ... the doctor's unconscious is able, from the derivatives of the
unconscious which are communicated to him, to reconstruct that
unconscious, which has determined the patient's free associations.

(Freud, 1912, pp. 115–116)

This openness to the process that occurs between two unconscious minds
leads Freud to present two other facets of the setting. One involves the
issue of the couch. While this can be seen as an example of the frame, I
think the idea of an atmosphere that creates a sense of the setting has merit
here as well. Freud wants to create an atmosphere of abstinent non-gratification where the patient is free to associate without being affected by
visual social cues that generate thoughts such as "what did the analyst
think of what I just said?" or "perhaps the look on his or her face shows I
shouldn't have said that," etc.

Among Freud's more controversial suggestions – especially given
today's emphasis on two people together in the consulting room – is the
idea that the analyst must function like a surgeon. Freud exhorts that
analysts should "model themselves during psycho-analytic treatment on
the surgeon, who puts aside all his feelings, even his human sympathy, and
concentrates his mental forces on the single aim of performing the operation as skilfully as possible" (1912, p. 115). While this idea has been much
criticized, it is important to include what Freud says right after the previous statement. Freud relates that, "A surgeon of earlier times took as his
motto the words: *'Je le pansai, Dieu le guérit.'*" [I dressed his wounds,
God cured him.] The analyst should be content with something similar
(1912, p. 115). Analysts interpret the patient's struggles but in the final
analysis the patient's mind has to heal itself. The procedure is in the
doctor's hands, while the healing is in the hands of the patient.

Finally, in conjunction with the foregoing quotes, the focus on creating
this kind of atmosphere eventuates in the formulation of one of the goals
of the process of treatment: "I require them to learn by personal experience" (1912, p. 120).

We can see that Freud's attempt to create a specific setting in which the
patient and analyst mutually engage reveals the patient's unconscious in
an atmosphere that is radically open to the potential emergence of what is
hidden deep inside, without the intrusion of the analyst's needs and desires
foreclosing the analytic space. Interestingly, this reading also shows that

Freud is patently the central precursor to several of Bion's innovations: the analyst's "reverie" that must dream the patient's experience (1962a) and the suspension of memory and desire in order to help the patient move towards the goal of *Learning from Experience* (Bion, 1962b).

Thus, the setting for Freud is an atmosphere that creates an openness that facilitates contact between patient and analyst on a deep level. The reference to being emotionally neutral like a surgeon is intended as a framing structure to hold the kind of setting that Freud enjoins. Even though Freud's psychoanalysis has been criticized as being a one-person psychology as opposed to the more current two-person intersubjective conceptualization, one can certainly see that Freud's focus concerns the creation of a setting that facilitates communication between the unconscious of the patient and that of the analyst.

In addition, Freud's idea here curiously balances his usually understood view of the countertransference, which he saw as something in the analyst that needed to be analyzed and kept out of the treatment room. While this may be true – in the sense that one should be careful about intruding narcissistically into the patient's mental space – the modern countertransference movement, largely inaugurated by Paula Heimann (1949/1950), was built on the "basic assumption ... that the analyst's unconscious understands that of his patient" (p. 82). Herbert Rosenfeld (1952) agrees with Heimann by invoking Freud's very metaphor. He tells us that working with primitive patients requires "the analyst's capacity to use his counter-transference as a kind of sensitive 'receiving set'" (p. 76) – an unmistakable resonance with Freud's "telephone receiver" analogy. Clearly we need to update our thinking about Freud.

Freud, then, establishes the classical – and yet not-so-classical – standard for the idea of the setting, defined by unconscious openness and neutrality on the analyst's part, and the commitment to free association and learning from one's own experience on the part of the analysand.

Klein

The expansion of Freud's view of the establishment of an analytic treatment was affected by Klein's object relations view of Freud's theory, as opposed to Anna Freud's ego psychology view of Freud (Tabakin, 2015). Klein built her theory on Freud's two principles of mental functioning – pleasure and reality – which became, in Klein's conception – phantasy and objectivity. Klein's technical procedure can be thought of as a tightening of the frame. In terms of the analyst's role, she focused on the analyst's interventions as primarily oriented towards the making of interpretations, while the conceptual setting for the patient – in the analyst's mind – is constructed around the idea that everything that takes place between the analysand and the analyst is grist for the analytic mill. With Klein's (1926) invention of the play technique in child analysis, she developed the idea that everything the patient says and does can be seen as potential free associations that require thought and interpretation by the analyst. So for Klein, the setting is the conceptual space wherein everything that comes from the patient is an association. She extends Freud's idea of the patient's free associations met by the analyst's evenly suspended attention into a much more pervasive concept.

Thus, the Kleinian frame is conceptualized as a representation of the patient's primary objects and becomes part and parcel of the analyst's interpretative focus. Based on this idea, Klein expands Freud's concept of the transference – which has vital significance for the expansion of the concept of the setting. If the frame represents the object, then the analytic setting is essentially an exploration of one's unresolved primitive object relations. From this follows another idea, that interpretations should be primarily focused on the transference of these relations into the setting. Thus the concept of transference is widened to include what Klein referred to as the "*total situations* transferred from the past into the present" (Klein, 1952, p. 55). Virtually everything that occurs between the analysand and the analyst is seen as a manifestation of the transference. This concept reinforces Freud's ideas about analytic neutrality, as the setting becomes – in Klein's theory – the space wherein the phantasy world of the internal objects of the superego are given the freedom to play.

This conceptualization of the Kleinian setting emanates from the fact that Klein deeply expanded Freud's concept of the superego, from Freud's (1923) theory of the superego as the internalization of the parents in union, to Klein's (1926) idea that every aspect of one's external object relations – from the parts of the object to its wholeness, its loved and hated aspects – are internalized, and in treatment projected into the figure of the analyst, or one could say into the setting. We see here the intimate relation between setting, frame, and transference. Thus, Klein's object relations and transference centered context requires even more that the analyst maintain emotional objectivity in order to allow the setting to become a theater in which the patient's internal objects can play their parts on the stage of the analytic frame. One might say that for Klein "the play's the thing, wherein I shall capture the conscience [superego] of the King" – the murderous, omnipotent part of the analysand (Shakespeare's *Hamlet*, Act 2, Scene 2, 1963, p. 42).

Klein's setting is a space of separateness and therefore weaning, where the attempts to merge with the primary object are analyzed so that the patient can learn to be separate and to develop his or her own mind. Klein's setting, building on Freud, is objective. Hanna Segal made this point in a conference in Los Angeles in 2000. She said, "psychoanalysis is a weaning therapy," a comment which created quite a stir in the audience – as James Grotstein later intoned, "What about attachment?" This anecdote brings to mind the tension in treatment between attachment and weaning. Tolerating absence and separation creates an objective frame that, in turn, creates an atmosphere of non-gratification. The Kleinian frame is also objective in that the analysis of the transference takes up both its positive and negative aspects, requiring the analyst to remain neutral in the face of the tangle of idealized and persecuting projections into the figure of the analyst.

Winnicott

While Klein was expanding Freud's classical view of the setting and the frame, Winnicott offered an alternative perspective. As discussed earlier, Klein's view of the setting can be summed up as a space of separateness, where the play of the unconscious phantasy of internal objects meets interpretation. Winnicott (1955) took a strikingly contrasting view. He tells us that there is a class of patients for whom "the setting becomes more important than the interpretation. The emphasis is changed from the one to the other" (p. 297). This class of patients is defined as people who have not been able to perform the foundational basics of mental development with their mothers. Thus, a sense of "primary integration" has never taken place, and they have instead developed "false selves." In Winnicott's view of psychopathology, the false self is created in response to environmental impingements which cause the nascent self to put up a false version to satisfy the demands of the environment, resulting in a loss of "going-on-being." It is the setting then that creates a specialized state wherein the patient can feel un-impinged. He tells us that the "individual psyche can only start in a certain setting. In this setting the individual can gradually come to create a personal environment" (Winnicott, 1952, p. 222). This creation of a "personal environment" occurs when the analyst attends to the setting:

> The behaviour of the analyst, represented by what I have called the setting, by being good enough in the matter of adaptation to need, is gradually perceived by the patient as something that raises a hope that the true self may at last be able to take the risks involved in its starting to experience living.
>
> (Winnicott, 1955, p. 297)

Winnicott's theory of the setting is based on his concept of "adaptation to need." The setting must be a safe space that allows regression of the patient back to a primitive un-integrated state – the original developmental task – so that development can be restarted with the sensitive analyst playing the role of the "good enough mother" who provides a "holding environment" where the "true self" can develop. This is in contrast to Klein, who places more emphasis on the resolution of anxieties than the fulfillment of needs. Thus, Klein creates an objective setting, while Winnicott creates a subjective one. Winnicott's conception of the setting is based on his idea that prior to all of the complexities that Klein sees in the infant, the infant needs to begin to exist creatively as it puts together the foundational parts of the self. As Winnicott (1962) tells us, "infant is not yet an entity having experiences. There is no id before ego" (p. 56).

Winnicott's atmosphere is infused with his belief that the infant cannot, and therefore does not, exist without the mother. Because of this idea, the setting is highly subjective and the analyst is, in Winnicott's terms, the "subjective-object" that reenacts the original infant/mother environment. While Klein's setting is based on the clarity of objectivity, Winnicott's is based on the nurturance of subjectivity. Winnicott's focus is on achieving a creative dependence. Quite different atmospheres, yet both create a setting designed to generate the experience and resolution of developmental conflicts and needs.

Bion

The concept of the setting was further expanded by Bion, who incorporated the ideas of Freud, Klein, and Winnicott while introducing some new, radical ideas of his own. As has been suggested, the setting is informed by one's theory and established by one's technique. There are two essential and interrelated aspects of Bion's theory that are particularly relevant to the discussion of the setting. The first involves his model of "container-contained"; the second concerns his concept of "transforma-tions in O" as distinct from, but related to, "transformations in K" – where O represents the patient's raw, unknown emotional experience and K represents thinking about and knowing that experience.

To explicate Bion's innovations it is important to understand what he added to Klein's concept of projective identification. Klein theorized that projective identification is used to get rid of intolerable feelings and parts of the self – sometimes good, sometimes bad – by means of a phantasy of aggressively intruding them into the object. While agreeing with Klein's conception, Bion expands her idea to include what he refers to as "normal degrees of projective identification" (1959, p. 102). Here, Bion posits a form of very early projective identification between the infant and the mother where the infant's intent is not to aggressively intrude into and attack the mother, but rather to communicate to her in its preverbal state. In order to receive these communications, the analyst must function as a container that can hold and detoxify the projections and then give them back to the analysand in an emotionally tolerable form. To perform this function of containment, the analyst must engage the patient in a state Bion (1962a) refers to as "maternal reverie," which he says functions as "the receptor organ for the infant's harvest of self-sensations" (p. 116).

Expanding on Freud's understanding of the dream-work as a crucial mental function that cryptically communicates the unconscious to the conscious mind, and Klein's interpretation of children's play as free asso-ciations or day-dreams, Bion builds his theory of the container-contained into a process wherein the analyst needs to dream the analysand's mate-rial in the session to facilitate the process of mental digestion. This state of "reverie" becomes the central point of Bion's technique. This implies a stage of the analyst's work that precedes interpretation, and thus becomes the central focus of the creation of the setting for Bion. To better grasp the implications of this idea we must consider Bion's second innovation to thinking about the setting.

The idea of the patient as that which needs to be contained, and the analyst as that which needs to contain the patient's emotional experience – through a process of receptive reverie – develops into Bion's (1965) more expansive theoretical landscape where treatment must effect "the transition from *knowing about* reality [K] to *becoming real* [O]" (p. 153). Bion's emphasis is always on the moment of experience, especially when the experience involves emotions that individuals try to get rid of reflexively. This emotional experience is referred to as the O of the session – an emotional fact that cannot be fully (K) known. Thus, for Bion, the model of interpretation creating insight is supplanted by the need to unearth the central emotional experience of the session – the O – without immediately transforming it into something that can be known (K), a knowing that can distract from "becoming real."

This state of reverie – essentially dreaming the session – challenges the idea of the "objective" analyst who "knows" what is wrong with the patient. The focus of Bion's technique is for the patient to discover what is really inside his or her self. That being understood, Bion (1963) still follows Freud in another component of setting up the analytic atmosphere, stating that "an analysis must be conducted in an atmosphere of deprivation [so that] at no time must either analyst or analysand lose the sense of isolation within the intimate relationship of analysis" (p. 15). It is important to take note of Bion's linking of an atmosphere of deprivation with a sense of intimacy. In this quote, Bion integrates the classical ideal of neutrality with the current ideal of intersubjectivity. Thus, a sense of intimacy in fulfilling the role of the container for the patient's unformulated emotional experience – signified by O – is linked with Bion's (1970) exhortation that the analyst abandon "memory and desire" – past and future – so that something new, perhaps unborn, might emerge *in the present experience.*

To summarize, while Klein creates an objective setting for instinctual-emotional conflicts to be resolved, and Winnicott creates a subjective setting for regressive emotional needs to be fulfilled, Bion conceptualizes the setting as a unique combination of both the subjective (reverie and intimacy) and the objective ("an atmosphere of deprivation") elements from which unknown emotional experience may emerge.

Meltzer

Continuing our review of different approaches to the frame and the setting, we must move forward to consider how the idea of the setting differs from, or is intermingled with, the concept of the transference. Let us look at Meltzer to delineate these concepts, utilizing his idea of the "gathering of the transference processes." In his book *The Psycho-Analytical Process* (1967), he discusses what he calls the "natural history" of the analytic process. According to Meltzer, this process is conducted by the analyst in order to slowly develop an analytic mindset in the patient. Of particular significance here is his differentiation of interpretation from the setting, method and purpose of the analytic process:

> But however important interpretation may be to the "cure" and the "insight", it is not the main work of the analyst as regards the establishment and maintenance of the analytical process. This is done by the *creation* of the "setting" in which the transference processes of the patient's mind may discover expression. The word "creation" stresses the nature of this technical part of the work, for it seems clear that a constant process of *discovery* by the analyst is required, referable to the modulation of anxiety on the one hand and the minimising of interference on the other.
>
> (Meltzer, 1967, p. xii)

Meltzer further distinguishes interpretation from the management of the setting by saying that an interpretation attempts to "modify" anxiety, whereas managing the setting "modulates" anxiety:

> Note that the term "modulation" of anxiety has been used rather than "modification," since the latter is surely a function of the *interpretive* aspect of the work while the modulation is managed as part of the *setting*. This modulation occurs through the patient's repeated experience in analysis that there is a place where the expression of his transference processes will not be met by *counter-transference activity* but only by *analytical activity*, namely a *search for the truth*.
>
> (Meltzer, 1967, p. xii)

The setting is a process of discovery, wherein the analyst presides, that allows for the development of the transference. Meltzer's concept is that the setting is the space wherein the transference can emerge. Meltzer refers to the creation of the setting as a process of discovery:

> This point will be clarified in the process of discovery with a patient, he must find through his sensitivity the means of modulation required

by that individual within the framework of his technique. In a word, he must *preside* over the setting in a way which permits the evolution of the patient's transference.

(Meltzer, 1967, p. xiii)

Setting calls on the analyst's subjectivity to construct the therapeutic space with the analysand, while the frame requires more contact with the analyst's objectivity in terms of maintaining boundaries. Setting is a subjective space-creating process; frame is an objective structure wherein the clash between the subjective and objective in the patient can be discovered, measured, and interpreted in the transference. In this idea, the transference represents the clash between subjectivities and objectivities.

Clinical examples

One

A new patient begins treatment. She says she is interested in working with someone who is "psychoanalytic." In the first few sessions she evinces a specific style of interacting. She and I sit face-to-face as she discusses her current family and relationship troubles. She tells me of her frustrations and then looks at me with great intensity and asks me, "So, what do you think?" I try to maintain the frame by redirecting her back to what's in her mind. She continues to talk in the same vein before returning to the same intense look and asking, "So what do you think about that?" I feel put on the spot. At another time she stops mid-association and says, "now it's your turn." Furthermore, she responds to my interpretations very quickly, averting her gaze for a second, as if rapidly evaluating what I said, before responding in a very clipped verbal style and saying either "Yes, I agree with that," or "No, that doesn't work for me." Each time after she averts her gaze and gives me a short, curt response she again stares at me intently, giving me the distinct impression that her evaluation of my inter-pretations is too quick and lacking unconscious depth. She seems to have the idea that therapy is a place to find validation for her feelings and to receive advice, and apparently not a place to feel frustration, an idea that controverts her desire for a "psychoanalytic" treatment.

This style of interacting continues for several sessions. In one session, as I am making an interpretation about her frustrations in relationships –

and preparing to address her similar frustrations in the transference – she interrupts me with a replay of her concern for somebody she had just been talking about. She asks me to repeat what I said. I tell her that before I do, I think it might be important to understand what happened in her mind to cause the interruption. She responds in an angry and disappointed manner, telling me, "I know you analysts try to analyze every little thing." When I address her view of analytic work her frustration heightens and she tells me that I'm stuck on insignificant details and that she just wanted me to repeat my interpretation. I feel we are on the brink of a mini analytic impasse that might balloon into premature termination of the treatment before it has a chance to get started.

This highlights an interesting and, I think, familiar analytic dilemma. A hostile transference seems to be showing itself. I could continue to try to unearth the transference in the hope of getting past a potentially fatal impasse. But I am also feeling that my back is being pushed up against a wall – perhaps this is how she feels in relationships. I am trying not to get riled up in a way that could cause me to make an aggressive, and therefore defensive, transference interpretation. In moments like these I often think that I might be missing a communicative projective identification – like the one I just mentioned about her relationship patterns.

However, it was my sense in that moment that there might be a different way for me to conceptualize and respond to the tense place we were in. I realized that this patient, even though she had some intellectual understanding of what it means to work with an analyst, really had no idea of what kind of experience analysis might be, and how different this experience might be from previous therapies, which were not analytic. I began to formulate the idea that we had not established the proper setting for an analytic investigation, and realized that if I doggedly pursued the analytic investigation without realizing that she has no true concept of it, I would simply be antagonizing her unproductively.

Though still in the heat of the moment, with these thoughts in mind I feel calmer. I tell her that I have observed that she has a specific style of relating in the sessions, that she is quick to express her frustrations and even quicker to respond to my interpretations, and that in this way she keeps the conversation on a visual and conscious level of action and reaction, which makes it difficult for us to go deeper into her treatment. She nods while turning away for a split second and returns to look at me intently again. In this particular moment, however, she appears less demanding.

At this point I realize that I need to continue addressing the creation of the setting. I tell her that we are both trying to find the best way to work with each other in the context of creating a relationship that can further explore the depths of her anxiety and anger. Based on the material she has provided concerning her mother, I now address both the setting and the potential transference. I say that I think she feels that she has never had a mother that could take in and hold her feelings for her, and that her intensity in our back-and-forth dialogue is a style that she has developed to compensate for this feeling of lack in her interaction with her mother. I add that she might feel that she never had a space in another person where her emotional experience could dwell without her having to take quick and curt actions. These interpretations broke the spell of the anxious intensity.

Two

The following case example expresses how the setting continues to evolve for long-term patients. In this case, an event occurred somewhere in the first third of a long analysis. This patient had been coming twice a week for many years, lying on the couch. She was very depressed. A common and oft-repeated association of hers was that "the sun is out today, but it's still gray to me."

After one summer break, by which time she was now coming four days a week – still on the couch – she came into a session, sat up on the couch rather defiantly, and announced – in a tone of intense anger I had never seen before – that she would not be lying down on the couch anymore.

This event presented a challenge to the analysis. I could have interpreted the breaking of the frame as an attack on the analysis – a clear expression of the negative transference. Instead I sensed that I could have been right in my interpretation but wrong for the moment, because it seemed to be a communication that needed to be taken up in the context of the evolution of the setting between us which, as it turned out, eventually led to an interpretation of the transference. In that moment, however, it seemed to me that it was the setting that most immediately required attention. Considering the patient's lack of observable emotion while she lay on the couch for so many years, I felt that this moment represented progress, as if the patient's emotional experience was beginning to emerge. (I might add that this patient had three younger siblings and often felt unacknowledged, and also that in being the de facto "babysitter" she felt she was not supposed to have feelings.) With this in mind, I commented to her that I felt she had burst into her analysis, and that her anger meant the arrival of her long-stifled emotional experience.

I accepted this change to the setting as essential for the patient's development. If I had interpreted the negative transference, based on her anger, I think she would have continued to feel unacknowledged in her life. This burst of emotion needed to be accepted and not interpreted in a way that probably would have caused her to take the emotion back inside and bury it under her persistently severe depression once again, as perhaps she had done throughout her life. Thus, in this instance, the patient's need for me to evolve the setting guided my approach.

The sequelae to this episode was the ushering in of several years during which the patient felt intense anger towards me. From her perspective, I was the mother that never allowed her to feel her emotion, in part as an identification with her "American pioneer background," and also in part because as the eldest sibling she had become the conscripted babysitter. Eventually, after several years of working through her anger, face-to-face, I felt that the time had come to reestablish the frame of lying down again, which I suggested would allow us to go deeper into the anger that had emerged. She assented and shortly after that requested a fifth analytic hour, with palpable emotional desire and need.

The intertwined nature of the frame, setting, and transference

While the second vignette involved the manifestation and working through of the patient's transference, it was also guided by the understanding that the setting is always in the process of forming. I could have seen her approach to me as an attack (Klein, 1946), or perhaps as necessary object-usage (Winnicott, 1969), or thought of it as a normal projective identification (Bion, 1959), all of which have merit. I believe, however, that the impact of that interaction occurred because I was helping her to develop a working atmosphere of the setting that allowed the analysis to move forward.

In reviewing these examples it is clear that these three clinical variables – the frame, the setting, and the transference – often intertwine in and around the same moment. This can create some conceptual confusion, but I think the value of these delineations lies in the fact that they can prevent technical errors, such as those I have mentioned, where an issue of the setting, for example, can be treated as a negative transference and create a therapeutic impasse. Mistaking one for the other can often become a significant technical error that can signal the premature end to a treatment.

In terms of the interrelationship between the frame, the setting, and the transference, the frame is easier to sort out than the setting. As I suggested earlier, the frame is a structure that represents the patient's transference to both reality and to primary objects. The relationship between the setting and the transference is more subtle, I think, for here one is building a relationship with the patient wherein psychoanalytic work can be done. As Meltzer (quoted above) says, the setting must be created wherein one can discover the transference. Meltzer applies this process to dealing with anxiety in the session, suggesting that while interpretation modifies anxiety, the setting modulates it. Interpretation addresses anxiety in order to alter it, while the setting provides the space wherein the patient can trepidly believe in the safe expression of his or her inner workings. One might analogize these three elements in terms of a painting – wherein the psychoanalytic frame corresponds to the frame of the painting, the setting resembles the scope, texture, and context of the scene that is represented, and the transference represents the meaning of the painting.

Concluding thoughts: subjectivity and objectivity

The concept of the setting, then, can be thought of as the subjective center of the relationship that the analyst builds with the patient, while the frame constitutes the objective center. The setting concerns the individual parameters for how one adjusts to the patient's needs, and how the patient can be helped to adjust to the needs of the analysis. Now, the question of adjusting to the patient's needs is one potentially fraught with technical peril, for one could use it to rationalize acting out one's countertransference desires and needs. To take a rather familiar example, analysts often unconsciously treat their patients as if they represent one's own wounded child, a child that the analyst – now identified as the mother/father – attempts to heal. This situation can be understood as a misuse of the concept of the setting to act out on the boundaries of the frame.

This brings up a technical issue for the analyst in managing his or her thinking of, and with, the patient. This technical issue involves what I think is a necessary process that must occur frequently in the analyst's mind, where the subjectivity of the setting must always be in dialogue with the objectivity of the frame. One can conceptualize this situation as representing one's internal parents (Segal, 1997) where the symbolized mother subjectively tunes into her baby – the setting – while the symbolized father objectively brings in language and the external world – the frame. (I say "symbolized" here to represent structuralized functions, not gender.) Hanna Segal (1997) suggests these functions when she states that "the father can be seen as protecting the mother and the child from a stream of mutual projective identifications, in phantasy and in reality" (p. 88) – projective identifications that are necessary for communicating on the preverbal level, but must be given up for separation-individuation to take place.

In this light, a continuous dialogue must always be occurring between one's objective and static frame for reality and treatment, and one's subjective and dynamic setting that adjusts to the patient. Too much focus on the frame and the atmosphere lacks humanity, while too much attention to the setting may gratify the omnipotent part of the self which can then dominate the treatment as a sort of negative analytic third – or "pathological organization" (Spillius, 1988) – that stunts growth according to the Freudian-Bionian injunctive to "learn from experience."

It is worth considering the conflicting theories of Klein and Winnicott in this light, as they seem to emblemize two fundamental ways of thinking about and conducting psychoanalysis. For the purpose of this paper, I would like to take up the "popular" characterizations of both. As these "popular" characterizations are reductive simplifications, usually rendered in negative form, they do not do justice to the complexities of these theories and techniques; nevertheless, these characterizations do exist in people's minds and are frequently exhibited in collegial conversation.

The negative reduction of Klein's theory is that her technique is too severe in its focus on weaning and separation, while the negative reduction of Winnicott's thinking is that his technique is too focused on attachment and is thus lacking in boundaries in its attentive concern for merging with the regressed patient in the maternal holding environment. If we superimpose the gradient of the frame and the setting on these two analytic positions or stances something interesting shows itself. We might then see Klein as primarily focused on the structure of the frame, while Winnicott could be viewed as primarily involved with the atmosphere of the setting. By thinking about these problems in this way we might be able to correct potential errors in technique that are often committed by adherents of these theorists.

This approach to thinking about treatment might help analysts to assess whether their patients are progressing, growing, stagnating, staying in treatment, prematurely terminating, etc. For example, I've noticed that supervisees with Kleinian leanings tend to push their interpretations prematurely and often force them into a transference context in ways that leave patients alienated. This of course is not necessarily easy to sort out because the interpretation may be right and the patient's reaction might be resistance; but the interpretation might also be poorly timed, too aggressive, or too focused on the destructive aspect of the personality, which ignores the ultimately most important aspect of Klein's theory – the constructive aspect where love ascends over hate in the depressive position. In other words, the interpretation is made "outside" the setting. So the problem may lie in the way a technique is employed, rather than in the technique itself. Realizing that one has focused too predominantly on the frame to the exclusion of the setting might allow analysts to see the problems in how they make use of technique.

The same critique can be applied to followers of Winnicott. While Kleinians are more likely to prematurely antagonize the patient, precipitating an early breaking off of the treatment, I've noticed in supervisees who resonate more towards Winnicott that they are more likely to gratify the patient without analyzing the frame of reality and the omnipotent attacks on it, leaving the patient in a long-term treatment in which they feel good about being with the analyst, but do not exhibit noticeable growth. In this sequence the relationship with the analyst seems to increasingly improve while external relationships deteriorate. I see this occurring in supervisees with Winnicottian proclivities, where they may be too concerned with the sensitive nature of the setting so that they become intimidated to make an interpretation that might create a moment of otherwise healthy separation and possibly painful growth. Where poor Kleinian technique might keep the patient at too great a distance, poor Winnicottian technique might hold the patient too close.

Seen from this perspective, one might consider the twin needs of attachment/feeding and separation/weaning in psychoanalytic treatment. The setting feeds, while the frame weans. Therefore the analyst must constantly sort out these matters in each individual treatment, as these needs surge and retreat constantly throughout the treatment. The inter-twining nature of these two concepts represents the ongoing dialogue that the analyst must engage in with both the patient's and the analyst's self in order to manage the treatment in the context of both variables.

References

Bion, W.R. (1959). Attacks on linking. In Bion, W.R., *Second Thoughts: Selected Papers on PsychoAnalysis* (1967). New York: Jason Aronson, pp. 93–109.

Bion, W.R. (1962a). A theory of thinking. In Bion, W.R., *Second Thoughts: Selected Papers on Psycho-Analysis* (1967). New York: Jason Aronson, pp. 110–119.

Bion, W.R. (1962b). *Learning from Experience.* New York: Jason Aronson.

Bion, W.R. (1963). *Elements of Psychoanalysis.* New York: Jason Aronson.

Bion, W.R. (1965). *Transformations.* New York: Jason Aronson.

Bion, W.R. (1970). *Attention and Interpretation.* New York: Jason Aronson.

Freud, S. (1912). Recommendations to physicians practising psycho-analysis. *Standard Edition*, 12, pp. 111–120. London: The Hogarth Press.

Freud, S. (1923). The ego and the id. *Standard Edition*, 19, pp. 3–66. London: The Hogarth Press.

Heimann, P. (1949/1950). On counter-transference. In Margret Tonnesmann (ed.), *About Children and Children-No-Longer: Collected Papers 1942–80* (1989). London: Tavistock/Routledge, pp. 73–79.

Klein, M. (1926). The psychological principles of early analysis. In Klein, M., *Love, Guilt and Reparation and Other Works 1921–1945* (1975). New York: The Free Press, pp. 128–138.

Klein, M. (1946). Notes on some schizoid mechanisms. In Klein, M., *Envy and Gratitude and Other Works 1946–1963* (1975). New York: The Free Press, pp. 1–24.

Klein, M. (1952). The origins of transference. In Klein, M., *Envy and Gratitude and Other Works 1946–1963* (1975). New York: The Free Press, pp. 48–56.

Meltzer, D. (1967). *The Psycho-Analytical Process.* London: Karnac Books.

Rosenfeld, H. (1952). Notes on the psycho-analysis of the super-ego conflict of an acute schizophrenic. In Rosenfeld, H., *Psychotic States: A Psycho-Analytical Approach* (1965). New York: International Universities Press, pp. 63–103.

Segal, H. (1997). The Oedipus complex today. In J. Steiner (ed.), *Psychoanalysis, Literature and War, Papers 1972–1995*. London: Routledge, pp. 86–94.

Shakespeare, W. (1963). *Hamlet.* New York: Norton Critical Editions.

Spillius, E. (1988). *Melanie Klein Today. Vol. 1: Mainly Theory.* London: Routledge.

Tabakin, J. (2015). The value of interpretation: Thoughts on its meaning, history and use. In F. Vaquer (ed.), *Contemporary Klein and Bion: Explorations in Clinical Practice*. London: Karnac.

Winnicott, D.W. (1952). Psychoses and child care. In Winnicott, D.W., *Through Paediatrics to Psychoanalysis* (1958). New York: Basic Books, pp. 219–228.

Winnicott, D.W. (1955). Clinical varieties of transference. In Winnicott, D.W., *Through Paediatrics to Psychoanalysis* (1958). New York: Basic Books, pp. 295–299.

Winnicott, D.W. (1962). Ego integration in child development. In Winnicott, D.W., *The Maturational Processes and the Facilitating Environment: Studies in the Theory of Emotional Development* (1965). New York: International Universities Press, pp. 56–63.

Winnicott, D.W. (1969). The use of an object. *International Journal of Psycho-Analysis,* 50: 711–716.

Chapter 5

Reconfiguring the frame as a dynamic structure

Peter Goldberg

Outline of a model

If the function of a frame is to secure a backdrop, demarcate a space, and provide a structure so that a distinct kind of experience can evolve within that space, it is usual to think of it as essentially inert. We assume that, as long as the frame stays in place, it should require little attention. This may account for why, until relatively recently and with some notable exceptions, the frame has received so little systematic attention in the clinical literature, especially when compared with the extensive focus on the analytic process that has dominated clinical theory in recent decades.

I would like to propose a model of the analytic frame that highlights its multi-faceted and heterogeneous make-up. This model recognizes that, far from being inert, the analytic frame is naturally always adjusting, its different components held at all times in a dynamic tension. In considering what the analytic frame is meant to do, we can see that, unlike a picture frame for example, the analytic frame must do more than demarcate a reliable boundaried space and must do more than remain fixed and unchanging. If the task of analysis is to sponsor new forms of psychical experience rather than merely reproduce existing psychical structures, the analytic frame must be capable of adjusting its shape, as it were, in order to facilitate these psychical transformations while continuing to provide the essential framing functions. In other words, the viability of the analytic frame depends upon the potential for *evolution in the framing structure itself*: it is less an unchanging structure than it is an always-evolving configuration.

So while the concept of a frame signifies something that is, by its very nature, a *limiting* structure, the work of analysis requires that the structuring function of the frame be capable of constant recalibration in response to the needs of the clinical process. The function of the frame thus appears paradoxical: it delimits and proscribes what can and should happen in the clinical situation, while at the same time facilitating disruption and change in the organization of psychical life.

This paradox can be seen in the natural tension that exists between the frame as an *objective* structure with fixed characteristics (physical setting, time, duration, rules of behavior, ethical practices, and economic arrangements), and the *subjectively* experienced work of *framing* – the way the frame functions and adapts moment-by-moment, constantly adjusting to the needs and demands emerging in the clinical field. If the objective, fixed, and tangible characteristics of the frame provide the clinical encounter with clear boundaries and with legitimacy as a social, legal, and professional institution, it is no less important that the frame operate as a living mutative structure.

It is clear, then, that the analytic frame must be capable of doing several things at once, staying true to the intimate framing requirements of a unique clinical encounter while at the same time upholding symbolic limits and instituting the impersonal requirements imposed by the surrounding cultural, legal, and socio-economic structures. The heterogeneous demands made upon the analytic frame define it as a complex and mobile structure whose different functions are perpetually held in a dynamic tension. In this picture of the frame as a dynamic structure, we can also see a precise reflection of the ethics of psychoanalytic care in action: the frame creates a space in which intimate psychical engagement is offered as a therapeutic tool and agent of change that must, however, always be oriented towards the specific psychical needs of the patient, and must operate at all times within the constraints of social and material existence.

In this paper, I will focus particular attention on the organic or *framing* dimension where, like a living skin, the frame adjusts to micro-changes in the clinical process. Operating like a shared sensorium, this organic dimension (or what I will call the *meta-framing* function of the frame) is where the moment-by-moment work of framing takes place – where structure is given to experience in the clinical situation through perceiving and sensing things. Here the frame works not just as a structure made up of symbolic and practical arrangements, but functions like a living membrane or *psycho-sensory contact barrier* through which patient and analyst together can sense the existence of psychical and external objects. When it is alive in this "meta-framing" way, the frame operates like a conductive membrane, making it possible for these psychical and external objects to be felt and experienced as *actual* presences in the clinical field. In this view, the frame's ambient responsiveness (its meta-framing potential) depends upon the degree to which therapist and patient *sense things together* – form a psycho-sensory bond. This joining of patient and therapist in a "sensory symbiosis" (Goldberg, 2012) is what animates the frame, lends the frame its organic character, keeping it tuned and responsive to the internal and external worlds.

The idea of the frame-as-contact-barrier has further implications: it implies not only that it serves to screen and protect the clinical situation and process from being flooded by objects and stimuli, but that it plays an active role in *organizing the perception of*, and maintaining psychosensory contact with, the world of objects (both psychical and external).

If the authentic potential of the analytic process depends at all times on the vital functioning of a living frame – i.e. on the effectiveness of its current dynamic configuration – then it is natural to ask: what is the analyst's ongoing contribution to keeping the frame alive and animated? While a fuller examination of the analyst's participation at the level of the frame is beyond the scope of this paper, I will briefly address a particular aspect of the analyst's therapeutic activity – an *inductive* mode of engagement in which the analyst implicitly joins the patient in *sensing things together*. This ongoing psycho-sensory engagement, which takes place entirely at an undifferentiated and non-representational level of mental functioning, constitutes an essential "framing" dimension of the analyst's activity. It is what animates the frame and keeps it alive to the clinical situation.

Heterogeneous functions of the analytic frame

By putting forward the idea of a living structure, I am proposing a model of the frame as something that, far from being static, has the character of a complex entity constantly micro-adjusting and "becoming" something new. In describing the different components of the analytic frame, I intend to highlight the inherent heterogeneity of its makeup – the fact that it operates simultaneously in material, social, and psychical reality; that it has features that are both tangible and intangible, inanimate and animate; and that it operates simultaneously as an "institution" and as an organic structure. Of fundamental importance in this multi-faceted model is the recognition that each of these diverse characteristics of the frame are *intrinsic* to its function – that none can be viewed as extrinsic.[1]

Several functional characteristics of the analytic frame can be outlined, ranging in order from the generic (necessary for any professional activity) to the most specifically psychoanalytic; from the tangibly institutional (i.e. situated in material and social reality), to the intangible, rooted in psychical reality and psycho-sensory experience. Thus, the frame functions as:

1   A *physical setting* that ensures confidentiality and a minimum of distraction, along with predictable scheduling and payment arrangements and reliable modes of communication.
2   A *social institution* that gives professional and legal standing, as well as cultural legitimization, to the practice of analysis.
3   A *psycho-social institution* (corresponding to the Oedipal situation) symbolizing the presence of a "third," thus marking the "law" of difference and establishing limits on desire in accordance with the societal "law" (Perelberg, 2004).
4   A *marker of the psychical boundary* differentiating inner from outer, separating the "dream space" of analysis from the spatial/temporal domains of social and material reality.[2]
5   A *non-process* or *meta-ego* that secures and "holds" the most primitive and psychotic anxieties, as described in the pioneering work of Jose Bleger (1967). This is comparable to the containing function of Bion (1970).
6   A *shared psycho-sensory contact barrier* (or *meta-frame*) operating at the non-representational and undifferentiated level of proto-containment or "sensory symbiosis."

Each of these diverse functions constitutes an essential aspect of what the frame is designed to do. None is more intrinsic than the others, and it is the complex interplay of these heterogeneous elements that gives the analytic frame its dynamic character and functional significance.

In this paper, I will focus on the last characteristic of the frame as listed above – the function of the frame as a shared contact barrier or membrane. This aspect of the frame is at once the most difficult to represent and the most crucial to its ongoing dynamic responsiveness in the analytic situation.

Fixed and mutative characteristics of the frame

In the context of pluralism in contemporary psychoanalytic theory, discussions have frequently revolved around the question of whether it is better to adhere to a strict frame, or to abandon this orthodoxy in favor of greater flexibility (Bass, 2007; Stern, 2009). But once we have a picture of the frame's multi-faceted makeup – the fact that it must do several different things at once – we will find that the simple choice between firmness and flexibility is spurious. Instead, it becomes clear that the viability and firmness of the frame depends upon the analyst's ability to deploy certain of its parts flexibly. Just as steel derives its strength from the alloys that lend it flexibility, so does the analytic frame gain its strength from the flexibility of some of its parts.

There can be no question that rigorous maintenance of the function of the frame is indispensable to clinical practice. Nonetheless, recognition of its dynamic structure suggests a different conception of what constitutes rigor in the maintenance of the frame. The effectiveness of the frame, in this model, would reside in the interchange between its fixed and its mobile characteristics, between its immobilizing and its mobilizing tendencies. Maintaining the rigor of the frame means working within the dynamism of its structure. It means maintaining its structural integrity, boundaries, and limits (in accordance with social, legal, and economic imperatives), while simultaneously adjusting its shape in response to the moment-by-moment psychical need for a shared psycho-sensory framework. The essentially bipolar reality of the frame (its existence both as a fixed entity and a shape-shifting configuration) means that there always exists the potential for segregation and even dissociation of the tangible, fixed characteristics of the frame from the organic sub-symbolic *meta-framing* level of psycho-sensory bonding. The work of the frame lies in the tension between these.

This view of the frame as a dynamic or "living" structure suggests that it is not just a sedentary set of fixed rules and professional arrangements that may occasionally become the object of displacements, projections, and transference-countertransference enactments (for example in the familiar instances of the patient "acting out around the frame"). Instead, the work of the frame is viewed here as pivotal to the clinical encounter, the vitalizing background function that defines what is possible in the foreground of the clinical process. While the clinical *process* is the object of our conscious attention, it is the quality of the framing function, working silently, unseen, and unrepresented in the background, that is the crucial underpinning of the clinical project. The essential factor is the frame's viability as a "living" structure rather than something dissociated or deadened.

Dual tendency towards boundary deterioration and bureaucratization

I have suggested that the vitality of the frame-as-contact-barrier depends upon the quality of an ongoing psycho-sensory bond (or sensory symbiosis) between patient and therapist. But when the formal superstructure of the frame (its professional, legal, material, and social aspects) becomes dissociated from its psycho-sensory (meta-framing) substructure, it becomes, instead, an *anti-contact* barrier, sealing off and removing the clinical space from the world of objects (both external and psychical). Divorced from its organic basis in embodied experience, the frame loses its dynamism, and when this happens, it inevitably begins to take on the bureaucratic character of a self-perpetuating institution, capable of upholding certain functions (the schedule, the procedures, the rules, the "law"), but no longer capable of adapting its shape to the immediate phenomenology of the clinical field. Under these circumstances, the frame becomes a formality, fixed in its ways, defined by its appearances, emptied out of its vital organic qualities. Under these conditions, the treatment process becomes servile to the dictates of the frame, rather than the frame serving the needs of the treatment.

The dynamic tensions within the frame between its fixed limits and its organic functions – between its institutional and its adaptive characteristics – makes it susceptible to "coming apart," either in the direction of undermining or dismantling the formal structure of rules and limits (resulting in oft-described role confusion, chronic enactments, boundary violations, etc.), or in the direction of a rigid and static structure, where the institutional rules and limits are maintained but are divorced from the organic dimensions of the frame. While we are likely to become aware of the first of these dysfunctions (i.e. those cases where coherence of the frame has become visibly compromised, leading to impasse or problematic enactments), it tends to be more difficult to recognize the dysfunction in the latter, where the frame seems to be stable and intact – where the deadening effects of the dissociation within the frame are hidden behind a superficial professional order and piety. Indeed, the "living" dimension of the frame is always prone to being eclipsed or effaced, since it is this dimension that disrupts the orderliness and fastidiousness of professional life, and which places a demand on the analyst to renew and re-animate the function of the frame. There exists, then, an inherent inertia, a tendency to resolve the dynamic tensions of the frame by ceding its definition entirely to its fixed formal characteristics, so that the life of the frame is seen as nothing other than a rote, reified, and unchanging set of policies and arrangements.

Consider a paradox that lies at the very heart of the clinical endeavor: if the analytic method is designed specifically to court the otherness (the unformed-ness, illogic, chaos, madness) of the unconscious, it is nevertheless essential that the frame should also preserve order and reason, and guarantee sanity in the clinical situation. If it cannot ensure sanity, the frame loses its therapeutic legitimacy, and the patient has no choice but to look elsewhere for help in finding an adequate shape for psychical life. However, in its role of safeguarding sanity, the frame inevitably trends towards a rationalized institutional structure, dedicated to its own orderly preservation, and as such is perpetually at risk of losing its specialized capacity as a mediator of "other realities" – those irrational forms and enigmatic messages emanating from unconscious life, and from the *real* of the external world. Designed to mount expeditions into unknown and anarchic terrain, the frame inevitably takes on the form of a bureaucracy.

Theory of the frame

Considering the changes that have taken place in clinical theory over the past half-century, and the diversity that now exists in models portraying the analytic process, it is odd how little variation has occurred in the tangible aspects – the institutional practices – of the analytic frame or setting. After almost a century, the 45–50 minute hour and the other *accouterments* of analysis remain remarkably unaltered. Freud's prototype remains the genotype, living on as the very institution of our daily practice, despite generations of veiled and explicit challenges from within psychoanalysis (Ferenczi, 1949; Fairbairn, 1954; Kohut, 1971; Winnicott, 1971; Bass, 2007; Stern, 2009, amongst others) as well as from without. Across the pluralistic landscape of differing theoretical persuasions, the institution of the frame may, in fact, be the closest thing we have to a defining blueprint of what clinical psychoanalysis actually is, or at least what it does. Yet it remains something of a neglected stepchild in our theories of clinical method. Once hardly spoken of at all, today "the frame" is used commonly in everyday clinical parlance, especially in America, where its meaning has largely been restricted to the management of the professional setting and procedures, contractual arrangements, and ethical boundaries of the clinical situation. Implicit in this usage is the assumption of the frame as a necessary professional structure that should remain steady and unchanging, held firmly in place while the real work of analysis (the analysis of the clinical *process*) is undertaken.

I will offer a contrasting picture of the frame as an animated structure that, beyond its role as an external superstructure demarcating and protecting the clinical process, plays its own distinctive part as an agent of the cure. In so doing, I follow another tradition of thinking about the frame in psychoanalysis, dating back to the post-war period when Marion Milner (1952) first identified the frame as playing a specific role in the treatment situation, and Winnicott recognized how the traumatized or psychotic patient will experience the setting (or frame) as a literal iteration of the holding environment and of the mother's body. It was Jose Bleger (1967), however, who developed the first substantial theory of the function of the frame in the clinical situation. It is only fairly recently that the role of the frame has re-emerged as a subject of study (Bass, 2007; Civitarese, 2010; Chetrit-Vatine, 2011; Lemma, 2014).

The role of the frame in the cure: Bleger's original contribution

In attempting to specify the role of the frame in the cure, I am building upon the original insights of Jose Bleger (1967), who saw the frame as fundamental in its role of securing the foundations of psychical functioning. In particular, he proposed that the primitive and psychotic parts of the personality are deposited in the frame and immobilized there. This makes the frame crucial to the ongoing "holding" function of the setting, as Winnicott (1960) described it. Winnicott indicated this function of the setting when he commented, for example, that if for the non-psychotic the couch *symbolizes* the mother's lap, for the psychotic it *is* the lap.

In conceptualizing the function of the frame, Bleger (1967) described it as a *non-process*, which he distinguishes from the analytic *process*. He points out that the frame does not present itself in the form of *variables in motion*, to be noticed and analyzed, but in the form of *constants* (Zac, 1972) within which the analytic process can unfold, a set of *invariants* in relation to which observable mental processes and data can be noticed, differentiated, categorized, and so on. In the analytic situation, these *constants* and *invariants* are present in the tangible and fixed characteristics of the setting (reclining on the couch, fixed duration of session, regular appointment times, constancy of the analyst's technical approach and neutrality, etc.).

Of particular significance is Bleger's identification of the function of the frame as emulating and securing the most primitive part of the patient's psychical life. In this regard, he described the frame as the "repository of the un-symbolized, mute repetition compulsion" of the earliest personality structure; the frame is where the "undifferentiated and non-solved part of the primitive symbiotic link" is deposited (Bleger, 1967, p. 518). The frame serves, then, to immobilize the "psychotic" part of the personality and keep it inert; but, by the same token, the frame is liable to become a stubborn, mute refuge for the disturbances of the self, a place where the pathological residue of the earliest damaged symbiosis is deposited beyond the reach of analysis, thus becoming what M. and W. Baranger (1983) call a "bastion." Bleger (2012) suggests that in these cases, the frame itself must become the object of attention and analysis – i.e. the way the frame operates must move to the foreground so that the "non-process" is disrupted and turned into a process that can be analyzed. The residual elements of the damaged symbiosis will be brought to light as the patient's relation to the frame is unveiled and analyzed. We are all familiar with tangible instances of this, for example on those occasions when we turn our attention to a pattern of behavior that has perhaps become routine, like a patient arriving slightly late for every session, or leaving the check on a side table, or straightening up the covers on the couch. It can be surprising how impenetrable to inquiry these things might be, and even more surprising when the enquiry opens up a hornet's nest in an otherwise reasonable and cooperative patient.

Frame as shared contact barrier: sensory symbiosis and beta-functioning

Bleger highlighted the way that the frame holds and immobilizes the early disturbance and unresolved psychotic elements of the personality, and in this way serves to prevent the outbreak of psychotic processes and frag-mentation (the setting functioning as *glue* or *suture*, as Civitarese, 2010, says). I would like to focus on a different aspect of what the frame does – the way it functions as a contact barrier that protects the clinical field while simultaneously facilitating moment-by-moment contact with the world. While Bleger's emphasis was on the *immobilizing* function of the frame, I am particularly interested in its capacity to *mobilize* the sensorial and perceptual dimension of experience, to keep the clinical encounter alive to the actual experience of objects-in-the-world. In this sense, the frame functions like a responsive and flexible membrane (analogous to the "skin" of the analytic setting) that keeps the analytic field alive to the sensation and perception of the world.

This contact-barrier function of the frame, which acts as a shared psycho-sensory membrane, operates entirely at a sub-symbolic level of mental functioning, where differentiation between self and other is annulled, and where something like a shared sensoriality is the decisive feature. Here analyst and patient join in a kind of sensory symbiosis, a sensing of things in common (Goldberg, 2012).[3] What is at stake here is not a fantasied merger or identification with an object, but an immediate sensorial registration of things-in-the-world, which Bleger describes as a "syncretic" engagement with the world, and which Ogden (1989) referred to in terms of sensory "contiguity". The formal, institutional, and symbolic functions of the frame are readily represented in thought and language, and are thereby capable of being repressed, dreamt about, and employed for various symbolic purposes (as demonstrated, for example, by the patient's struggle over arriving at the appointed time, or being early or late). By contrast, the ongoing activity of *meta-framing* is a psycho-sensory activity that occurs at the level of *presentation* rather than representation, and is therefore felt as something that is *happening*, rather than something thought about or represented in a symbolic register. In terms of Bion's (1970) conceptual system, I would suggest that framing does not entail the transformation of *beta* to *alpha* elements, but relies upon what I would like to call a *beta-function*, i.e. an entirely non-repre-sentational mode of psychical organization that shapes psychical existence through a direct syncretic patterning experienced in terms of movement, rhythm, shape, consonance and dissonance, prosody, intensity, and other qualities of experience that give a sense of the immediacy or presence of objects in the world – the sense of unmediated being in the world. The normative symbiotizing or psycho-sensory bonding function of the frame operates here, where patient and analyst are undifferentiated, registering things together as if through the same eyes. And here we see the consequences of the failure or inability of analyst and/or patient to forge an adequate psycho-sensory bond: it deprives the frame of its quality of being a "living membrane" that makes the clinical field alive to the world of objects, and that infuses the analytic space with the living quality of a virtual reality. This impairment in the function of the frame can only be repaired through re-engagement at the level of shared psycho-sensory experience, rather than at the differentiated level of object relationships which lend themselves to transference analysis and interpretation of wish and defense. Here the emphasis is on the meta-framing function that continually operates as a *non-represented background structuring presence*, constructing at every moment the space/time in which the clinical process can be experienced and observed.

Regressive and progressive developments in the function of the frame

In considering the makeup of the analytic frame, I have described an ever-present tension that exists between its institutional and animating aspects. Dysfunction within the structure of the frame (i.e. dissociation of its various functions) can take various forms, the most obvious of which are those tangible failures (unreliable arrangements, confusions of role, blurring of temporal, physical, and social boundaries, breaches in confidentiality and physical intimacy, etc.) that result in the frame's definition and functionality being *explicitly* compromised. These dysfunctions call for a tightening up of the tangible dimensions of the frame and greater consistency.

Far more difficult to discern is the kind of frame pathology that leaves the formal and tangible elements intact but dissociated from the level of shared sensoriality. It is of special significance, in this regard, that the more tangible professional functions of the frame may remain intact even while the organic psycho-sensory aspects may falter, leaving an empty professional shell. While the institutional dimension is by its nature robust and fixed over time, the organic dimension of the frame is always tenuous, constantly having to be renewed and re-animated in the present moment. If the psycho-sensory (meta-framing) dimension is impaired, dissociated, or goes "dead," the frame is immediately impeded in its psychoanalytic function, even if it continues to operate at the level of a professional and social institution. Thus there is always a contest over whether the quality of animation is eclipsed or sacrificed in the service of order and predictability (something I alluded to earlier in terms of a tendency towards bureaucratization).

When its dynamic or animated quality frame is attenuated or sacrificed, the frame tends to become a self-perpetuating "empty institution"; its essential meta-framing function of being a "living membrane" withers away. Here the frame not only fails to serve its vital function of being a live contact barrier, but it becomes itself an *anti*-contact barrier, keeping the clinical situation sealed off from real contact with the other worlds of internal and external objects. In trying to portray this kind of pathological regression in the structure of the frame, it may be useful to refer by analogy to Ogden's (1991) distinction between, on the one hand, the defensive use of the sensorium to form an adhesive barrier against contact with the world (what Bick, 1968, referred to as the formation of a "second-skin" autistic defense); and, on the other hand, the role of the senses in building an experiential matrix based on *contiguity* and live contact with the world (through periodicity, rhythm, symmetries, etc.).

The point here is that the clinical frame may itself become a calcified psycho-social structure, an inert institution that forms a barrier to contact with the world of (internal and external) objects, rather than bringing objects to life in the analytic situation.

In opposition to this regressive inertia, there exists a progressive tendency in the life of the frame – albeit one that entails active work on the part of the analyst – where it takes on the qualities of an *animated structure*. Here the operation of the frame, rather than serving as an inert barrier, instead functions more like a flexible psycho-sensory membrane or contact barrier, providing a stable structure while affording a novel responsive contact with the world of objects. Under these conditions, where the frame operates as a dynamic and mutative structure, the clinical field will tend to feel naturally alive, and the clinical process unfolds almost of its own accord. From this vantage point, we could say that the restoration of the vitality of the frame is foundational to our clinical work at all times.[4]

Maintaining the frame's dynamism requires of the analyst a certain kind of participation, an active or "inductive" engagement at the psychosensory level, which I address below.

The frame and clinical technique

I have proposed that, when it comes to providing an analytic frame fit for unconscious experience and communication, what holds things in place is not something static and detached, but, on the contrary, must be animated and engaged. What does this imply for analytic technique? What does it mean for the analyst to be engaged in "animating" or building the frame?

This is an underexplored topic in clinical theory, in that it constitutes a barely theorized but pivotal dimension of our clinical presence. Beyond the establishment of tangible arrangements (including ground-rules and material aspects of the setting), the analyst is also always engaged unconsciously in establishing a particular kind of "contact" at the level of shared experience. *Sensing things together* is basic to the operation of a viable clinical frame, reflecting as it does a fundamental drive towards a pre-subjective, symbiotic registration of experience (Goldberg, 2012).

Framing as an active ongoing dimension of analytic technique

The dynamic model being proposed here has implications for how we think about clinical technique. It calls into question the presumption that our technique should be relatively fixed and unchanging. Instead, we may think that what is likely to keep the frame alive and responsive to the clinical field is an experimental propensity, a certain mobility in technical approach, including an ability to employ different modes of attention and alterations in consciousness. For the same reason, it is important for the analyst to maintain a psycho-physical responsiveness, so as not to collude in a straitjacketing or deadening of the organic matrix of the frame, which depends for its vitality on the presence of living bodies.

In this view, a truly alive clinical frame is constantly being reconfigured – a moment-to-moment recalibration of the frame's pragmatics in accord with the current demands of its various heterogeneous functions. This involves an implicit (and sometimes explicit) kind of *calculation* of what is possible at any given juncture in the clinical encounter: the frame is constantly being reframed.

In any given case, many factors go into the calculation of how to engage the patient and set boundaries, and in the context of an established analytic practice, these calculations may follow a fairly standard protocol, according to the analyst's customary way of dealing with things. But the analytic frame is inherently tendentious, is constantly being reconfigured, and so the idea of its routinization is a mirage. Calculations concerning the combination of various functions of the frame (the need for a fixed setting, for the "law," for the demarcation of inner and outer, but also for a kind of bonding at the psycho-sensory level) may not be carried out consciously, but they are nonetheless constantly being made.

It is only rarely that the frame is recalculated in deliberate fashion, entailing explicit changes in formal arrangements – in length of session, frequency, use of chair or couch. For the most part, frame recalibrations take place pre-consciously, or sub-symbolically, at the level of micro-adjustments in the analyst's psycho-physical *presence* and *active technique*. "Active technique" (or what I will describe as the *inductive* dimension of technique) is the part of our technique that is performative rather than receptive or interpretive: it is the aspect of our clinical activity that is embodied in the actuality of our presence (in contrast to what we may *represent* in the transference, in a dream, in a phantasy, and so on). These elements of the analyst's *actuality* and *presence* – the way we speak, move, and react – have a formative role in the ongoing configuration of the frame, become part of the living body of the frame, "before" our presence is captured in the web of representation and transferential objectification. So, while at one level we are participants in the field of object-relational exchanges and meaning creation (transference-counter-transference, projective identification, etc.), we are also involved in the background activity of building and maintaining a living psycho-sensory framework.

The "inductive" dimension of the analyst's presence and its framing function

The analyst, in addition to providing holding and containing functions, will inevitably also serve *as initiator of qualities in the bipersonal field*. The analyst's actual participation as an aspect of the framing environment – his performative reality as a psychophysical presence – directly affects the shared psychosomatic matrix that constitutes the "living" dimension of the frame which underpins everything that happens in the clinical process. Engaging the patient at the level of shared sensory perception forms an essential *inductive* dimension of the analyst's technique (as distinct from the *interpretive* and the *receptive* dimensions we usually emphasize).[5] This "inductive" dimension of the analyst's activity, which tends to operate unnoticed at a "procedural" level, depends upon an implicit improvisational propensity towards engagement in the analyst's psycho-physical posture, in his states of consciousness, and in his modes of speech – adjustments in prosody, tone, rhythm and timing of speech, non-verbal sounds, and gestural cues, all of which act to catalyze or revitalize the sub-symbolic domain of mental functioning in the clinical encounter (Bucci, 2001). Together, these forms of interaction bring the bodily and sensorial domain into contact with the more differentiated mental functions associated with representational thought, language, and higher level affects. In this respect, the inductive dimension of the analyst's activity may be viewed as a specialized "frame-building" or frame-revitalizing dimension of technique.

I have suggested that there is an ongoing "syncretic" activity (a non-differentiated sensorial engagement with the world) that accompanies and underwrites the work of analysis – a kind of "proto-containment" (Cartwright, 2009) located in the "living" frame that perpetually generates a common ground of apperception and sensory engagement with the world of objects. Under normal circumstances, this joint participation of analyst and patient in a kind of ambient communal perception (Goldberg, 2012) or *sensing things together* carries on entirely in the background as an implicit or "mute" dimension of the work of the frame. However, it moves into the foreground on those occasions when there is an obvious breakdown of the implicit function of the frame. This is perhaps most evident in extreme instances of breakdown of shared psycho-sensory experience, as in cases of dissociative detachment or autistic encapsulation, and of course in psychosis and borderline conditions. Here there is no escaping the need for technical innovation; the "framing" or inductive activity of the analyst, usually operative invisibly in the background, comes to the foreground. Now the presence or "presencing" (Eshel, 2005) of the analyst counts for more than the representational impact of the words spoken (Alvarez's 2010 conception of "reclamation" is relevant here). The performative impact of the analyst's non-verbal activity, posture, and movement takes a central role, along with the performative aspects of the analyst's speech. The emphasis now falls on building a shared framework, a re-finding or revitalization of a psycho-sensory bond.

I would like to suggest that, while the analyst's framing activity is carried out largely unconsciously, it is crucially facilitated by the analyst's *conscious willingness to maintain a mobile attention and an experimental attitude towards technique.* In terms of clinical theory, I have suggested that the "framing" function of the analyst takes place not in the "space of absence" that gives rise to the transference relationship, but in the analyst's adaptive *presence* and psycho-sensory engagement at the level of proto-containment.[6]

Summary

I have proposed a model of the analytic frame as a "dynamic structure" serving a variety of functions that are constantly being reconfigured. A crucial aspect of the analyst's activity involves a kind of "frame-building" through psycho-sensory participation and technical innovation. Building on Bleger's conception of the frame as the repository of the psychotic parts of the personality and the earliest symbiosis, I suggest that the most important (but also the most inscrutable) aspect of the frame is its "meta-framing" function of providing a shared contact barrier or psycho-sensory membrane, which serves both to protect the analytic situation and to bring the clinical field into live contact with the world of objects (both external and psychical). In its meta-framing function, the frame, as embodiment of the non-differentiated (symbiotic) sensorial dimension of psychical life, makes possible the immediate perception of the presence and actuality of objects, so that they become available for experience in the clinical field. Where this meta-framing activity of shared psycho-sensory engagement is divorced or dissociated from the institutional, symbolic, and formal functions of the frame, the frame as a whole begins to take on the character of a bureaucratic institution, or alternately loses its coherence and breaks down.

Notes

1   In this respect, my view differs from Gill, Bass (2007), Stern (2009), and others who have made the case that the integrity of the analytic frame lies in its *intrinsic* qualities, rather than the *extrinsic* definition of analysis (imposed institutionally in terms of session frequency, use of the couch, etc.). In my view, both the (inherently psychoanalytic) "holding" function of the frame and the institutional "external" characteristics are intrinsic to the workings of

the frame, giving the frame its complex and dynamic hybrid quality of being both a psycho-social and a psycho-sensory structure.

2   Andre Green (1975) gives a vivid description of how the frame (or "setting," in his terminology) constitutes both a *symbolic* and a *psychical* boundary. The setting, he says, is "necessary in order to maintain the isolation of the analytic situation, the impossibility of discharge, the closeness of contact which is restricted to the sphere of the psyche, and the certainty that the mad thoughts will not go beyond the four walls of the consulting room. It ensures that the language used as a vehicle for the thoughts will remain metaphorical; that the session will come to an end; that it will be followed by another session and that its weighty truth, truer than reality, will be dissipated once the door shuts behind the patient" (p. 17).

3   Bleger tended to see treatment in terms of "de-symbiotization" (i.e. gradually undoing the symbiotic links), and this does aptly describe one direction of the treatment – towards differentiation and the integration of a viable internal world. But he also suggests the ongoing importance of experiencing a bond at the symbiotic level, and in this vein he speaks of the importance of the analyst's "syncretic participation," and the notion that the ego makes a "primary identification" with the world. The idea of a necessary access to states of de-differentiation or "one-ness" is strongly present in Milner (1952) and Little (1960).

4   This would accord with Ferro's (2005) observation that, today, our clinical approach has shifted from the analysis of the *contained* to the analysis of the *container*.

5   The analyst's "inductive" activity should be seen as operating in conjunction with the interpretive as well as the receptive or "reverie" activity of the analyst which has been so fruitfully explicated in recent decades (Bion, 1970; Ogden, 1997; Ferro, 2006).

6   The tendency towards merger and symbiosis has, with some exceptions (e.g. Milner, 1952), been viewed in clinical theory as regressive, defensive, and antithetical to the processes of separation, individuation, and development. Yet for some patients, the difficulty lies in an *inability* to experience a satisfactory symbiosis at the sensory level. In fact, this deficit in shared sensory experience may constitute the greatest impediment to a patient's well-being.

References

Alvarez, A. (2010). Levels of analytic work and levels of pathology: The work of calibration. *International Journal of Psychoanalysis*, 91: 859–878.

Baranger, M., Baranger, W., Mom, J. (1983). Process and non-process in analytic work. *International Journal of Psychoanalysis*, 64: 1–15.

Bass, A. (2007). When the frame doesn't fit the picture. *Psychoanalytic Dialogues*, 17: 1–27.

Bick, E. (1968). The experience of the skin in early object-relations. *International Journal of Psychoanalysis*, 49: 484–486.

Bion, W.R. (1970). *Attention and Interpretation*. London: Tavistock.

Bleger, J. (1967). Psycho-analysis of the psycho-analytic frame. *International Journal of Psychoanalysis*, 48: 511–519.

Bleger, J. (2012). *Symbiosis and Ambiguity: A Psychoanalytic Study*. New Library of Psychoanalysis. London: Routledge.

Bucci, W. (2001). Toward a "psychodynamic science": The state of current research. *Journal of the American Psychoanalytic Association*, 49: 57–68.

Cartwright, D. (2009). *Containing States of Mind: Exploring Bion's Container Model in Psychoanalytic Psychotherapy*. London: Routledge.

Chetrit-Vatine, V. (2011). The frame, the analyst's passion, and the ethical seduction of the analytic situation. *EPF-Bulletin*, 64: 247–260.

Civitarese, G. (2010). *The Intimate Room: Theory and Technique of the Analytic Field*. London: Routledge.

Eshel, O. (2005). Pantheus rather than Oedipus: On perversion, survival and analytic "presencing". *International Journal of Psychoanalysis*, 86: 1071–1097.

Fairbairn, W.D. (1954). *An Object-Relations Theory of the Personality*. New York: Basic Books.

Ferenczi, S. (1949). Confusion of the tongues between the adults and the child: The language of tenderness and of passion. *International Journal of Psychoanalysis*, 30: 225–230.

Ferro, A. (2005). *Seeds of Illness, Seeds of Recovery*. New York: Brunner-Routledge.

Ferro, A. (2006). Clinical implications of Bion's thought. *International Journal of Psychoanalysis*, 87(4): 989–1003.

Goldberg, P. (2012). Active perception and the search for sensory symbiosis. *Journal of the American Psychoanalytic Association*, 60: 791–812.

Green, A. (1975). The analyst, symbolization and absence in the analytic setting (on changes in analytic practice and analytic experience) – in memory of D.W. Winnicott. *International Journal of Psychoanalysis*, 56: 1–22.

Kohut, H. (1971). *The Analysis of the Self*. New York: International Universities Press.

Lemma, A. (2014). The body of the analyst and the analytic setting: Reflections on the embodied setting and the symbiotic transference. *International Journal of Psychoanalysis*, 95: 225–244.

Little, M. (1960). On basic unity. *International Journal of Psychoanalysis*, 41: 377–384.

Milner, M. (1952). Aspects of symbolism in comprehension of the not-self. *International Journal of Psychoanalysis*, 33: 181–194.

Ogden, T.H. (1989). *The Primitive Edge of Experience*. Northvale, NJ: Aronson.

Ogden, T.H. (1997). Reverie and interpretation. *Psychoanalytic Quarterly*, 66: 567–595.

Ogden, T.H. (1991). Some theoretical comments on personal isolation. *Psychoanalytic Dialogues*, 1: 377–390.

Perelberg, R.J. (2004). Narcissistic configurations: Violence and its absence in treatment. *International Journal of Psychoanalysis*, 85: 1065–1079.

Stern, S. (2009). Session frequency and the definition of psychoanalysis. *Psychoanalytic Dialogues*, 19: 670–675.

Winnicott, D.W. (1960). The theory of the parent–infant relationship. *International Journal of Psychoanalysis*, 41: 585–595.

Winnicott, D.W. (1971). *Playing and Reality*. London: Tavistock.

Zac, J. (1972). An investigation on how interpretations arise in the analyst. *International Journal of Psychoanalysis*, 53: 315–320.

Chapter 6

When the frame doesn't fit the picture

Anthony Bass

A patient, Helena, came to see me for consultation and let me know right away that she was flat broke. Atypically, she raised concerns about the way we would handle some of the arrangements that analysts consider to be part of the "frame" of the work even before she began to tell me why she wanted my help. Usually such discussions take place after I have spent at least a couple of sessions listening carefully to the prospective patient, trying to grasp something about what has brought her to see me. By then, the patient and I have started getting to know each other and have some beginning sense of how it might be to work together. Indeed, the work is already underway. But for Helena, the troubles for which she was seeking help and the ways in which we could approach the work were inextricably intertwined, making it important to consider some of the ground rules right away. A recovering addict, she could commit to only one session at a time. She proposed paying at the end of each session, in cash. In her view there could be no question of paying for missed sessions, which, in response to her question, I had told her was my general and preferred practice, because between any missed session and the next one she attended, she would owe me the fee for the session. To be in debt to me would constitute a slippery slope, which she had reason to fear could send her sliding back into serious trouble, the kind that she cautiously, somewhat skeptically hoped analysis might help her to transcend. With a history of extreme debt that went along with poly-drug abuse, her view, based on agonizing experience, was that to owe me money would be akin to using cocaine. She had been over her head in debt and variously addicted, and knew all too well the seductively compelling sirens that had repeatedly lured her to self-destruction. To allow her to owe me money would also implicate me in a codependent relationship with her, which would threaten to bring us both to our knees. She told me that in debtors anonymous meetings that she attended, therapist/addicts regularly spoke about how their patients owed them thousands of dollars, enacting collusive code-pendent relationships in which the therapists themselves would incur great debt while waiting impotently, pathetically, for their patients' ever-elusive, tantalizing payment. For these therapists, each session was a roll of the dice, a chance to hope once again that their ship was about to come in and finally get them out of the debt, both literal and symbolic of the morass in which they lived with their patient, that they had themselves incurred. Professional therapists who couldn't collect fees from their patients would sit together with patients who owed their therapists money at these meet-ings, telling their stories, helping each other with the shared problem that they had often found themselves helpless to conquer in their own personal therapy. She wondered if I had trouble collecting money from my patients, having come to believe that such forms of codependence were a difficulty shared by many therapists. She could not afford to risk enacting that type of emotional choreography with me. I paused, thought about that for a few moments. She waited.

I inquired as to whether she had picked up something about me that worried her that way, wondering to myself whether her psychic radar had already homed in on a disavowed part of me that would be receptive to engaging in the very enactment that she both dreaded and unconsciously sought. I wouldn't have necessarily wanted to reassure her about how I would be able to handle our financial affairs in any case, preferring to first explore her apprehensions and her fantasies, but there was something about her and her question that had me feeling insecure on the point right away, imagining that in certain states of mind quite likely to emerge with her I would become part of the problem before, and hopefully on the way to, contributing to some solutions.

Her vivid descriptions of the meetings led me to sense that perhaps she had put her finger on an occupational vulnerability suffered by many who had gone down the path of becoming professional therapists. My thoughts turned to recent threads on my institute list serve, in which distressed, frustrated, angry therapists shared experiences about trying to collect fees from runaway patients. "Were small claims court and collection agencies advisable measures to take?" they queried one another on the list.

Discouragement, anger, guilt, and fear emerged in these conversations, as some advised against taking such measures lest they stir up a hornet's nest of trouble in the form of dreaded malpractice suits. "Better just leave well enough alone and write it off," some advised. These conversational threads were generally of a concrete, practice management sort, reflecting anxiety, and did not engage the unconscious enactments and personal vulnerabilities on both sides that had led to a breakdown of the therapeutic process symbolized by the stemming of the flow of money for the unique and complex set of experiences that psychoanalysts offer.

Though I had not regarded collecting fees from my patients as a chronic problem, as Helena spoke several situations began to come to mind in which a patient seemingly "suddenly" owed me several months' worth of fees, enacting a problem in the transference-countertransference field that remained dissociated from my awareness until it became large enough to threaten the analytic work itself. I recalled one patient, like the cartoon character Wimpy, who would famously say, "I'd be glad to pay you Tuesday for a hamburger today." She uttered the constant refrain, "Well, you know I'll pay you eventually, don't you?" shaking her head in considerable umbrage, rolling her eyes in long-suffering, irritated impatience as she read my concern about her mounting bill as a sign that I actually distrusted her. She was mystified at the source of my distrust that kept me from relying on her evident integrity. I didn't distrust her in the way that she assumed, knowing that ultimately she would pay her fees, but I felt thwarted nevertheless, wanting her to pay her fee today so that I could pay for my hamburgers today. It took years of analysis before my point of view about payment became of interest or concern to her.

On at least one of the occasions of mounting debt that Helena's description was bringing into focus for me, the therapy ended when the patient and I belatedly realized that she could simply not pay my fee as a result of some career change choices and the related, not consciously anticipated termination of a generous insurance policy. A large debt has yet to be paid off, though once or twice a year a hundred dollar check still floats in, folded into a flowery, perfumed greeting card with a brief note that she intends to resume therapy one day, a sign that she hasn't forgotten me and doesn't want me to forget her either.

In Helena's view, even paying me by check would constitute too great a risk to take, because a check can bounce, falsely symbolizing money that isn't actually there. Technically, then, paying me by check would be tantamount to owing me money, pending the check clearing, existing until then in a potential space of bad faith. Even paying my bill at the end of the month, my usual practice, represented a form of debt, because Helena would always be in the position of owing me money for services provided until the end of any given month when payment was due.

We faced a paradox from the opening moments of the first session. We couldn't really begin our work until we reached an agreement on essential ground rules, because the ground rules themselves threatened to become implicated in an immediate collusion and enactment of threatening symptoms. Our negotiation, including our joint reflection on the establishment of these ground rules, had to be our point of entry into the work. We learned a lot about each other in the first few sessions.

An atypical set of ground rules began to emerge. If she had money that day for a session, we would work. If not, she would let me know that she was tapped out, and we would forego sessions until she could pay for one. Missed sessions would not be charged, but she would not miss any session that she could afford to pay for. We would both have to understand and bear the knowledge that any session could be our last. She would do her best to make enough money that week for a session or two (she was talented and savvy, having a track record of making a very good income when she was not spiraling out of control), but she had come to recognize that her life was best lived as a one-day-at-a-time proposition, and if I were going to be able to help her, I would have to live with that as well. Her analysis would happen one day at a time or it wouldn't happen at all, a useful life lesson that Helena began to teach me beginning with our first encounter, more than three thousand days ago.

But the plan that was beginning to take shape in those first exploratory meetings was leaving me feeling uneasy. How would I feel having her terminate the sessions on the spot if she found that she could not pay for sessions? I worried, based in part on past experiences that she described to me, that Helena would sabotage herself and our work at a difficult or a promising moment by seeing to it that she couldn't pay. A dysfunctional week in which she wasn't earning money would immediately translate into the suspension of sessions, which could intensify her sense of failure and shame, leading to even greater paralysis and a potential spiraling into destructive self-states that had been part of the fabric of her experience.

The prospect of beginning to work together under these circumstances didn't feel altogether responsible, yet I could sense a bind. She wanted to work with me, and I felt both game and apprehensive. I imagined finding myself having to choose between leaving a patient in trouble in the lurch because of what amounted to a temporary cash flow problem and playing a role in an analysis whereby my patient and I found ourselves in the grip of a mutually destructive enactment in which her seeing me for sessions she couldn't afford led us down the road to perdition. We spoke about many of these concerns in those first few days of sessions.

I had never worked with a patient under such circumstances, and indeed, when it came to my own financial needs, I preferred a more predictable approach to structuring my practice and planning my income. Yet if I wished to work with this patient I would have to change my way of doing business. And I would have to bear the anxiety of working in a new way. So I did, and these arrangements (about payment and missed sessions) were made in a quite concrete way initially, without a great deal of attention to the meanings and symbolism held in our choices. Once we agreed on the basic ground rules for the therapy, there was a lot Helena needed to tell me about what brought her to this point in her life.

As is often the case in situations in which idiosyncratic frame arrangements take hold, aspects of the way Helena's therapy was structured helped illuminate aspects of her emergent history as well as elements of the shifting transference-countertransference field. In our work together over time, particular features of the cocreated frame and the meanings associated with them furthered exploration of analytic material as it evolved, material that illuminated features of her history as well as features of our relationship as it developed.

For example, three years into the therapy, the choreography of payment became once again a subject of discussion. For a woman who had difficulty with closeness to men and whose sexual history had included considerable trauma, the exchange of cash at the end of each session was a subtle maneuver. The daily handoff of money brought us but an inch or two from each other, carefully, never actually touching, a complex physical and emotional balancing act, which eventually became of interest to both of us, providing access to fantasy material that never before had been discussed and that took us to unanticipated depths.

Our awareness of the delicacy of such moments, apparently mutually dissociated until this juncture, and our newfound capacity to think about them together in the context of emerging aspects of her history and the evolving state of our relationship had not been accessible to us until much had been accomplished. Two years further into the therapy, Helena found that she preferred that I bill her at the end of the month and began paying her bill with a check, which impressed both of us as a meaningful marker of change.

The "frame" remains an essential reference point throughout any analysis. Although in one sense it is meant to create and stand for, both practically and symbolically, a therapeutic structure with clear and safe boundaries in which the process of therapy unfolds, the establishment of a frame is, at the same time, paradoxically an integral part of the process itself. That is, the establishment of the frame serves both as a relatively fixed, clearly defined container for the therapeutic work and as a point of departure for the negotiation of transference-countertransference elements, and enactments, and the working through of such enactments in an intersubjective field. Aspects of the patient's and analyst's psychic lives, and the way their relationship is taking shape, are expressed and negotiated through the establishment of a frame for their work together.

The essential shape of any given psychoanalytic process, given definition by the frame, is often set forth by the analyst as "rules" or "policies," typically most explicitly delineated at the beginning of an analysis in the first few sessions. The frame is constituted of the various arrangements that define the unique shapes, functions, and boundaries of an analysis, differentiating it from other sorts of interpersonal relationships. Although Freud never utilized the concept of the frame per se, and study of his published cases and reports from his patients reveal a more flexible approach to technique in his own clinical practice than his theorizing suggests, the frame of traditional psychoanalysis includes many of the elements set forth by Freud in his technical papers.

Freud recognized the necessity for establishing the frame early on in the treatment in his oft-cited metaphor of clinical psychoanalysis as a chess game, in which rules for the opening moves are more systematically formulated and easily mastered than approaches to the far more complex middle game, where play becomes increasingly subtle and the successful player relies increasingly on experience, intuition, and creative breakthroughs rather than preconceived rules to move the play forward.

The experienced psychoanalyst, like the chess master, knows the "book moves" well, and in the asymmetrical roles that analyst and patient typically assume, the analyst bears the lion's share of responsibility for managing the proceedings with these rules in mind. (It should be noted, too, that the book moves, whether in chess or in psychoanalysis, do change over time. Creative breakthroughs in technique lead to innovations in theory, which open up new possibilities for technique, eventually leading to alterations in what is regarded as standard procedure.)

Equally important, though, as Hoffman (1998) pointed out, is the option to toss out the book from time to time, to respond with spontaneity and creativity to unique features of any given patient, to feel one's way in the immediacy of experience, and to free up what may have become the constraints and rigidities of "policy." Such "acts of freedom" (see also Symington, 1983), crucial to the analyst's repertoire, are highly personal, expressive of the analyst's personality as well as his understanding of the patient, and integral to the analyst's art. Indeed, I believe these rogue interpretive moments lie at the heart of therapeutic action.

Although Freud did note that subjective factors guide each analyst's preferences regarding technique and the structure of the psychoanalytic situation, starting with his own, there has been a tendency—at least among traditional American analysts who have taken up the question of the frame explicitly—to favor a relatively fixed and definitive structure for psycho-analysis. Perhaps the most prolific theoretician on the subject of the frame as an explicit reference point is Robert Langs, from whose perspective an unvarying frame must be set and maintained actively by the analyst, holding the shape and structure of the analysis and carefully interpreting any threat of compromise.

For Langs (1982), modifications of the frame, departure from classical technique (e.g. making noninterpretive interventions or indulging in extraneous or social remarks, or any form of self-disclosure), are likely to generate what he called a "misalliance" with the patient and always reflect disturbances in the analyst (countertransference difficulties) that the patient takes note of consciously or unconsciously and responds to by trying to cure, virtually always to the detriment of the process and the patient's own best interests. In such a model, self-disclosure, noninterpretive forms of participation, or varying kinds of participation in transference-counter-transference enactments are regarded as destructive because they compromise traditional framing principles of anonymity, neutrality, and non-gratification—all key shibboleths of Freudian analysis.

The use of the metaphor of the frame was probably introduced into psychoanalytic discourse in 1952 by the artist/analyst Marion Milner, evoking the image of a picture frame:

The frame marks off the different kind of reality that is within it from that which is outside it, but a temporal spatial frame also marks off the special kind of reality of a psychoanalytic session. In psychoanalysis it is the existence of this frame that makes possible the full development of that creative illusion that analysts call transference.

(Milner, 1952, p. 182)

So in Milner's usage, the creation of a frame represents the analyst's activity in marking off a special kind of space in which certain unusual, quintessentially "psychoanalytic" kinds of experience may occur—potential space, to use Winnicott's term. Loewald (1980), in elaborating his view of psychoanalysis as an art, and the fantasy character of the psychoanalytic situation, compared psychoanalysis to a dramatic art, in which the analyst and patient conspire in the creation of an illusion, a play (p. 355). Patient and analyst are, in a sense, coauthors of the production. If analytic work is conceived as an artistic creation fashioned by analyst and patient together, the frame, or the set design in the theatrical metaphor, also lends itself to collaborative creative effort, patient and analyst working on and with each other to achieve the right blend of materials to achieve their joint vision. As Loewald felicitously put it:

in the mutual interaction of the good analytic hour, patient and analyst—each in his own way and on his own mental level—become both artist and medium for each other. For the analyst as artist his medium is the patient in his psychic life; for the patient as artist the analyst becomes his medium. But as the living human media they have their own creative capabilities, so they are both creators themselves.

(Loewald, 1980, p. 369)

Whether visual or dramatic, the artistic metaphor suggests that "function," the actualization of the shared creative effort, is paramount, whereas specific, concrete elements of frame or set are secondary, playing a supportive role to the unique therapeutic vision created by the therapeutic dyad. What are the rules, elements, shapes, and structures of the psychoanalytic situation that make for the most powerful and effective therapeutic transformations in any given collaborative process? To a great extent, the answer to the question lies at the heart of the work of any given psychoanalytic couple. Indeed, the negotiation of framing activity may, itself, be a medium carrying potential therapeutic action, in the patient's discovery of a negotiable relational world, or the development of competence in negotiation, both of which carry interpersonal and object relational implications for change (S. Pizer, personal communication).

The interpersonal and intrapsychic negotiation of how we find ways to be ourselves with one another and accept others on their own terms is a developmental achievement that psychoanalysis may be uniquely situated to facilitate through attention to the vicissitudes of the ongoing negotiation and analysis of that negotiation in the analytic situation. In the living, unfolding quintessentially generative relationship with each patient, different structures or different ways of negotiating the rules that sustain an analytic setting and process may be more or less suited to the task in any given dyad. Milner's use of the concept of "marking off" areas in which different kinds of reality operate presaged extensive theorizing in other fields about the nature and function of frames.

Gregory Bateson's influential anthropological and ethological studies on frames as containers for divergent realities led him to conceptualize psychotherapy as a kind of frame-repairing enterprise (Bateson, 1972; Bromberg, 1982). By comparing the rules of psychotherapy to that of more formally structured games, Bateson suggested that the:

> process of psychotherapy is a framed interaction between two persons, in which the rules are implicit but subject to change. Such change can only be proposed by experimental action, but every such experimental action, in which a proposal to change the rules is implicit, is itself a part of the ongoing game. It is this combination of logical types within the single meaningful act that gives to therapy the character not of a rigid game like canasta but, instead, that of an evolving system of interaction. The play of kittens or otters has this character.
>
> (Bateson, 1972, pp. 191–192)

In other words, in Bateson's view, the rules of psychotherapy, like that of other forms of structured but free play, cannot be clearly distinguished from the process itself. The rules are themselves in play.

Goffman's (1986) sociological study *Frame Analysis: An Essay on the Organization of Experience*, in which frames are defined as containing the rules and practices that create the context in which everyday experience is understood, introduced ways of thinking about frames well suited to considering the forms and functions of psychoanalysis. Goffman's work provides us with more flexible paradigms capable of holding and engaging the complex intrapsychic and interpersonal experiences we regularly encounter in analytic work.

Frames generate what Goffman referred to as "guided doings" in his model, any act or behavior can only really be understood within the context of the particular frame in which it takes place, and confusion is inevitable when we try to understand experience without reference to its framing context. For example, in observing one man pointing a gun at another, Goffman observed that it would be crucial to recognize that the context of the act is a movie set rather than an actual bank robbery. Any observer's response to the scene will necessarily be different given that important piece of framing information.

Similarly, psychoanalytic moments, interactions, and choices can be understood only in the context of the particular psychoanalytic frame in which they take place. Failure to take such variables into account has frequently led to the unfortunate fruitless but familiar form of psychoanalytic discourse and dissing that typically takes the form of suggesting that what the other person is doing is "not psychoanalysis." We know that many innovations in psychoanalytic technique were originally dismissed as not psychoanalytic. That is, they could not be understood without reference to the newly developing paradigm that framed them.

For example, the analyst's self-disclosure was regarded as problematic because it transgressed fundamental traditional psychoanalytic principles of anonymity and neutrality. But contemporary psychoanalytic frames of reference reconsider that prescription and replace it with a principle that suggests that self-disclosure can be helpful to the patient in psychoanalysis or problematic, depending on the specific context in which the moment is framed (Bass, 2001, p. 721). There are times when self-disclosure—especially but not exclusively of one's experience or state of mind in relation to the patient—is useful, opening up new possibilities, enriching and shaping new forms of experience of self and others while further elucidating established forms. And there are times when self-disclosure simply reenacts and reinforces entrenched ways of being, nipping change in the bud. The art of psychoanalysis resides in how well we go about trying to tell the difference and how resourcefully we are able to manage to move forward with the work when we are unsure.

When Freud (1913) set forth his own recommendations for technique, he wrote that whereas his suggestions might seem like mere details, their justification was that they were the rules of the game, acquiring importance through their connection to the whole game plan (p. 342). His rules—captured in rich metaphor of the analyst as mirror, surgeon, and interpreter of patients' dreams and unconscious life—served his plan exceptionally well, generating a unique and powerful psychoanalytic reality designed to highlight the unfolding of transference experience as drive derivatives from deep inside the patient, with minimal "contamination" by the analyst.

A century later, we are in a position to observe that psychoanalysis does not take place in a vacuum but rather evolves in particular cultural milieus, social, and intellectual contexts (J. Davies, personal communication). New frames of reference that apply to physical reality (by way of contemporary physics and field theories) and psychic reality (reflecting a variety of two-person relational and interpersonal perspectives) have changed our vantage point for considering a number of psychoanalytic assumptions. Freud developed his approach in a time and place in which the analyst's authority enjoyed a different, perhaps less ambivalent standing. Parents were themselves seen as absolute authorities, and the ideal "child/patient" was expected to follow the analyst's/parent's rules as prescribed. The capacity to negotiate rules in appropriate ways, emphasizing an intersubjective field of experience, was not yet understood or valued as it is today.

From another perspective, the movement from omnipotence to an appropriate form of self-regard, for analyst and patient alike, in which both triumphs and disappointments were not only possible but also necessary, was not yet theorized. Social, cultural, and intellectual trends during the past century have contributed to the creation of new norms and therefore different analytic goals and expectations. We would expect that the rules and frames of analysis would shift to reflect such changing mores.

We have observed that different values, sensibilities, and ways of understanding the psychoanalytic project generate different psychoanalytic realities, alternate frames, other "doings." In Mitchell's (1998, p. 170) terms, "each analytic tradition has its own notion of what it is that the analyst should try to do and be: neutral, empathic, holding, containing, authentic." Analytic rules are relative to analytic goals. Each analyst must define and refine the relationship between the particular qualities of the frame that he creates with his patient and the goals and values that guide his psychoanalytic vision. And each analyst will construct a personal map in accordance with the particular vision that guides the doings. Each analyst's work is guided by a particular, personally constructed set of intentions.

In describing his own analytic intentions in relation to his management of the frame, Mitchell (1993) suggested that:

> what is most important is not what the analyst does, as long as he struggles to do what seems, at the moment, to be the right thing; what is most important is the way in which analyst and analysand come to understand what has happened. What is most crucial is that, whatever the analyst does, whether acting flexibly or standing firm, he does it with considerable self-reflection, and openness to question and reconsider, and most important, with the patient's best interests at heart. If the patient and analyst together find a way to construe the event constructively, as an opportunity, the process opens up and is enriched. If both end up experiencing the event as the defeat of either the patient or analyst, the process closes off and an opportunity is lost … In short, the process itself is more important than the decision arrived at. And the process does not end at the point at which the analyst makes a decision with regard to the analysand's request … A critical dimension of making constructive use of these situations is an openness to a continual reevaluation of their meanings over time.
>
> (Mitchell, 1993, p. 196)

Similarly, Coltart (1992) noted that although attention to general principles of technique is essential,

> we must recognize the ever-present phenomenon that every patient is unique, and any generalized statement about how to do what, when, where and why, must always be subject to modifications in the light of the patient's uniqueness and our unique developing relationship to him and our personality.—The atmosphere of the analysis is the joint creation of the patient and analyst, and between this unique pair it grows and happens. In fact, if I were to settle for which of the pair in the therapeutic dyad has more influence than the other on the whole way of being of an analysis, I would say it is the patient.
>
> (Coltart, 1992, p. 99)

From the latter vantage point, I find it helpful to recognize that I will most likely participate in the cocreation of and be guided by quite different frames of analysis in a day's work, each frame containing, reflecting, and blending aspects of the two separate and unique subjectivities engaged in an analytic process. My unconscious life with any given patient is implicated, and the unique construction of any given frame for analysis is likely to carry with it enactments of aspects of our experience that will be unlike that with any other patient. This process is itself likely to become the subject of joint analytic consideration and is often highlighted when aspects of the way a frame is constructed change over time in the course of an analysis.

Because analysts work within different frames over the course of a day's work, and because different analysts work with different intentions in mind, a notion of the analytic frame is misleading and may work to the detriment of the process. Rather, analytic frames come in many different shapes and seem to be constructed out of a variety of materials, varying in intent as well as the technical details that express that intent. The notion that "one size fits all" doesn't quite fit anyone, and enacting and eventually understanding and articulating the particular ways in which the frame doesn't fit inevitably becomes an integral aspect of an evolving therapeutic process. A patient with whom I recently began to work commented in the midst of some negotiation of the fee that his grandfather, a wise and successful entrepreneur, used to say that a good negotiation is one in which no one is entirely happy. In our case, meeting his grandfather's criterion for good-enough negotiating, we were both sufficiently satisfied with the outcome of our negotiation, neither of us getting exactly what we wanted.

Just as physicists came to understand that light has properties of both particle and wave, psychoanalysts began to see that a frame for analysis has properties of both process and structure (Bass, 2001, p. 718). Technical issues related to the management of the frame are therefore always contextual and can never effectively operate according to "received" doctrine or prescription. Elements of process and structure move from foreground to background as the analysis unfolds.

The patient's conscious and unconscious observational and interpretive work on the analyst is an ongoing dimension of the psychoanalytic experience, whether the analyst recognizes it or not. Presumptions of a patient's naivete, regarding his analyst's psychology notwithstanding, the analyst's relation to the setting and rules of engagement with any particular patient provide a rich source of data for the patient about aspects of the analyst's personality and character as well as about the analyst's unconscious life as it shapes the contours of his relationship both to his preferred theory and to the patient.

Sometimes the process of frame construction occurs in a relatively seamless way, only faintly observed, whereas in other analyses or at other points in the same analysis, the shaping of a frame becomes a more central, consciously negotiated, or contentious aspect of the process. A frame functions to define where attention is to be directed. In the case of the picture frame, it is what is inside the frame that is worth considering. Sometimes strong differences of opinion between analyst and patient regarding what is inside the frame and what is outside become the source of impasses, stalled or failed analyses, or mutually mystifying enactments in the transference-countertransference. Sometimes they lead to fruitful working through of differences, moments of mutual analysis of transference-countertransference processes or enactments.

In one such moment in my analysis, as I anxiously pressed my analyst about his contribution to what I regarded as a disturbing enactment in our work, Benjamin Wolstein encouraged me to press on with my analysis of his unconscious countertransference by recounting a story from his own analysis with Clara Thompson. He reported that he has raised a pointed question about the meaning of something she had done in a session. She told him that its meaning was something that didn't belong there, that it was for her to sort out privately, in her own self-analysis. He quoted himself as having said to her, "Well, if it doesn't belong in my analysis, what is it doing in here?"

Impasses in analysis often represent the emergence of an incompatibility of frames; bringing such incompatibilities into joint awareness is frequently the first step toward inquiring into the possibility of a negotiation of the frame activity that can become an important part of the psychic work for both participants. Such phases of analytic work often generate considerable anxiety in both participants, as mutual blind spots and dissociative processes may begin to come into awareness in ways that can be quite disorienting at first while holding considerable potential for mutual growth.

In such situations, it can seem as though the patient and analyst have come to be living in different analyses altogether. This may have something of the feeling of a couple in a long marriage recognizing that they need to work on their marriage following the recognition that they have grown in different directions, or that they no longer want the same things in the relationship as they had in the early years of their marriage. With many psychoanalyses today lasting longer than average marriages (it is not unusual for analytic relationships to outlast the marriage of both analyst and patient), changes in the relationship over time are often reflected in the need to reconsider aspects of the way the relationship is structured. Sometimes such junctures lead the therapist to seek consultation or the patient to confer with another analyst on the state of his therapy. "Can my therapeutic relationship be saved, or is it time to cut my losses and move on?" is a common theme in analytic consultation. I have heard of cases in which a patient and therapist go together to a consultant in a kind of therapeutic "couples" session. Either participant in the analytic couple may initiate a change in the frame, as either patient or analyst may be the first to feel the need to break out of a frame that no longer fits (see Symington, 1983, for some examples of this). Over the course of any long analysis, both patient and analyst will inevitably grow and change, and most likely they will have contributed in no small way to the changes each have been able to make. The relationship must grow to encompass these changing needs or it can be at risk.

Fixed and rigid frame constructions can become impediments to necessary changes in the relationship. Indeed, they are frequently implicated in the failure of an analysis to get off the ground in the first place. Too rigid a sense of the necessity of a particular kind of frame has all too often taken the form of an assessment that the patient is "not analyzable." I have seen in my practice a surprising number of patients (frequently psychoanalysts) who carry with them the scars of having been told while applying for analysis at classical institutes in New York that they were unsuitable for analysis, a diagnostic prediction that almost invariably turns out to be premature and incorrect, more a statement about disclaimed incompatible frames of reference than a genuinely psychoanalytic assessment.

My own approach to participating in the establishment of a frame in which psychoanalytic work can be initiated and has the opportunity to flourish has become increasingly elastic over these past twenty years of practice. Over time I have come to recognize that any frame for an ever-deepening analysis benefits from allowing more play to stretch and fit the unforeseen.

As the patient and analyst change, learn, and grow, the frame for analysis is likely to prove unwieldy unless it is built to accommodate surprises.

Too fixed a frame may take on a Procrustean rigidity, constraining, even perverting the process, which may require struggling to cast off one carapace so that another more suitable might grow in its stead. However, too loose a frame or one too quickly abandoned might fail to provide proper engagement and traction in the process, producing a flaccid, deadened experience ill-suited to helping the patient negotiate the inner obstacles to further self-differentiation, individuation, and self-awareness.

The process of negotiating such transformations is an essential part of an approach to analysis that regards "enactments" not as pathological junctures to be avoided but as a necessary part of the creation of a therapeutic environment through which heretofore unformulated aspects of inner life and experience come into being in new ways in the immediate shared experience of patient and analyst. In other words, each unique frame construction will inevitably reflect enactments in the transference-countertransference field. But in putting too fine a point on the external characteristics that constitute an analytic frame, we threaten to turn the frame into a kind of fetish, limiting the scope, flexibility, and full potential of the intrinsic process, thereby thwarting the possibility of a living, changing, mutually engaging, and mutually transforming relationship.

In his 1928 paper on technique, Ferenzci introduced a phrase coined by his patient, "elasticity of technique." "A patient of mine once spoke of the elasticity of technique," he wrote. "The analyst, like an elastic band, must yield to the patient's pull, but without ceasing to pull in his own direction, so long as one position or the other has not been conclusively demonstrated to be untenable" (Ferenzci, 1928, p. 95).

The yielding and pulling in Ferenzci's metaphor captures something of my experience of how a frame, or more aptly a series of transformations of framing elements, is cocreated in any given analytic process. The shape of the frame that my patients and I create both performs its function in defining the work's boundaries, and its establishment also becomes at the same time an essential part of our experience together and of each other, and so part of the data of analysis. In other words, the frame embodies the paradox of being both structure and process simultaneously.

I generally prefer to see a patient at least three times a week, with payment expected for missed sessions. I sometimes prefer that a patient use the couch (though this is less of a preference now than it was several years ago) and begin sessions telling me what is coming to mind, following with associations. Yet I find that each preference that I hold evokes recollections of multiple exceptions to any given "rule." In one case with a patient who became frozen at the beginning of sessions shortly after we began, we agreed that I would begin sessions for a period of time. A few weeks later, she resumed her initiating position and we were able to gain some understanding of the context and meaning of her temporary paralysis. Different arrangements concerning the payment of fees, physical positions on the couch, in the chair, standing, in one case lying on the floor; arrangements about phone contacts and phone sessions, phone analyses, most recently email contacts, arrangements about payment, vacations, missed sessions—are all variables rather than constants.

As Pizer (1998) averred, the nonnegotiable realm in psychoanalysis is quite limited, except when a history of trauma complicates the field with the detritus of dread, hopelessness, and exploitation, creating a sclerotic condition that can be enacted at the heart of the analysis itself. Appropriate nonnegotiability is easily defined. We don't have sex with our patients or go into business together, although we all know of too many unfortunate and mutually destructive exceptions to these rules. We commit ourselves to work with our patients' best interests in mind and at heart. As best we can, we pay attention to whatever evidence we can find of our patients' and our own unconscious experience with one another, using it, ourselves, and the evolving relationship we offer in the service of deepening and enriching the process and bringing about growth and healing change.

A man came to see me following a long classical analysis in connection with a long-standing symptom that was once again plaguing him after some years of control. The context of his concern currently, however, was that he was living with cancer that had metastasized to the lung, and so his life was at a particularly vulnerable and uncertain juncture. He was seeing another therapist, a cancer specialist, for help coping with his illness, and she had concurred that he might find someone to help him with this other symptom, as they had agreed that it was important to keep on living and working out his life issues as long as he could.

He very quickly plunged into what impressed me as a remarkably deep analysis, in which some of these ground rule arrangements became the subject of a good deal of attention. Talk of an eating disorder (the presenting symptom) led to talk of sexual practices and problems, to mother, to incestuous feelings and behaviors, to mother's controlling personality, to his difficulty separating from her, a dawning recognition that he had only ever seen his father through his mother's eyes so that he never could really have his own relationship to him, and so on. The transference-counter-transference field was rich and intense from the get-go. He was angry with me about my fee (higher than his psychiatrist's, a younger woman toward whom he felt a great deal of rather paternal affection) and about my stopping sessions more or less on time (which she did not and which he felt expressed her love for him, but at the same time he somewhat patronized her about it). He had a great deal to talk about and an awareness of the limits of time, and he was put out when I would stop a session before another patient had rung my bell. "Your next patient isn't here yet," he would protest.

He was drawn to and envied my relative youth, apparent health, and presumed virility, a quality he believed he lacked and about which he harbored enormous shame. Despite his protestations and his annoyance and hurt feelings with me, and perhaps because of them as well, he became deeply engaged in our sessions, deciding to stop seeing his cancer therapist so that he could devote his full energies to our work. He pushed and I pulled. Exploring his response to my fee, time arrangements, and other manifestations of boundaries to which I felt it important to hold firm for my sake, as well as for his, the frame became an important aspect of our conversations, and little by little he began to see changes in himself in relation to his own boundaries. We both came to believe that these changes, his increasing sense of self-differentiation and individuation, had something to do with confronting our differences, our unique ways of being, forged under the pressure of time constraints.

He began to respond to friends differently. He took enormous pleasure from the way in which old acquaintances were now becoming real friends, showing up at his house for visits that really meant something to him and, he knew, to them. He told me with a sense of wonder that he had many more real friendships than he had ever had before, and he knew and took pride in his sense that these changes started with the changes in himself that he was beginning to feel from the inside out. He was able to be clearer with his wife about his own needs, and his relationship to food began to change. He was developing a new (his own) relationship to his father and separating from his mother, both long dead. He was becoming more open with his wife and friends, finding bittersweet richness in his life and in our psychoanalytic explorations.

After awhile, his illness progressed further. The cancer metastasized to the bone, breaking some of them so that he was in great pain, and he couldn't get around anymore. He wouldn't be able to come to sessions. Would I consider coming to his house to continue the analysis, he wondered. Now questions pertaining to the ground rules for analysis existed in a different context, as a new set of meanings took central stage. Intimacy, love, and loss became central themes, and my presence at his bedside as he approached death became an enormously important symbol of where he and we had come to.

He recognized that he had become important to me and that my coming to his house for sessions was now a necessity that we both felt. Our relationship no longer seemed defined by the particular asymmetries that defined some of our earlier discussions of ground rules. Sensing that I was struggling with feelings about losing him, he asked me if I had someone to talk to about all this, my own therapist or supervisor.

I felt grateful for his recognition and sensitivity to my feelings for him, and I said that I would have access to that sort of help when I needed it but that it was also helpful for us to be able to talk about what we were feeling and going through together in our sessions. He came to feel that I had changed as much in our time together as he had and that the changes that our sessions along with his life circumstances had brought about in him had had a complementary and positive affect on me. He could see that I had changed too. My flexibility and responsiveness to his needs regarding how we could conduct our sessions were only part of what he had observed in me that he felt reflected my own growth with him. And, of course, I knew that he was right.

Each psychoanalytic relationship carries with it the potential to engage and promote newly evolving aspects of both patient and analyst, which may be reflected in transformations of an evolving analytic frame. This may be particularly the case in long analyses in which the extended deep and intimate engagement of two personalities at conscious and unconscious levels brings about mutual personality change that is felt at the heart of the process and that reverberates at the very core of the structure of the work itself.

The following vignette is intended to capture something of the complex and evolving shaping and reshaping of a custom-made frame meant to provide a full-enough context for an analysis that spanned many years of change. A striking young woman, Nicole, started treatment some years ago. Recently relocated to New York City, she let me know in the initial phone conversation, as she (accurately) heard in my voice some uncertainty as to whether I could begin with a new patient, that she could be quite flexible about time and that my fee would not be a problem either. She was anxious to work with me because of a strong recommendation that had come from a trusted friend who also told her that I tended to be busy and might not have time available, so she wanted me to know that it would be worth my while to work with her.

Several elements of the frame of Nicole's analysis became of interest early in the consultation and quickly came into play in enacting various aspects of our psychic life together in what would become an extensive exploration of the role of money, boundaries, exploitation, control, need, and power. She reported an erotic dream in the second consultation hour in which I appeared undisguised as a workman in her apartment whom she paid for sex. She made it clear that she was quite prone to "acting out" and that traditional therapeutic frames had failed to hold her in the past. She had an affair with a former therapist, initiated by her as she reported it, one that she reported as having been in no way disturbing, let alone traumatic.

Surprisingly, she appeared to regard the experience as quite positive, with no hard feelings or any sense of betrayal, though it later emerged that she herself had used sex on a number of occasions to betray her partners. In fact, she grew impatient and frustrated with my apparently uptight attitudes about such arrangements and my tiresome, irritating need to clarify with her that my approach to analytic work excluded them.

Her frame and mine often seemed distinctly at odds, leading to conflict in early sessions, at times to disturbing effect. One day I was blinded at her arrival, seeing nothing but spots as I opened the door, stunned, disoriented, and upset as I took a moment to realize that she had taken my picture with a flash camera as she entered the room. She told me she intended to use the photo so that she could look at it and soothe herself at night in bed when she was feeling stressed and lonely. She could use it to help her go to sleep. She felt that my presence in this quite concrete form would provide necessary relief, better than taking a Valium. She was perplexed and more than a little wounded by my less-than-enthusiastic response to her snapping my picture, a unilateral act, neither negotiated nor discussed. She wasn't sure if my difficulty with it stemmed from some personal difference between us, or something about my view of analysis, or maybe I felt that she was just "acting out." Like my original ambivalence on the phone, my response suggested to her that she loved me more than I loved her, wanted me more, something that she often felt in her relationships.

We had agreed to begin analysis three times a week, and though she could easily afford my fee, she did have some concerns about spending that much money on herself. She had access to considerable financial resources, having inherited a substantial amount of money, and lived a lifestyle that included expensive apartments and vacation homes, but she had presented among her initial self-reflections the paradox that despite great resources and expenses she would have enormous difficulty spending a few hundred dollars on a handbag that she liked. Although enormously wealthy, she didn't believe she deserved to spend money on herself, because not having earned the money, she didn't really think it was hers to spend. Nevertheless, she agreed to pay my fee.

A complication arose, however, as we tried to work out arrangements about missed sessions. She had houses in a number of vacation spots around the world and liked to use them for a couple of weeks at a time. When I told her that I generally charged for missed sessions, she let me know that arrangement would be impossible for her. It was not that she couldn't "afford it," but psychologically, to pay for a session that she was already missing would be adding insult to injury, somehow like missing a session twice. It was bad enough to be missing it once. This concern became an occasion for some exploration of her somewhat dissociated sense of agency, as it was difficult for her to fully identify with the fact that she could choose to stay in New York for sessions if she preferred. Her traveling schedule was a given, organized by a part of her that had quite different needs from the part of her that would have a terrible feeling of loss about missing sessions.

Efforts to explore her experience of this and to grasp the distressing meanings associated with "choosing" to travel and yet acknowledging the missed sessions (and my missed income and my economic needs) in the form of payment to me didn't take us very far, other than to highlight some aspects of a kind of dissociative quality to her experience. In Bromberg's (1998) terms, she was having some trouble standing in the spaces between her loss of the session and her need to be away, and perhaps the reality and impingement of her analyst's economic needs. As we considered our options, I felt that we were facing a possible impasse. I did not relish the idea of holding hours open for her for a couple of weeks at a time to accommodate her traveling schedule, and she could not bear to pay for sessions that she had already "paid" for by "having to miss."

I felt stumped, holding my ground for the moment but wondering whether I would feel impelled to draw a line in the sand about my typical preference that patients pay for missed sessions, which could threaten to terminate the work before it had begun and before either of us were in a position to understand what is was that we might be enacting. Out of an extended silence, uncomfortable (at least for me) she proffered a novel suggestion, one I had never encountered in the first fifteen years of practice. Could she "make up" sessions in advance? If she knew she would be away, could she put in extra sessions in the weeks prior to her leaving?

As we explored the concrete practicalities as well as the more nuanced meanings to her of this arrangement, the following proposal began to take shape. Because she would often be away a couple of weeks at a time, it wouldn't be practical to make up that many sessions in the week or two prior to her trip. So, she suggested, what about the idea that we could meet four times a week rather than three, with the fourth session each week being banked as a make-up session against future misses. She would, under that arrangement, technically still be in a three-time-a-week analysis but stockpiling make-up sessions against future absences.

Having some hours open, I agreed to this arrangement, though not without considerable reflection, with her, both prior to and following the change, on some meanings and feelings associated with our new approach. Did her making up the sessions in advance provide a magical solution to the problem of loss or the terrible sense that she was missing out on something? Did our arrangement mean that she didn't have to feel those feelings, that she wouldn't have to take responsibility for her choice to travel and miss sessions, or that she could avoid feeling angry with me for my greed and stubbornness? Did it take me off the hook of feeling that I was exploiting her by charging her for so many unused sessions, enforcing a unilateral paid vacation policy for me that I secretly relished? Did it mean that I could avoid feeling guilty about charging her for many sessions that she would not use or that I could elude being the object of her anger and disappointment, depriving her of the opportunity to express such feelings? Were we colluding in dissociating feelings that might have arisen about missing sessions on the weeks that she was away by treating the "extra" sessions as substitutes rather than fully facing and acknowledging the reality that we were doing analysis four times a week? Much ground was covered in these explorations, while I sensed that other soil remained untilled.

Nevertheless, it wasn't evident to me at the time that her suggestion was any less tenable, to use Ferenzci's guideline, than my preferred approach, and I could find no compelling reason not to arrange things as she required. She seemed pleased and surprised that I took her experience of the matter and her suggestion seriously, and analytic work continued, including, of course, some ongoing exploration of the experience of our way of negotiating and working out what had seemed to be a difficult problem. She was moved to feel that I was taking her needs seriously and that I could modify my approach in response to her creative solution, about which she felt considerable pride and gratitude. She was pleased that she was able to provide a solution that both of us could accept. It brought to mind and into the analysis other successful solutions that she had found in the past and became an occasion for her filling me in on forms her creativity had taken in successful business ventures as well as exploring how it was that her creative assertiveness had gone missing in recent years. Her pleasure gave way to intense sadness as she came into contact with what an unusual experience it was for her to get what she needed and to participate actively in negotiating a solution that could potentially work out well for her.

After a couple of years, the work had deepened. Nicole began to feel that the arrangement no longer felt right to her. After all, it was now clear to her that a four-time-a-week analysis is what she needed and counted on. It didn't really hold water any longer to operate under what now seemed clearly an illusion of a three-times-a-week format, with make-up sessions. Fewer than four sessions a week no longer felt that it met her needs, so now the fourth session no longer felt valid as a make-up session. It was not fair to me then to regard it as such. She wondered whether the solution might be to start coming five times a week, the fifth session playing the role of the extra make-up one, but that didn't feel quite right or necessary to either of us. By now she was opting to be in New York more so as not to miss sessions, and our relationship had evolved to the point that missed sessions no longer evoked the same anxiety that they had earlier, and so we agreed that she would now pay for missed sessions, as was my usual custom.

That worked well for a while, but then we entered a period in which she would miss sessions with some frequency for one reason or another, and I could rarely make them up due to a very busy clinical schedule; I never had an hour available on the only day that she did not have an appointment. When she realized that I was thinking in terms of making up sessions on days that we had not already met, she questioned another fixed aspect of frame: once-a-day meetings. It had never occurred to me to meet with a patient twice on the same day, with the occasional exception of double sessions when conditions warranted it, unless he or she was in special need or crisis and a second session seemed crucial. But in response to her suggestion that two sessions in a day could be just as useful to her as two on contiguous days, we did try that on several occasions when an hour became available. It generally turned out to be extremely fruitful, an alternative that never would have occurred to me without her direct intervention and one that I have subsequently integrated into my repertoire of clinical options.

But because even that solution was most often impossible to arrange, she was again feeling disturbed by my inability to offer make-up sessions. By now it was becoming increasingly clear that the issue was not really about money at all. She realized that she felt tantalized by my policy that I would make up sessions when able. We discovered this by way of her associations to an older sister (and later to her father as well), who had always promised to be there for her in a variety of ways but who, when push came to shove, would invariably let her down.

This issue was further elaborated in yet another transference-countertransference enactment. Nicole expressed interest in taking a painting class that would interfere with one of her sessions, about once a month or so. She wished to change the hour on a regular basis to make it possible to take the class, but no alternative hours were open. As we explored the situation, her distress mounted about having a regular hour that she would once again face missing on a regular basis. Perhaps she would just drop the class (which I hoped she wouldn't do) or drop the session altogether (for what seemed like complicated and overdetermined reasons). After several sessions of exploration of the problem and its meanings, seizing on one of the several obstacles that had come up in our exploration of the matter, I was finally moved to say "OK, how would it feel if when it comes to that particular event I won't charge you for those sessions you miss to attend it?"

To my surprise (obviously a countertransference blind spot in its own right, as retrospectively, it is surprising that I was surprised), this was far from a satisfying solution, as she realized immediately that every month or so she would have to choose between the class and our session and go through the anguish of giving up one or the other. Either way it was spoiled. If she chose the seminar she wouldn't get as much out of it because of the feelings of loss regarding the session, and vice versa. In either case, she would be tantalized, frustrated, and ultimately saddened by the sacrifice. What I consciously intended as a flexible solution that would meet both of our needs (I was happy to have an occasional open hour) turned out to be a much more complicated matter that brought into focus unattended aspects of the transference-countertransference and the fact of loss and the inevitability of her mourning.

She found my proposed solution to be quite tantalizing and frustrating to her and expressed a preference that I simply stop attempting to make up sessions altogether, the most galling part of my "policy," and that rather than charging for them, I should simply raise my fee to the point that the economics of it would not be burdensome. Her suggesting that I raise my fee brought into focus another complicated issue that I had avoided up to this point. I became aware on her suggestion that I had indeed not raised her fee in quite some time, as fees for new patients and other ongoing patients had in fact gone up. It wasn't clear to me exactly why I had hesitated to raise hers, but I did reveal to her as we explored our experience of this situation that I would actually like to raise her fee but that that would not resolve the issue of how we should handle missed sessions.

The disclosure that I had delayed raising her fee led into what seemed like a most revealing exploration of the ways in which she recognized that subtle suggestions on her part might have contributed to discouraging me from raising her fee. She also hypothesized that I might have held back because my full fee at four sessions a week would mean that she would be paying me a really substantial amount of money every month and that I might have hesitated to create a situation in which I would feel so dependent for income on a single patient. This impressed me as an intriguing and quite plausible bit of analysis. But she also viewed my semiconscious responsiveness to her pressure not to raise her fee as a reflection of my concern about her, and the outcome of our mutual analysis at this juncture was that she agreed to the fee change and was able to separate its meaning from the question of how missed sessions would be managed. But as the work proceeded, other dimensions of this enactment came into focus, and more work on the various forms of mutual care, control, suggestion, tantalization, dependency, and loss followed. Explorations of all of these themes weaved back and forth between her life with me in the transference-countertransference field of our experience and many places in her relationships outside of analysis.

During this same period, while these changes and the work that was taking place around them were leading me to think more about how we might gain access to the meanings of complex enactments and the potential for therapeutic gains in the context of fluid and changeable frames in the analytic situation, what appeared to be an uncanny moment transpired, which suggested to me the title for this essay. As my patient lay on the couch, gazing at the painting on the wall in front of her—a painting showing several different doors off a hallway, some slightly ajar, some closed, others ambiguous—she suddenly said, "Is that a new frame for that picture? The frame seems different." How do you mean, I asked. "It seems somehow lighter. Has it always been that light wood. I have never noticed this before. I know I have seen that picture and frame a thousand times, but somehow, now it doesn't seem to fit that picture."

Indeed, this interaction took place at a moment in our work in which the particular arrangement about missed sessions and how they were being handled felt to her that it was not quite right anymore. It just didn't seem to fit, and her projection of that feeling onto the literal frame that had been hanging on the wall in front of us both since we had started our work together several years earlier became a point of entry into the question of what sort of frame fit our picture best at this particular juncture. As I recognized that there was something about our arrangement that perhaps we had both outgrown and no longer seemed to fit either of us, Nicole felt extremely relieved and felt that I had understood something about her that had not been recognized before. A few days later, she looked at the picture again and couldn't remember what had felt wrong about the frame such a short time before.

The lack of fit between the frame and the picture could then be explored, not simply as a concrete illusion perhaps attributable to the change of light and shadow in the autumn afternoon of her session but as a symbolic representation of our work that seemed to have something to do with changes that had taken place in her, that allowed greater freedom and flexibility. She was also convinced that changes in me as a result of my work with her were also being reflected, and she spent some time enumerating the ways that she had seen me change and grow and what she had contributed to these changes. In one of several notes that she wrote to me for the first couple of years after ending her analysis, she told me that her life was going well, that she had married, was happy, and looked upon our work as having helped her in many different ways. But she also observed that one of the things that had been especially helpful was her sense that I had changed too and that there had been ways that her insights into my personality had helped me as well.

Each analysis bears innumerable roads not taken, and it is of course one of the existential realities of our work that it is impossible to know how any analytic relationship would have evolved given different choices along the way. In every analysis worth its salt, both participants change along the way for having encountered one another. Nicole expressed a sense that her analysis with me, with all the shifting arrangements of frame that marked different phases of the work, had made possible deeper and more transformative experiences than many of her past therapeutic efforts had yielded. In accordance with what I have discovered about myself with my patients over the course of these extended relationships in analysis, analyses guided by principles of elasticity and flexibility of a frame intended to facilitate ongoing development and negotiation of a relationship seem to offer the greatest opportunity for mutual personal transformation. I believe that within the surface negotiation of the frame, deep consolidation of a wide variety of intrapsychic and intersubjective elements are being created, worked through, and recreated, to the ultimate benefit of both participants.

References

Bass, A. (2001), Mental structure, psychic process, and analytic relations—How people change in analysis. *Psychoanalytic Dialogues*, 11: 717–725.

Bateson, G. (1972), *Steps to an Ecology of Mind*. New York: Ballantine.

Bromberg, P. M. (1982), The supervisory process and parallel process in psychoanalysis. *Contemporary Psychoanalysis*, 18: 92–110.

Bromberg, P. M. (1998), *Standing in the Spaces: Essays on Clinical Process, Trauma, and Dissociation*. Hillsdale, NJ: The Analytic Press.

Coltart, N. (1992), On the tightrope: Therapeutic and non-therapeutic factors in psychoanalysis. In: N. Coltart, *Slouching Towards Bethlehem and Further Psychoanalytic Explorations*. London: Free Association Books.

Ferenczi, S. (1928), The elasticity of psycho-analytic technique. In: M. Balint (ed.) (1955), *Final Contributions to the Problems and Methods of Psychoanalysis*. New York: Bruner/Mazel.

Freud, S. (1913), Further recommendations in the technique of psychoanalysis. In: *Collected Papers*, Vol. 2, The International Psychoanalytical Library, No. 8, 1959. New York: Basic Books.

Goffman, I. (1986), *Frame Analysis: An Essay on the Organization of Experience*. New York: Harper and Row.

Hoffman, I. Z. (1998), *Ritual and Spontaneity in the Psychoanalytic Process*. Hillsdale, NJ: The Analytic Press.

Langs, R. (1982), *Psychotherapy: A Basic Text*. New York: Aronson.

Loewald, H. W. (1980), Psychoanalysis as art. In: H. W. Loewald (ed.), *Papers on Psychoanalysis*. New Haven, CT: Yale University Press.

Milner, M. (1952), Aspects of symbolism in comprehension of the not self. *International Journal of Psychoanalysis*, 33: 181–194.

Mitchell, S. A. (1993), *Hope and Dread in Psychoanalysis*. New York: Basic Books.

Mitchell, S. A. (1998), *Influence and Autonomy*. Hillsdale, NJ: The Analytic Press.

Pizer, S. A. (1998), *Building Bridges: The Negotiation of Paradox in Psychoanalysis*. Hillsdale, NJ: The Analytic Press.

Symington, N. (1983), The analyst's act of freedom as agent of therapeutic change. *International Review of Psycho-Analysis*, 10: 283–291.

Part II

Frame, culture, politics, terror

Chapter 7

When we frame

Stephen Hartman

Private terror/social terror

As Adam Phillips writes, we psychoanalysts surf in our patients' waves of terror:

> Each psychoanalytic theorist, starting with Freud, describes a set of essential terrors; that which, it is assumed, people cannot bear to remember, experience, or know. These essential terrors define what it is to be human; or what, in order to be human, one feels obliged to exclude.
>
> (Phillips, 1995, p. 13)

We lend our "expertise" in mostly private interactions, and we try to be ever aware of our own terrors: primal phantasies, sequelae of developmental mishaps, and traumas intergenerationally transmitted. Often, our private terrors are for the most part unspeakable. Wordless, they elude representation but surface in rhythmic registers (Blum, 2016) and interpersonal enactments that position private experience in a social matrix giving private terrors a "social" flare. These are the unbearable terrors that others are unable to give voice to except perhaps through projective identification. These terrors manifest in the intersubjective project that psychoanalysts of diverse schools call *transference*.

Not all terrors refer to a personal past or an originary phantasy, that is, to a "source object" that marks an unbearable experience and allows it representation as the source of innocence lost (Jacobs, 2015). These social terrors are collective in origin yet, as affect, social terror assumes an as-if intrapsychic form. When it emerges from the shadows it attacks each of us en masse. Not only do these waves of terror evoke associations to a private source in the past (which they cannot help but do by unconscious association), these social terrors unfold as the public spectacle of more terror to come writ small in each of our guts. Distinctly different from private terrors that circle back to definitive moments in *nachtraglichkeit*, these social terrors lay in store for us together but are felt by each of us alone. There may be an inkling that something is awry, but no one names that feeling as "terror" quite yet since we cannot yet apply that terrible feeling to a direct attack. Alone we feel ill at ease; together we harbor innocence.

We will lose our innocence though, soon enough. Equally unbearable to private hells, these social terrors are presented to us *avant la lettre* as horror unfolds and before we (place yourself in the scene upon hearing of school gun violence for example) know the terrorists' identity or affiliation. Suddenly, in the very same moment that social terror acquires afterwardness, we worry that we should have known it all along. Perhaps we couldn't know, couldn't see it coming, as we didn't know prior to 9/11 that there was even a war?

Social and political terrors such as these tax the discursive practices that we fashion, called "the frame," to protect our selves, our patients, and the integrity of our work as we mull through multiple registers of conscious and unformulated experience. Unlike terrors that seem private and allow us to assume a source (as in the primal scene, the Oedipus Complex, or various types of trauma) that we explore to model past experience, social and political terrors emanate from a threat that has yet to take form. The unspeakable has yet to become so, by virtue of the same *unfoldingness* that renders social and political terror collective, this lack of a private source gives social terror a not-as-of-yet quality. Social terror is not readily framed by an analyst who is as much subject to the surprise of terror as her analysand. When working in a traditional frame, she can't do much with social terror—other than wait, defensively talk politics, or source the terror both analyst and analysand anticipate in the patient's intrapsychic space.

If the terrors Adam Phillips described are named in hindsight, social and political terror, terrorism for short, is utterly virtual. It emerges as real. It spreads. It goes viral. It has an *open source* rather than a source object. There are no rules. As terror for the digital age, social terror's codes can be adapted and changed at the terrorists' whim. There need be no honor among thieves because the crime can be constantly reinvented and the locus of terror renamed in each iteration.

Terrorism in the field

Social terror appears as an interloper rather than a constituent feature of most psychoanalytic sessions just as it does in a well-defended, everyday life. We meet our patients in safe, protected settings, and it is understandable that we habitually focus internally and interpersonally while relegating the intrusions of social terror to the margins of therapeutic space. Terror may be intrinsic to many aspects of being human, but terrorism, political and social terror, is harder to place in a one-on-one interaction because it is virtually diffuse.

By habit, psychoanalysts relegate social terror to private space in order to grasp it among source objects rather than the virtual ones that have yet to be named. In this way, we evade terrorism and "the political" by discerning the presence of terror only after it falls upon the unconscious and strikes the ego with unceremonious links to primal fears. ("If I hadn't xyz when …, I could have known that that kid was strange"; or "if I hadn't wished to SEX I might have known that that immigrant was hiding something"). We pasturize terror and individuate it to be able to think it through.

As was the case of Dzhokhar Tzarnaev, the Boston Marathon bomber, intergenerational traumas are attributed to identified patients whose ever-present histories eluded us just the day before. Warning signs take root in private reactions to public events and unthought knowns that we collectively ignored. Then, in our personal reflections on public *nachtraglikheit*, social terror moves into personal space. This melancholic scenario keeps the imaginary source of terror (the "xyz" I couldn't bear or didn't believe I could do anything about) close by in me. At the same time, it absolves the collective unconscious of complicity in fomenting terror that is yet to come. Confused and dislocated, I protest my innocence amid the collective: governments irked them, the terrorists, or demagogues like Donald Trump, or fanatics of one sort or another, or no one—certainly not me. Any complicity I have in arousing terror as a member of a culture or society or polity is pushed into the psychoanalytic past as inchoate terror issues a summons to *my* past fears by associative links. Thus externalized, terror lingers as if unawares until some attack somewhere out *there* has effects in *here* on me. Now we can know terror as *mine* in a field that is frame-ably *ours*.

Culture and politics thus come upon the intimacy of "the setting" *foreign* and, like a tsunami, mostly unannounced (though ever present in hindsight) and then vastly overwhelming of the landscape we thought we knew. In its aftermath, we debate divergent views of what counts as the proper discourse of "psychoanalysis" *per se* to account for the encroachment of the external political *upon the field*. We broaden our catchment to recruit the "unanalyzable" and our field grows, yet terror remains inside the patient. Rarely do we understand terror or politics *as the field*: how would that work? A field composed only of ideology with no symbolic or semiotic register? A setting made entirely of *beta* with no *alpha* function? A digital fantasy coded with no analogue source (Jacobs, 2015)?

The social that was thought "private" becomes political

Terrorism poses theoretical questions about the nature of the psychoanalytic frame on two counts. It launches *the setting* into the social without us even having to move (or notice that we have been moved) out of our private space into a different kind of intimacy, an intimacy that knows not the difference between the psychic and social, for there is no longer a space between them. We are in terror together: conscious or unconscious, and we have to deal with its stark now-ness despite reality—memory, desire, and all—even if our theoretical preference for dealing with "the social" dwells in the "the dream." Enter "the political."

Secondly, terror has no respect for analytic structures or functions. Terror defies representation for lack of a source to copy. No matter if we have terror in our family lineage or in our personal history, if we are waylaid by the psychic weight of terror when trying to put it into words, thrown off-kilter by terror in the political State where we live, driven mad by the state of the world, unhinged by our patient's state or by our own state of mind, *social terror is always new.* It becomes our job to look deep within and cast a broad net that allows terrors to be represented in the space between our patients and our selves even though terror mounts in rogue practices that at best resemble a psychotic transference.

Ours would be a relatively easy job if terrors were the predictable product of structural psychic phenomena as was deemed the case during the heyday of the Oedipus Complex. Technical moves such as the negotiation of a well-considered frame would equip us just fine if terror, articulated idiosyncratically, nevertheless unfolded in a reliable sequence of moves that respected the asymmetrical alignment of transference. But it does not.

Terror, at least terror as we know it in 2017, is unreliable; it lacks structure altogether.

Structure and function vs. terror

When terror emanates from institutions of State power (as in Argentina during the dictatorship of 1976–1983), it falls back on the structural logic of institutions. Even though it "adopts a causal logic based on false hypotheses, supported by perverse ethical values which promote corrupt actions" (Puget, 2002, p. 621) it has a structure that supports regressive fantasy. With such logic, no matter how perverse, terror gathers a kind of predictable structure provided by history.

History gives us a referent that terror otherwise lacks. The referent then serves the frame. Dictatorship. Apartheid. AIDS. Donald Trump. Historical events such as these are remembered to have a source that structures how each of us encountered them when, in lived experience, these events were polymorphous and confusingly impossible to pin down. Social memory is infinitely unstable and constantly in search of a unified structure (Coman & Hirst, 2015). This mutability in memory is an understandable collective defense that paradoxically splinters the collective: "I could have avoided terror *if only* we had let ourselves know." "I wouldn't have been infected among *them* were we more *self*-conscious." This kind of defensive manoeuver structures the social as if private. I (not we) couldn't know. It allows the analyst the safety of a fictive but mutative function: the "re-fashioning of ready-made material" (Freud, 1908).

Under these circumstances, the analyst works with the possibility of marshaling recognizable defenses against terror as one might do *vis à vis* primitive phantasy. The analyst has recourse to method, which is in and of itself a defensive operation. As Cairo (2010, p. 22) explains, "resorting to ideas that simplified our task, with the illusion of being artisans of the extraction of the presumably static internal world of our patients, maintained for us a sense of relative individual intactness and an implied experience of power in the task."

Defenses thus travel from the *interpersonal field* to the professional psychoanalytic field and back to the *interpersonal field* as standards that structure practice. Psychoanalytic institutes and journals dwell on matters of orthodoxy (Aron & Starr, 2013) without espying how theoretical moves to define the discipline and close ranks around method and technique are a reactionary defense in a context of political estrangement and terror. When our functional roles are preserved, our profession becomes an organizing structure to fall back on no matter how chaotic the world around us is.

The analyst's functional role

The analyst adopts a reliable role or frame "to constitute a process that is studied, analyzed, and interpreted" (Bleger, 1967). He becomes an identifiable *character*, as philosopher Alasdair MacIntryre (1981) elaborates the term, whose ethical position is taken to be a constant and not, like a *role* that he may don in the transference/countertransference, an element of the process. Structure is restored (epistemologically and ontologically) because of the link that is forged during the session and in "the setting" (both fixed) between the analyst's functional character (taken as a relative constant) and the patient's variable role. The structure of ongoing work both defends against structureless terror and allows the analyst to interpret formless terror as it overflows within the analyst's frame, a frame that can barely contain the patient's terror.

The discursive function of "the frame" as a disciplinary structure (Foucault, 1979) that defends against social and political terror by individuating the terrorized person gets lost because the frame appears home-grown, even domestic after a heredity fashioned by transference. Then, when the analyst as participant-observer interprets a structural irregularity in the intersubjective field, the analysis fosters the illusion that the analytic function ensues in a necessary relation to the functional articulation of that structure (Geertz, 1973). We rely on the analyst to know what to analyze and then we may feel secure in our analysis. The functional role of the analyst, then, is to frame the source and represent it contextually (with reference to the transference) even though "the source" defies context and remains open.

As a constant, the frame restores structure and function

A fine example of this defensive summoning of the frame to rejuvenate structure and function and thus sustain analytic work is provided by Puget. When the analyst recognizes the other to be isolated in a state of "social pain" (Puget, 2010), she "opens the space for the creation of the links that will help solve the common problem or situation. This approach adds a social dimension to the construction of subjectivity" (Sosnik, 2010, p. 29) in the familiar manner that "intersubjective" approaches are described as "social."[1] Here again, at the level of method, in the constant that is provided by mutual recognition (Benjamin, 1988; Hartman, 2013), structure is restored and participant observation may continue unabated despite the terror surround. Meaning is somehow illustrated by the practice of holding the frame, and the frame becomes a structure that protects against terror.

But when terrorism loses its face and becomes a "social state of threat" structure collapses to a point that threatens the analyst's position as a helpful character. This occurs when terror erupts with what I am calling an "open source" because there are no "rules of the game" from which to infer structure or meaning. As Puget (2002, p. 624) has stated, "This is a mental condition in which the ego loses the ability to recognize those signs which enable it to perceive and to classify, hierarchically, dangers from the outside world and to distinguish between imagination and reality, life and death." When this happens, time is altered because there is no if/then relationship with which to distinguish among symbolic, imaginary, and real registers. Puget continues:

> The code of rules of the game are unknown. When this occurs at the macro-social level, the ego feels that the points of identity on which its social identity is based are undermined. Uncertainty and its associated anxiety become a state whose disorganizing force attacks those reference points which previously gave consistency to identity and the feeling of belonging.
>
> (Puget, 2002, p. 623)

Techniques and strategies that psychoanalysts have developed to plumb these "reference points" in the unconscious rely on some measure of consistency so that the frame can be a constant in view of which the process can be interpreted by an identifiable character, the analyst. A steady technique, in turn, allows the analyst to interpret structural irregularities in what she observes even though the world around us is unpredictable. Thus restored as both a character who is constant and a role that is variable in the transference, the analyst can interpret structureless terror by likening its lack of structure, time, and orientation to the timeless unconscious (about which the analyst's expertise, given Freud's discovery, may be taken as a constant). The unconscious made conscious, in turn, offers up examples of terror's effects after the fact. A certain order is restored in the reciprocity of structure and functions that are held in place by "the frame."

The frame as bulwark of knowing

The frame, as described by psychoanalysts of diverse theoretical orientations, thus offers a baseline of reliability that provides a "bulwark" for a basic functional configuration of roles that are contained in the initial commitment and agreement to enter treatment (Baranger & Baranger, 2008). It elevates function, associating it with reason and the epistemophilic instinct (Klein, 1932). When we frame, we adopt functional roles that we then position in a reciprocal relationship to the structures we are now equipped to observe.

The frame becomes a practice with a social history, turning to an Other for care (Westerman, 2015), and as such, it has been theorized in the lineage of parental functions that much of psychoanalysis models itself upon. Bleger (1967, p. 513) argues that the frame has a similar function to *maternal symbiosis*, "it acts as support, as mainstay, but, so far, we have been able to perceive it only when it changes or breaks. The most powerful, endurable, and at the same time least apparent 'bulwark' is, then, the one that lies on the frame." Given the double character of the frame, it provides reliability as well as a measure of inevitable and necessary unreliability.

Bass (2007, p. 9) wisely adds that "in the living, unfolding quintessentially generative relationship with the patient, different structures or different ways of negotiating the rules that sustain an analytic setting and process may be more or less suited to the task in any given dyad." We would expect that the rules and frames of any therapeutic practice would shift to reflect the social conditions in which analyst and patient meet and provision is delimited to enable optimal impasses and enactments (Carnochan, 2001). So, adds Bass, (2007, p. 14), "a frame functions to define where attention is to be directed." How, then, do we understand the frame when there are no clear roles and structureless terror yields no direction other than ever-present threat? There is no *good enough* terrorist.

Some limitations of the frame defense

Inevitably, reliance on the frame in social states of threat falls short of achieving its ideal variable yet homeostatic state and has a defensive quality. Given the frame's structural and functional relation to an imaginary and originary source object or context, the frame always looks backward in a present that has been jolted forward. The frame also defensively treats terror as an artifact of psychic economy in an equally defensive effort to retain a functionalist justification for psychoanalytic work. Most significantly from a "social" perspective, the frame is ill equipped to describe aspects of experience that are social in our deepest sense of being, modes of relatedness that might offer analyst and analysand as only-human-together a structure prior to the individuating effects of terror on which to depend (Rozmarin, 2009, 2010) and a collective unconscious to lean into (Doi, 1989).

No structural logic (such as that which Freud located in primary bisexuality) or set of functional roles (that are not subject to Oedipal order and *The Real* [Butler, 1995]) can quite describe the randomness of terrorism as it guts the public mind, turning the social private and creating paranoid schizoid object relating at the macro-social level—now the sum of individual parts (Deleuze and Guattari, 1983). *Us* becomes you and/versus me. There is no emotional corrective inherent in the structure of terror that compels us to form working groups in the way that neoliberals wistfully wish for there to be a trickle-down effect in the structural logic of capitalism.

The frame and the collective unconscious

Although terror strikes us collectively, we become isolates in the effort to represent terrorized affect. If, as Puget (2002, p. 618) writes: "each individual carries a code which is related to her or his participation in the social structure" (be that code a signifier of enigmatic transmission, a trace of *The Real*, or a marker of ideological reference), and "the infant is the subject of the social structure into which it is integrated before it is the subject of its relations with its parents," terror is prior to anything we know except, perhaps, the under-theorized and little considered collective unconscious.

If indeed the social code is prior to the family code of discursive instructions that hail the subject into normative roles (Guralnik and

Simeon, 2010) then the question is: how ought the analyst frame the session so as to hear terror in the unconscious social code without inferring as if it were an obvious result of the structures of psychoanalytic lore that posit universal conflicts among isolated individuals?

If the frame is to account for terror that strikes the analyst and analysand together at a preverbal level in a collective register that is prior to parental contact, it must account for the practices that bring two vulnerable participants to a scene of care where, paradoxically, for each character to play her role, any primordial link between them is deferred in a way which mirrors the effects of political terror that transform collective bonds into individual terrors. This is particularly urgent because of analytic asymmetry, as Bass (2007, p. 14) writes: the analyst's unconscious and experience "shapes the contours of his relationship to his preferred theory and to the patient." The analyst must be all the more relationally minded when the frame commands a collective strategy for containment and original thought.

When we frame

I wish to avoid prescribing any technique that might guide *how* we frame or *what* happens within the frame and turn instead to suggest we focus on how constant characters and variable roles interact recursively with individual and social aspects of being human *when* we frame. I propose that interest in the frame coincides with the experience of living fearfully alone in the plural scene of terror (Rozmarin, 2009). Furthermore, while living with terror, deracination from the social is combined with the chilling sense that terror can neither be known nor stopped. We are helplessly alone together.[2]

We frame in response to an upsurge in incidences of State-sponsored violence and in the New World "Order" of terrorist threat. Both scenes of terror aggregate and isolate us simultaneously. Container and contained become objects subject to the same threat but separated objects nonetheless. Mounting concern with the frame reflects a sense of hopelessness about the insidious and ubiquitous threat of terror that cannot be contained by the psychoanalyst either in a fantasy about psychoanalytic technique, in concrete reality, or by the society in which we live.

Terror eludes us. In moments of terror, we wish for regularity, for a constant frame in which we may delimit the limitless and re-socialize the space between us. We turn to government institutions for confidence only to feel alienated when political discourse is hijacked by rogue politicians and media frenzy. Though I see psychic life and social life in a recursive relationship (each creating the other in an ongoing chain of being) and Puget describes two intertwined lines of contact with (what Winnicott, 1988, called) "the soul," I agree with Puget's assessment that: "We are not talking here about disavowing, excluding the other's unbearable foreignness; it is the *problem* that determines the nature of the situation. *Doing with others* becomes the *drive* that constitutes new groups" (Puget, 2010, p. 9, ital. added).

Doing with others

"New groups" are best constituted through participatory, democratic social experience (Dewey, 1916). By contrast exercises in social engineering and public policy mostly benefit a neoliberal economy and its functional agents: bureaucrats, technocrats, the military, the wealthy, and policy makers themselves (Brown, 2015). In the United States and many other parts of the world, psychoanalysts and other mental health professionals have experienced the devastating effects of neoliberal economics on their ability to construct a viable frame in which to practice, necessitating analytic self-care all the more (Harris, 2009).

Daniel Butler (2015) makes the strong case that young psychoanalysts in particular meet their patients already somewhat traumatized by working in a precarious professional context while having to precociously juggle their personal needs with the demands of treatment. Butler emphasizes how the neoliberal context isolates individual clinicians from one another and pits them in competition to garner the scare clinical resources necessary to establish themselves in the profession. *Doing with others* quickly becomes doing what it takes to survive in a psychic landscape overcome by precarity. In the aftermath of terror, as Judith Butler (2004) eloquently describes, precarity is all the more ubiquitous.

Theories of the frame cannot rely on analytic function alone and still take an honest account of the political and economic structure wherein clinicians practice. Given the context of social terror and the overarching structure of neoliberal public policy and economics that we work in, it is essential that doing with others in analytic space be able to address the isolating effects that result from terror. This problematic challenges a certain bias in the frame literature toward wanting psychoanalysis, and the unconscious in particular, to stand somehow aloof from politics (Goldberg & Sekoff, 1980) as if one could minimize the effects of ideology and more accurately hear the individual. In this more classical form of psychoanalytic practice, "the psychic" is given a priority that demands "the social" yield to the margins even as its importance is recognized.

The apolitical social frame

With great certainty, Bleger (1967, p. 514) observed that: "social institutions are unconsciously used as a defense against psychotic anxiety." Aggregates of "the social" become the repository for undifferentiated symbolic links. Turning the lens away from social structure toward analytic function allows for what is properly psychoanalytic material: psychic bits and undifferentiated links that analytic function restores. Bleger adds: "psychotic anxieties take place within the institution, and in the case of the psycho-analytic situation, within what we have described as the process—what "is in motion" against what is not: the frame" (p. 514).

Bleger's detailed account of the frame provides a contextually broader complement to the Barangers' (2008) description of "temporal ambiguities" and "points of urgency" that connote psychotic regression within the frame/institution but it does not account, however, for the psychotic nature of institutions under the conditions of precarity in which we live and symbolize our experience.

In principle, in a democratic society, participation is a constant equal to if not recursively entwined with the development of the individual psyche. Although in "democratic" societies under neoliberalism, doing with others becomes increasingly rare. Decisions about the provision of social services are routinely divested from practitioners and out-sourced to administrative agencies such as we regularly see under "managed care" in the health insurance industry. With the growth of a highly administrative governmental sector as well as the professionalization of philanthropy, the streamlining of heath care as per insurers' biases against psychoanalytic treatment, and the requirement of "empirical validity" for reimbursable treatments, psychoanalysis becomes an increasingly privatized consumer affair accessible mostly to a privileged class of patients and clinicians. Workers in community mental health agencies struggle to provide services, and even when they are psychoanalytically trained, their work is not recognized to be equal to the hours accrued in private settings. Individualism flourishes, communities collapse, and we witness the demise of the social container (Layton, 2009).

The frame is held collectively

In order to adapt the psychoanalytic frame to best allow the experience of terror to emerge under circumstances that reduce what is properly social to the province of individual achievement, one has to reconsider the notion that the frame is held in the mind of the analyst (Rosenfeld, 1980). At the same time, one has to factor into the clinical mindset that doing with others or, as Puget (2010) calls it, the social drive, is a repressed if not terrorized aspect of collective memory and desire. One must amend Bion's dictum that the psychoanalyst eschew memory and desire in the radical present of "the field" to allow that *one* is always in the presence of *our* past. The traditional, functionalist emphasis on the analyst's constant manner of participation should shift to a broader analysis of the dyad's discourse and participation in discursive regimes.

To account for the ubiquity of terror and its individuating effects, the analysis has to allow for the collapse of the sense of doing with others in the very language of interaction. *Terror* (by which I mean the expectation of terror's effects) would be iterated as an element of constant structure (rather than an *après coup*). When the social is instituted within the structure of the frame, rupture in the analytic process stands equally in relation to a social drive and to its individuating effects. To return to a point I made earlier in this chapter, terror *as the field* opens the door to the view that our deepest sense of being has a collective structure which has been disrupted. By contrast, when terror is iterated *in the field* by virtue of its effects on the analysand and analyst as isolates, the frame seizes upon "the social" only after it has already become an artifact of the precarious subject's condensed intrapsychic need.

Furthermore, when seen as "a functional field" in which "the two persons expect from each other very determinate behavior and the maintenance of the basic commitment, whatever the content of momentary modifications may be" (Baranger & Baranger, 2008, p. 798) the frame is constrained by structural-functionalist principles of reciprocity and homeostasis. Thus, many efforts to frame "the setting" can be viewed as efforts to institute and structure the uncontainable and the untamed within a set of functional procedures and epistemological guidelines that render the unthinkable coherent enough for the individual to think. Upon finding a link between a disturbance in the frame and an archaic source object, analytic function demonstrates that which is "structural" to the individual psyche via an interpretation of a disturbance in the frame. It's a circular logic that nonetheless reassures. *One's* mind is put to rest and the frame is restored.

The danger in a structural-functionalist method that links thinking to functional roles is that the frame carries a homeostatic burden in order to do its work. It risks becoming a defense against structural evolution in collective experience of culture and discourse and, consequently, against the broader culture wherein terror is experienced and the society wherein psychoanalysis, as a professional discipline, is practiced.

A detour in structural-functionalist anthropology

Structural-functionalist theory in social science unwittingly worked to bolster colonialism by making it possible to intervene in local customs that were the bulwark of social structure.[3] The functional roles of village elders, if held constant, were seen to guide the indigenous system to homeostasis. To observe how rituals supported characters and roles that could stabilize local cultural structures was to know how to co-opt communities and introduce sympathetic characters into roles that rendered a stable field. The theoretical emphasis on homeostasis in systems theory provided a frame for governance much as the psychoanalytic emphasis on the "implicit rules" in the psychoanalytic situation allows for the emer- gence—and interpretation—of "points of urgency" that render the analyst's role its healing "art" (Baranger & Baranger, 2008).

British colonialism created what we might call a container/contained relationship with "native" cultures. By learning how a traditional culture developed in the presence of British tutelage, one could identify the struc- tures and functions necessary to groom that society for "indirect rule." Generally, kinship structure was respected, allowing local customs to flourish and granting local communities some purchase on self- government albeit at the behest of colonial administrators.

The critique of structural functionalism and Franz Fanon

Inevitably, after the fall of colonialism, structural functionalism was criticized for its inherently tautological nature. Functionalism explained the particularities of societies through recourse to the effects that were derived from the same functions that were used to describe how cultures achieved homeostasis. Structural functionalist theories were inherently circular and esteemed the functional importance of the observer without accounting for his manner of scripting the setting that he or she participated in (Geertz, 1973).

From the perspective of social theory, the psychoanalytic frame operates as a set of functional roles that cohere in order to allow for the articulation of variable local structures. Talcott Parsons (Parsons & Shils, 1976), influenced by Max Weber's emphasis on ideal types, observed how the behaviors of certain fixed characters were repeated in regular interactions. This had the effect of generating expectations for what would happen in a setting as it became entrenched and institutionalized. Roles were created that guided subsequent interaction and a kind of coherence was produced that maintained a functional equilibrium in the social system. In this way, framing behaviors among constant characters inhabiting framing roles created a sense of "organic solidarity" that was the antidote to urban alienation or *anomie*. Yet, at the same time, framed observations tended to yield what they expected to find rather than what was already latent and emergent in local custom and politics (Cohen, 1969).

Franz Fanon (1952/2008) grew weary of the functionalist bias in psychoanalytic concepts. Suggesting that stringent belief in the Oedipus Complex would ultimately fail psychoanalysis just as assumptions about the primitivity and exteriority of native cultures doomed colonialism, he wrote:

> We too often tend to forget that neurosis is not a basic component of human reality. Whether you like it or not, the Oedipus Complex is far from being a black complex. It could be argued, as Malinowski does argue, that the matriarchal regime is the only reason for its absence. But apart from wondering whether the anthropologists, steeped in their civilizations' complexes, have not done their best to find copies

in the people they study, it would be fairly easy for us to demonstrate that in the French Antilles ninety-seven percent of families are incapable of producing a single oedipal neurosis. And we have only to congratulate ourselves for that.

(Fanon, 1952/2008, p. 130)

Indeed, Fanon (1963) explained, people of color were terrorized by the colonial gaze. He felt the only recourse left to the wretched of the earth was to form "new groups" and recoup individual integrity through a mass turn to violence. Violence, he concluded, was the only language the colonizer spoke. Any psychic transformation in the mind of the colonized would entail a transformation within the discourse of violence. Quite ahead of his time in his emphasis on discourse (and albeit the discursive effects of violence), Fanon located psychoanalytic intervention in a profoundly social register, turning our attention to framework in discourse.

Toward a discursive rather than functionalist frame

In the linguistic study of discourse, speech activity becomes a homespun and emergent frame for collective action. As Tannen (1993, p. 4) explains: "conversational inference, a process requisite for conversational involvement is made possible by contextualization cues that signal the speech activity in which participants perceive themselves to be engaged." Frames provide "structures of expectation" that lead participants in a conversation or readers engaged in a semiotically rich event to anticipate the next move in the text (Goffman, 1986). One plays a game by intuiting the rules of the game and then changing them as the game evolves (Winnicott, 1971). These rules are always shifting in a sequence of moves that reveal the shifting expectations that make a game *play* and doing with others *doing*.

Bateson (1972) explained that play references the structure or *metamessage*: "this is play." Monkeys could differentiate between hostile gestures and playful ones because they were able to access a social structure—play. The rules of play are thus *"in play"* (Bass, 2007, p. 10). Bateson believed this to be true in psychoanalytic process as well, as Bass (2007, p. 11) elaborates: we expect that the rules and frames of analysis shift to reflect changes in the course of the analytic relationship. All the while, these changes bring us back to the place where we began. The frame, then, evolves and looks back simultaneously, much as Bleger described, though not because of the analyst's function so much as the expectation of care that brought the players together in the first place. This may seem a very subtle difference, but it is an important one nonetheless. The frame resides in collective experience and is described discursively not functionally.

However, discourse is never value neutral. As Foucault (1980) demonstrated in great detail, discourse circulates through social institutions in structural practices that site power in normative practices. Foucault's critique of psychoanalysis hinged on his understanding that Freud initiated a discourse regarding "the subject" wherein mythic structures, the Incest Taboo and Oedipus Complex, created (what analysts of discourse call) the framing expectations from which the *Law of the Father* gathers its unknowable power. The frame is held as a constant in order that the Real, the symbolic, and the imaginary may mix in such a way that sexuality can be practiced within a discourse of health. The observational capacity of the psychoanalyst is then instituted in psychiatric practice on the regulatory model of the heteronormative family. Knowledge that accrues on the model of maternal care and phallic power thus define maternal care and its ability to represent symbolic order. Practices empowered by participation in discourse thus define knowledge.

Foucault (1980) championed "resistances to discourse" that were found in practices that revealed discursive regimes and offered some purchase on multiplicity. Postmodern psychoanalysis attempts to find footing, consequently, in the twin practices of resisting the always already present quality of discursive regimes and in decentering the expert role of the psychoanalyst (Fairfield et al., 2002). As Puget's (2002, 2010) writing on social pain beautifully describes, social terror embeds us in a discourse with expectations that can be discerned within practices that displace doing together. To deconstruct those structures of expectation in psychoanalytic space is to begin to frame the transference in a socially meaningful way.

Conclusion: risk and uncertainty

Terror turns the citizen into a vehicle. She becomes an at-risk member of society whose risk status is then referenced by demagogues to justify isolating a liminal group of potential terrorists who come only vaguely into focus: immigrants, people with mental illness, the disaffected, the ones who went astray or were seduced by another, even worse, Other. A pervasive sense of risk mixes with nameless dread.

The terrorist over there and the liminal group over here become interchangeable in the unconscious mind no matter how much thinking people try not to collapse the two. Wars begin abroad and then find their way home. Terror is *Us*. All space is *here*. This is the cynical ruse a of neoliberal ideology that actually cares little for individuals except insofar as the nation of terrorized individuals enables political, corporate, and military entities to identify and target the types of people who infringe on *our* right-making State. The neoliberal State asks the individual to sanction interventions as obvious and psychically necessary. Soon we have lost personhood to necessity.

In due course, as the wish to frame terror expands to the means by which terror circulates at large, there is the call for internet providers to track digital footprints and shut down the email accounts used by would-be terrorists or to somehow decipher terrorists' encrypted communications and turn them over to the State, even though it is not technically possible to isolate terabytes of suspicious data that might distinguish terror speech from free speech. It's a big mess in reality and havoc in the psyche.

Internal objects appear that seem to belong to the terrorized individual whereas internal objects born of terror, of history, exploitation, segregation, and inequality are rightly collective objects that implode for fear of dominant practices of social organization and State terror.

Even for psychoanalysts who take strong political positions, it is not quite obvious how and when to address the individuated collective objects of terror in the privacy of the consulting room. When "the setting" is held in the mind of the analyst who interprets resistances to the practice of analysis (Rosenfeld, 1980), the diffuse nature of terror is denied. A false equilibrium is reached by streamlining the vulnerable analyst and analysand into roles framed around the articulation of source objects and idiosyncratic phantasies. Even when the frame is seen as malleable or negotiable, the frame post-9/11 lacks the same reference point in object relations that it had prior to the new state of social terror making it difficult to identify who might have had the capacity to protect the other from becoming a victim.

Sometimes, there is a present eruption of the always already that terror has become in the framed-off analytic setting. But more and more often, terror melts into obviousness and can be easily overlooked. Even when terror appears naked in the session, we lack a ready language to describe its murky boundaries other than the ideological one given by the State. The "field" created between analyst and patient recognizes terrorized objects more easily than it does those objects' liminal origins (McGleughlin, 2015) or social accent (Puget, 2010).

The risk of a psychoanalytic technique that relies too heavily on the frame to render the treatment intelligible is that it proffers the fantasy that terror can be thought about if the space of interaction is limited, even though terror has unlimited access to the liminal crevices of the collective mind.

Coda: open source

Open-source spaces such as online communities that flourish with infinite access are often greeted with suspicion by many psychoanalysts who prefer treatment, even online treatment, to have a traditional frame even though new forms of potential space spawned online may provide the best *cyberframe* we have to think about the experience of terror in psychoanalytic space.

With the rise of the internet, *Open Source* describes an effort to embed doing with others in computer code. As we use computers and encounter open source code, *how we think* is altered via a process that Katherine Hayles (2012) calls "technogenesis." An evolution takes place where participation in *searching* forges new possibilities of meaning as it also returns us to the guiding terms with which we searched. Open source is a thus a developmental model based on principles of recursivity wherein universal access to the code or information that structures a product's design or blueprint allows it be to further developed.

In an open source computing model, a principle of universal redistribution guides how subsequent improvements to a source may be accessed and revised by anyone. Searching drives the elaboration of content and the structure wherein content is searched. Open source code is meant to be decentralized, participatory, and collaborative. Users can appropriate the code and change it to suit their needs and to form online communities. Whether or not this is actually achieved at the level of ownership of internet technologies (even open source search engines are "owned" by a corporate entity. Mozilla, for example, owns the open source web browser Firefox), within online spaces there is tremendous psychic mobility and room for creativity.[4]

Communities of information sharing evolve in cyberspace that are guided by the principle that access, not loss or the limitations imposed by a static frame, fosters development (Hartman, 2011). This has had tremendous, if not controversial, influence on how individual psychologies evolve. Internal source objects will always be part of our analog experience, but digital objects that have an unfolding, progressive, and collective flare increasingly share psychic space with intrapsychic and regressive ones (Hartman, 2017). Leaving aside critiques of the internet that describe social isolation, addiction, and the implosion of The Real in The Possible (see Hartman, 2011 for review), there can be little doubt that even regressive online practices contain within them the aspiration to contend with relational drives (Lingiardi, 2008).

Were we to conceive of the psychoanalytic frame on an open source model, I argue, the experience of "doing together" would become the structure that elaborates what we may search for as it also returns us to the original source terms with which we search. The analog/digital binary is, like most binaries, a false dichotomy. The open source nature of new technology, in a sense, guarantees that any new development will refer to a prior effort.

The project of framing is emergent because it is relational, not because it has functional value. The relational experience of the frame reminds us of the lost collective experience that is the source of our search for more meaning and more life (Corbett, 2001). To the extent that terror creates an isolative closed loop, participation in an open source frame expands our expectations for mutual influence and brackets the terms of a social life that recursively allows us independent experience.

Notes

1   As I will soon argue, this view of the social assumes that our deepest sense of being does not have a collective structure to being with (Rozmarin, 2010). State terror only serves to demonstrate how a primarily social state of being has already been routed by neoliberal ideologies of individualism and the structural logic of capitalism.

2   I'm borrowing the phrase "alone together" from Turkle (2011), even though I disagree with her assessment of new technology, because it aptly describes the condition one lives with under terror.

3   Influenced by such theorists as Emile Durkheim, Herbert Spencer, and Alfred Radcliffe Brown, anthropologists (most notably Bronislaw Malinowski and

E.E. Evans Pritchard) scattered their graduate students across the globe to observe elaborate rituals and decode how societies were organized and what relations of kinship and mercantile exchange held them together.

4   Here are two lists of open source resources available in the US and UK alone:
www.neteasy.us/technology/open-source/examples-of-open-source-software
www.datamation.com/osrc/article.php/3925806/Open-Source-Software-Top-59-Sites.htm

References

Aron, L. & Starr, K. E. (2013). *A Psychotherapy for the People*. New York: Routledge.

Baranger, M. & Baranger, W. (2008). The analytic situation as a dynamic field. *International Journal of Psychoanalysis*, 89: 795–826.

Bass, A. (2007). When the frame doesn't fit the picture. *Psychoanalytic Dialogues*, 17: 1–27.

Bateson, G. (1972). *Steps Toward An Ecology of Mind*. New York: Ballentine.

Benjamin, J. (1988). *The Bonds of Love*. New York: Pantheon.

Bleger, J. (1967). Psycho-analysis of the psycho-analytic frame. *International Journal of Psycho-Analysis*, 48: 511–519.

Blum, A. (2016). Rhythm nation. *Studies in Gender and Sexuality*, 17: 141–149.

Brown, W. (2015). *Undoing the Demos: Neoliberalism's Stealth Revolution*. New York: Zone/Near Futures.

Butler, D. (2015). Falling through the cracks: precarity, precocity, and other neoliberal pressures. *Fort Da*, 21: 33–52.

Butler, J. (2004). *Precarious Life*. New York: Verso.

Cairo, I. (2010). My colleague, the other. *Psychoanalytic Dialogues*, 20: 21–26.

Carnochan, P. (2001). *Looking for Ground: Countertransference and the Problem of Value in Psychoanalysis*. New York: Routledge.

Cohen, A. (1969). *Custom and Politics in Urban Africa*. Berkeley, CA.: University of California Press.

Coman, A. & Hirst, W. (2015). Social identity and socially shared retrieval-induced forgetting: the effects of group membership. *Journal of Experimental Psychology*, 144: 717–722.

Corbett, K. (2001). More life: centrality and marginality in human development. *Psychoanalytic Dialogues*, 11: 313–335.

Deleuze, G. & Guattari, F. (1983). *Anti-Oedipus: Capitalism and Schizophrenia*. Minneapolis: University of Minnesota Press.

Dewey, J. (1916). *Democracy and Education*. New York: Macmillan.

Doi, T. (1989). The concept of amae and its psychoanalytic implications. *International Review of Psycho-Analysis*, 16: 349–354.

Fairfield, S., Layton, L. & Stack, C. (eds) (2002). *Bringing the Plague: Toward a Postmodern Psychoanalysis*. New York: Other Press.

Fanon, F. (1952/2008). *Black Skin, White Masks*. New York: Grove Press.

Fanon, F. (1963). *The Wretched of the Earth*. New York: Grove Press.

Foucault, M. (1979). *Discipline and Punish*. New York: Vintage Books.

Foucault, M. (1980). *Power/Knowledge*. New York: Pantheon Books.

Freud, S. (1908). *Creative Writers and Day-Dreaming*. The Standard Edition of the Complete Psychological Works of Sigmund Freud, Volume IX (1906–1908): Jensen's 'Gradiva' and Other Works, pp. 141–154.

Geertz, C. (1973). *The Interpretation of Cultures*. New York, NY: Basic Books.

Goffman, I. (1986). *Frame Analysis: An Essay on the Organization of Experience*. New York: Harper and Row.

Goldberg, P. and Sekoff, J. (1980). Ideology and the question of the subject. *Canadian Journal of Political and Social Theory*, 4: 23–43.

Guralnik, O. & Simeon, D. (2010). Depersonalization: standing in the spaces between recognition and interpellation. *Psychoanalytic Dialogues*, 20: 400–416.

Harris, A. (2009). You must remember this. *Psychoanalytic Dialogues*, 19: 2–21.

Hartman, S. (2011). Reality 2.0: when loss is lost. *Psychoanalytic Dialogues*, 21: 468–482.

Hartman, S. (2013). Bondless love. *Studies in Gender and Sexuality*, 14: 35–50.

Hartman, S. (2017). The poetic timestamp of digital erotic objects. *Psychoanalytic Perspectives*, 14(2): 159–174.

Hayles, N. K. (2012). *How We Think: Digitial Media and Contemporary Technogenesis*. Chicago, IL: University of Chicago Press.

Jacobs, A. (2015). The demise of the analogue mind: digital primal fantasies and the technologies of loss-less-ness. In S. Frosch (ed.), *Psychosocial Imaginaries: Perspectives on Temporality, Subjectivity, and Activism*. London: Palgrave Macmillan, pp. 126–144.

Klein, M. (1932). *The Psycho-Analysis of Children*. The International Psycho-Analytical Library. London: Hogarth.

Layton, L. (2009). Who's responsible: our mutual implication in each other's suffering. *Psychoanalytic Dialogues*, 19: 105–120.

Lingiardi, V. (2008). Playing with unreality: transference and computer. *International Journal of Psychoanalysis*, 89: 111–126.

MacIntyre, A. (1981). *After Virtue*. Notre Dame, IN: University of Indiana Press.

McGleughlin, J. (2015). Do we find or lose ourselves in the negative? *Psychoanalytic Dialogues*, 25: 214–236.

Parsons, T. & Shils, A. (eds) (1976). *Toward a General Theory of Action*. Cambridge, MA: Harvard University Press.

Phillips, A. (1995). *Terrors and Experts*. Cambridge, MA: Harvard University Press.

Puget, J. (2002). The state of threat and psychoanalysis: from the uncanny that structures to the uncanny that alienates. *Free Associations*, 9: 611–648.

Puget, J. (2010). The subjectivity of certainty and the subjectivity of uncertainty. *Psychoanalytic Dialogues*, 20: 4–20.

Rosenfeld, D. (1980). The handling of resistances in adult patients. *The International Journal of Psychoanalysis*, 61: 71–83.

Rozmarin, E. (2009). I am yourself: subjectivity and the collective. *Psychoanalytic Dialogues*, 5: 165–180.

Rozmarin, E. (2010). Reflections on Janine Puget's paper. *Psychoanalytic Dialogues*, 20: 32–39.

Sosnik, R. A. (2010). Reflections on links and linking. *Psychoanalytic Dialogues*, 20: 27–31.

Tannen, D. (1993). *Framing in Discourse*. New York: Oxford University Press.

Turkle, S. (2011). *Alone Together: Why We Expect More from Technology and Less from Each Other*. New York: Basic Books.

Westerman, M. (2015). Constructivism: what are our alternatives? *Psychoanalytic Dialogues Blog*. https://psychoanalyticdialoguesblog.wordpress.com/2015/12/21/by-michael-a-western-phd-constructionism-what-are-our-alternatives/

Winnicott, D. (1971). *Playing and Reality*. London: Routledge.

Winnicott, D. W. (1988). *Human Nature*. New York: Patheon Books.

Chapter 8

The frame as a border in a variety of settings

Yolanda Gampel

An analytic process confronts both patient and analyst with a heterogeneous range of sensations, perceptions, emotions, and fantasies emanating from within. A determination not to experience anything coexists with an inability to reject or ignore any stimulus, as well as with the limitations of our instruments – dreams, every human act – and the constraints imposed by every prediction. The diversity of images generated by death, which becomes disembedded from the body, emotions stirred by catastrophe, circumstances that return to the mind (scenes that were not evacuated), internal images, fear, the vicissitudes of relational life, all generate a tension that is inscribed in the body at every level. These elements scare us and prompt us to establish a kind of artificial order.

For this reason, the creator of psychoanalysis developed a framework that establishes constants whose boundaries make it possible for the analytic process to unfold both in the analyst's and in the analysand's minds. Patients will thus find the unity of the self through the variety of images, sensations, and emotions that emerge in the sessions, and become their own witnesses through the presence of an other, the analyst. A contemplative movement develops that entails observing and listening in a process that shifts from instant to instant and surprises us.

Freud (1912, 1913) established the importance of boundaries early in the development of the "talking cure." He understood the powerful forces unleashed within the intimacy of the therapy as well as the therapist's ability to rationalize the countertransference. He was aware of the fact that the relationship with the patient was both real and symbolic. Freud offered the components of the frame as recommendations, and they were established as constants. He did not use the word *frame*, even though psychoanalytic authors who discuss this term refer to it as "the traditional Freudian method." Generally speaking, the frame is the framework that promotes the development of the analysis. It serves as a support for patients' psychotic aspects (Bleger, 1967), their formal or affective signifiers (Anzieu, 1987), and the fears caused by their own psychic content, as well as psychoanalysts' own fears as to their ability to be receptive to patients' turmoil, to face their own, or to deal with their own blindness or deafness.

The frame protects the two participants in their vulnerable positions, circumscribing a room where two people can listen to each other's thoughts and share feelings and the movements of the unconscious. When the unknown or unthinkable, the non-ego, phantoms (Bleger, 1967), or transmitted radioactive residues (Gampel, 2005, 2013) emerge, they revive traumatic experiences and break the frame and the continuity of the process. Such breakdowns open the possibility for the incorporation of what had been rendered inaccessible into patients' thoughts and feelings and hence for the restoration of the analytic frame.

The "frame" of the psychoanalytic session is detached from ordinary life insofar as it embodies a unique contractual arrangement between the participants. Bleger describes the analytic frame as "a 'non process', in the sense that it is made up of constants within whose bounds the process of analysis takes place" (1967, p. 511). Winnicott (1955) had already expanded the role of this boundary from protecting the transference to providing a holding-facilitating environment without which the therapeutic process could not occur. Bleger (1967) further extends the concept of frame to include the meta-behavior that forms the backdrop for the contents of the therapy. It is a frame around the therapy. If it changes, the therapy becomes severely compromised. The frame is perceived only when it changes or breaks, and patients will repeatedly put it to the test in order to reenact neurotic childhood interactions.

I believe that Bleger's conceptualization constitutes a qualitative leap that enables a different view. The frame, he asserts:

is an institution within whose bounds certain phenomena take place which we call behavior ... What became evident to me was that each institution is a portion of the individual's personality; and it is of such importance that identity is always, wholly or partially, institutional, in the sense that at least one part of the identity always shapes itself by belonging to a group, institution, ideology, party.

(Bleger, 1967, p. 511)

Patients transfer onto the frame their indiscriminate aspects, which, in this author's view, are either psychotic or correspond to the non-ego of the personality. According to the classic notion used in all psychoanalytic institutes affiliated with the International Psychoanalytic Association (IPA), the fixed, stable, and reasonable qualities of the frame, or the fact that it cannot be easily moved, provide an environment for deep ego development. The frame would be the setting, the background where the psychoanalytic treatment takes place. This process corresponds to the level of secondary symbolization, which is represented by the formulation of the basic rules and by everything that can be made explicit regarding the reasons for the frame's specific structure.

As secondary symbolization grows more flexible and complex and primary symbolization is worked through, the gap between them will gradually narrow. At the same time, the right conditions will emerge for a tertiary (Green, 1972), intermediary (Freud, 1913), or transitional (Winnicott, 1953) symbolization that will allow subjects to overcome the split between two irreconcilable levels of representation. The psychoanalytic process is situated in this intermediate space between the two ways of symbolizing the frame and the psychoanalytic situation, and reduces the gap between them.

All these reflections on the dynamics of the analytic process bear the stamp of private practice. The environment considered is always the private office. The literature on the frame rarely takes into account the sociocultural, political, and economic context, which forms the backdrop for the development of the frame in an individual analysis. What happens if we leave the office and go to work at hospitals, schools, or *favelas*? What if we bring a psychoanalytic perspective to our work with the homeless, with people living in the street? How do we create a mobile frame? How do we create a frame in situations of war, of political and social violence, where the so-called "external world of reality" is always imbalanced, always in crisis? If we thought of psychoanalysis as a device, which device would we choose?

With a late-twentieth-century worldview, Deleuze presents a matrilineal psychoanalysis that does not form a system; it goes in different directions, mutates, is unstable, and what it narrates is always in crisis. This author advances a psychoanalytic device that focuses on the event, and where subjects develop from upheaval to upheaval rather than following a pre-established direction. What would result from the implementation of such unconventional devices? This approach allows me to define the frame as a border and to reflect on how to handle this border in a variety of settings.[1]

When we are faced with our patients' human pain, we learn that besides listening and intervening in a timely way whenever an unconscious formation appears, we must play a supportive role that is very necessary for individuals who may be alone – immigrants, the unemployed, those suffering post-traumatic stress due to social or political violence. Furthermore, it is when we take on this supportive role that listening and intervening become possible.

The work on borders, boundaries, and frames is a major concern not only for psychoanalysis but also for political geographers, whose research is no longer limited to issues related to territorial demarcation in a geopolitical sense. Geographers now inquire into the role of borders in defining and negotiating social, cultural, and economic differences, and investigate the changing nature of these borders. Boundaries are seen as impermanent, contested, and dependent on historical and political contexts. An interdisciplinary approach has enabled the development of research on borders and their relevance in the context of social inequality, ethnic rivalry, and different identity constructions.

I started writing this article in early 2015, having in mind my work experiences in different cultural contexts and in different political, social, and historical conditions. At that time events were succeeding one another ceaselessly, and I felt I was losing both the frame of my reflection on collective or social trauma, and the frame of my psychoanalytic work. If an event (*événement*) stands out from a background of uniformity, it is a difference, something we cannot foretell. Yet since January 2015, their rapid succession turned these events into an undifferentiated background and, at the same time, shaped them into a single event that we knew would continue even though its nature and location might surprise us. It is as though events had changed meaning and function and had become a part of life (Deleuze, 1990). What we were experiencing was a form of surviving rather than living.

Alain Badiou, a French philosopher who has built on Deleuze's ideas, distinguishes event from situation. The event is the moment of excess, the utterly unpredictable invasion of the extra-ordinary. It constitutes subjects and demands loyalty (Badiou, 2005). In this sense, events should be conceived of as sequences of occurrences that result in the transformation of structures. They cannot simply be forgotten and put out of mind; they cast a shadow over people's ability to go into their present and envision a future free of the events' debilitating effects. They "press upon the world with the same insistence and obstinacy with which the real creates holes in the symbolic" (Das, 2007, p134).

The massacre at *Charlie Hebdo* in Paris, the violence and political unrest in Israel, and the so-called "refugee crisis" – the large number of people fleeing war, terror, and persecution and seeking a better future in Europe, has generated an incredible wave of solidarity on the part of civil society but, at the same time, has triggered an intense debate on security policy and border control. This "crisis" has contributed to the reemergence of debates on boundaries as lines of demarcation of authority, law, and identity and, overall, has led to the sealing of external borders and, at the same time, to the challenge of internal ones.

Then the stabbings began in Jerusalem. If Israeli authorities think it is worthwhile to keep Jerusalem united, they should act to unite it. What the stabbings have shown is how quickly a few incidents can raise walls and divide the city. And then there was the mass shooting at the Bataclan in Paris at 10:30 p.m. on November 13, 2015. Such events have fueled and been fueled by the loss of rational thought and the rise of populism, Islamophobia, and anti-Semitism. According to Clotilde Leguil:

> hatred leads to the persecution of suspects, the legitimization of terror, conspiracy theories, and the identification of the enemy among us. It is always about taking on "an enemy hidden behind the appearance of Good" and endlessly punishing the Other, who would be responsible for all human suffering.
>
> (Leguil, 2015, p. 1)

I decided I would use clinical experience as the starting point of this paper. I would gather material from sessions and supervisions that had taken place at different times and historical events would serve as symbolic capital that transcends spatial and temporal coordinates, as a referent that helps organize memories and experiences: what went through my mind and what I learned when I was teaching or was asked to intervene. I would narrate the experience, the process, and the various moments of political and social tension that distinguish these events from simple occurrences. What follows are examples of interventions in groups, in an individual therapeutic encounter, in a psychoanalytic session, and in supervision when the traditional psychoanalytic frame has been challenged.

One

I was invited to work with a team of mental health professionals who were volunteering their services at a refugee camp in Germany. Fourteen mothers and their children had been brought from Bosnia when the conflict in the former Yugoslavia had reached its peak. The therapists described how this group of women and their children would sit closely together, resembling one consolidated, undifferentiated mass. Each of these women, sitting with her own children, created yet another smaller mass within the bigger one. They were all afraid of speaking. Their mood was very sad, and they would not respond when the therapists encouraged them to express their thoughts and feelings. Furthermore, they all refused to participate in any kind of group work.

These women were Muslim and came from rural areas. In their culture of origin problems are resolved within the extended family. The Western practice of psychotherapy, where we talk to someone who is an "outsider," who is not a relative, was foreign to them. In some cases it might even be considered bizarre or translated as an act of treason. In this specific sociopolitical context, in which they were accustomed to seeing neighbors and friends betraying one another, they did not even trust each other enough to talk among themselves, since their husbands, fathers, and sons were still in the former Yugoslavia. We also had to consider the different ways in which people go through mourning processes.

By way of a translator, I invited the entire group of women to stay with me for half an hour while the rest of the team were taking care of the children in a nearby room. I talked a little bit about their losses, the fear they had experienced, and especially about their sadness and I asked them, in this half hour, to scream and cry out all together everything that "worried their hearts." When the half hour was over, I told them I would be there for five days and would come to meet with them every day for half an hour to accompany them during this ceremony of grief.

The volunteer team reported that in the aftermath of that meeting the atmosphere in the camp had changed. The women had started working on their very special handicrafts, and the children had started using the spaces designated for play. Acknowledging their state of mind and offering them a space-time to mourn together and feel supported, a space in which to think and express themselves in their own way through acts had allowed them to regain their specificity and subjectivity (Gampel, 2005). The implications of this example point to the fact that we can and do exert influence over people's reactions to their terrible wounds. They will not necessarily remain in a stance of survival or act in a very aggressive style. Instead, they may continue to be creative and thus let their capacity to think and grow emerge. Only a society that recognizes and takes responsibility for its actions may truly influence and promote the healing of psychic wounds.

Two

The Friday after the murder of three young people who were celebrating a birthday in a bar in Tel Aviv, I receive a request for an urgent visit. A young woman who had come to Israel to visit friends and family started having panic attacks accompanied by shivering, crying, distress, and moments of paralysis. Opale relates that she traveled to different places on business and in each of these places a terrorist attack took place. She was in Paris on November 13, near the site of the massacre. The next week, after taking the train to Belgium and being forced to remain in it because the city had been closed off, she arrived in Israel a day before the attack on Dizengoff Street.

She asks me if I know of a place anywhere in the world that is truly peaceful (a background or frame of safety!) (Gampel, 1999, 2000). The trauma she went through due to social and political violence can be viewed as the outcome of a constellation of life experiences narrated within a violent social context. Besides its quality as event, for Opale violence is a *persisting condition* rather than simply a serious occurrence.

I will briefly recount what I learned from her story as I continued to see her every day that week. Our conversation was disrupted by inner turmoil at times, and at other times her narrative was strongly associative. Critical, painful, unthinkable moments linked to political and social violence emerged through connective thought. These moments had been impossible to contain and work through; they had acted as cumulative traumas that led her to go into exile in search of a transitional space somewhere on planet Earth. Opale is from South Africa, where rape and murder happen all the time. She and her co-workers were attacked with knifes at the office. Other people died, but she was spared. Yet a week later she left her home country and started wandering around the world.

The shivers have decreased. Distress and fear remain but are less intense. She is once again able to work and communicate with others. During our fifth meeting the tone of anxiety has diminished but she still shows great fragility. She relates a dream, and a sad state of mind emerges. I point out that she seems sad to me today, and we talk about it. She bursts into tears and slowly starts talking about how hard it is not being able to live in South Africa. It is a beautiful country with a magnificent landscape, with mountains and forests. She had thought she would always live there, but this no longer seems possible. She recounts two other horrible episodes of attacks on remote houses by gangs that rape and murder their victims. She will never be free to make a decision.

The next Saturday, while I am writing about Opale, I get a Skype call from a colleague in Gaza with whom I have worked for many years. He does not look good. He is at home, wearing sweaters and a hat and covered in blankets. I ask him if he is sick. "I'm cold," he says. "We don't have enough electricity to heat the house, and it's awfully cold." (They receive electricity from Israel and Egypt, which is problematic. They have a small power plant but it is overstretched.) He is also worried because he is not getting enough financial support to pay his colleagues at the new clinic.

During the 1989 Intifada, a Palestinian uprising against the Israeli occupation, a group of mental health professionals, myself among them, wanted to establish a link, a connection based on professional affinity. The group we formed is called IMUT, a Hebrew word meaning "confrontation." This link opened an exchange of words and thoughts between Israelis and Palestinians in spite of the breakdown of political links, in spite of the Israeli occupation in the Territories, in spite of the mass movement of the Intifada, and in spite of terrorism. It took us four years, from 1989 until the spring of 1993, to start carrying out activities that would support mental health services in Palestine. The main goal of the partnership was to facilitate training and specialization for psychologists, social workers, and psychiatrists. In this way, we would help develop a cadre of Palestinian professionals to meet the needs for mental health services in Gaza.[2]

I would like to share with you some of the dilemmas that we, Israelis and Palestinians, faced and still face. We needed to find a way to respect the other side's identity and space and the wide variety of reactions determined by sociocultural ideals, and to transmit knowledge while taking into account the significant difference between fantasies and intentions, on the one hand, and accomplished actions, on the other. Our Palestinian colleagues felt that they must be heard and that we, the Israelis, were there to listen to their testimony. The great challenge, however, lay in going beyond sociopolitical testimony and creating a professional working alliance that could focus on psychic reality. Thus, the greatest fear on both sides was the fear of betraying the "sacredness of the subject."

Our Palestinian colleagues wanted to be heard in their experience of suffering a primordial damage. Their account was a manifest expression of the chilling desecration of a sacred value, a narrative of an awfully destructive social process, and a demand for emotional, institutional, and symbolic reparation and reconstitution. To discuss the inviolable and violation would put us in a different conceptual realm from the one pertaining to the discussion of the possible and the impossible. Violation is linked to desecration. One desecrates something enshrined by the law or something holy. The act of desecration breaks a taboo. It contradicts the life drive; it is contrary to the construction of a link and to the psychic function of representation and symbolization. Symbolization nurtures psychic life. Violation destroys the symbol and turns it into raw, fragmented matter that fails to encourage thought. Nevertheless, inviolability means accepting symbolization and the link that extends "beyond any conflict" (Gampel, 1998, 2002, 2009). In this way, the link is grounded in the roots of being and becoming – in the future, in the law, and in human ethical consensus.

It is worth illustrating these questions with some cases that unfolded on both sides of the border during Israel's attacks on Gaza in 2014.

Three

Clinical work during these months challenged me day after day, mobilized my emotions, and taught me about aspects of life in Israel that I had not experienced before. In this intertwining of overlapping worlds (Puget and Wender, 1982) in which patients and therapists coexist there is and there isn't a caesura, a link, a synapse, a transference-countertransference dynamic. There is a passage from an inside to an outside where one must act; there is the siren and the need to go to the shelters and then back to the session. Simultaneously with these experiences, we had to keep in mind what was happening in Gaza – how children and women without shelter were being attacked by Israel from the air and, at the same time, forced to remain in place by men whose extremist ideology of sacrifice demanded that they accept death. What is left? The bond, the bridge, makes it possible to move from one side to the other. It grants mobility (Puget, 2013).

What follows is the account of a session during the first days of the war. Avi is 54 years old, and the session discussed here took place on July 21, 2014. Avi starts by strongly criticizing the government's decision to enter Gaza. He asserts that Israel must find a way to start a dialogue. He discusses a suitable military strategy. While I point out that he is talking in an assertive, confident, controlled way, I think of the fear, of the great dread he feels that his son will have to go to Gaza (his role in the army is both necessary and dangerous), and of the threat to his son's life.

Avi says his son is waiting to receive the order to rejoin the army, which is called Order Number 8. All his son talks about is how all of his friends on his team have already gone back. By law, a person who has just finished his time in the army cannot rejoin for at least a month, even if there is a war. "That's reassuring, but my son is going from office to office to convince them to let him go back and be with his teammates." It is clear that as a father, Avi does not want this to happen at all; he is terrified. Fear, pain, and déjà vu converge:

I understand him, I understand, because if I were his age I'd do the exact same thing, and I understand that to him, this is the most important thing in the world. How can I beat that?!

Avi has been involved in several very difficult wars, and his role in the army was as dangerous as his son's. His unit did very courageous things. He asks himself:

How can you overcome this? How can you overcome the fear of killing and being killed, the tension between wanting to be with one's friends and cooperating, and wanting to live? My son did everything he did, but he doesn't know what war is like, and I dearly wish he didn't have to go.

My patient wants to protect his son from himself and from the context surrounding him.

Without transition, he starts talking about the woman with whom he is currently involved. Things are not going that well, and he feels very lonely. She needs his support, and he needs hers really badly. I tell him that he asks women for help but feels that we cannot provide it because we also need support. He returns to discussing the war and the strategy the military should use. With great sadness, he states that he has no confidence in the people giving orders. He recalls episodes from the war where his superiors' commands and indications led to the loss of lives. He keeps remembering different war experiences, what he did as a soldier and as a lieutenant. At times he is an expert giving advice, and at other times, thinking about what his son will undergo if he rejoins, he is a father/mother full of sorrow and pain who simply wants his child to live.

I point out the difference between the emotions he conveys when he speaks as a former lieutenant colonel and the emotions he expresses when speaking as the father/mother he has become. In the next sessions I learn more about combat, about the army's rules and lies, how soldiers must respond to orders. Because, for instance, it is a good thing that Amir Peretz (the former Israeli Minister of Defense) approved and promoted the installation of anti-missile defense equipment, developed by a young man, without the consent of those who think they know what they're doing. The young man worked without any help. Only Amir Peretz understood, and that's why we are protected. On the one hand, Avi talks about listening to young men and appreciating their skills; on the other, he criticizes soldiers' lack of maturity to think for themselves, and claims that this is why they need experienced lieutenants.

And in Gaza, he continues, Hamas invested everything they had, all their money and energy in building tunnels. It is a poor city, where citizens live with basic lacks. They are poor because Hamas invested in one thing only. They invested in fighting, in rebellion, in war, which is what they think life is about, and did not invest in life.

> And I get really mad at those Israelis who say we shouldn't invest in them, we shouldn't help them, we shouldn't give them electricity and water, send them food. That is such poor thinking! On the contrary, we should give it to them, and do things differently so that some day we'll be able to talk.

I keep learning about war tactics, about Avi's experience as a soldier, about what is going on with his son. In the meantime, something terrible happened in Gaza due to one of the big mistakes Avi so feared. Hamas had built houses on a road they knew the Israelis would take. The houses had been wrecked, but they seemed to be inhabited. Hamas thought the Israeli army would go into these houses to order the residents to leave and then destroy the buildings. Four members of the team that had been under his son's command (under the command of that young, inexperienced lieu-tenant) went into the houses and were killed. They had received the wrong order.

Those were terrible days. Avi's son went to all the funerals, and Avi went along so that the young man would not be on his own. On the one hand, Avi was pained by the parents' suffering; on the other, he was happy that his own son was alive. One of the mothers approached his son and said to him, "How lucky your mom is that you're outside; she doesn't need to worry." "My mom hasn't worried for a long time," he answered. Avi's wife and the mother of his children had died ten years earlier. He wondered how he could save his son from all the pain, the guilt, and everything else. There was so much suffering on both sides … How can one keep going? And yet we do.

When I asked for his permission to publish material from our sessions and explained what the book was about, Avi reminded me that because of my work in Gaza, I had been unable to sustain the frame; at the beginning of his analysis, he had come to my office to find I was not there.[3] I had gone to Gaza and forgotten to let him know that I needed to cancel the session. The next day, among other things, he wondered what he had done to me. He felt guilty. I told him he was not responsible for my absence. I was the one to blame for not letting him know I would not be there. He asked me where I had been that I had forgotten about him. I told him I had been in Gaza.

That day he said to me, "It was hard for you to be here and there!" I think I am not always aware of the nature of my presence with patients in relation to my presence in the context of social violence that affects us both, even if I am not acknowledging this context. It is hard to assess where and when external reality becomes overwhelming.

What follows are two cases that I discussed on Skype with Gaza colleagues during the period when this session was taking place. When the ceasefires started, the entire team of psychologists took to the streets, which were full of people. They started looking for places where those who had nowhere to go could find shelter and food. Some had lost their homes, some had not. People told them about the pain of their loss, their panic, the feelings caused by losing everything. Mothers had lost their children; children had lost their parents. Several psychologists were particularly affected by these conversations, and asked to supervise with me. I told them that all I could do was have a conversation with them so that we could think together, because I had not experienced anything similar to what they had gone through. These situations were new, and we needed to create a mode of presence as therapists for which no theoretical framework had been developed.

Four

In the first days of the truce the therapists on the team showed great apathy and pain. They did not know what to say in the face of such suffering. They listened and tried to find something positive to which people could cling so that they would keep looking for food, shelter, a home. Then the team started getting requests for intervention from families that were in a much better situation. A family had taken in some relatives who had lost their home. The host called one of the psychologists and asked him, "Please, I need you to talk to my brother's family, the parents and two teenage children. They are staying with me. There are terrible fights and scenes going on, and I don't know what to do. I need help."

The team met with the parents. Their children were being very aggressive with them; they claimed that the parents had not been able to defend them, had not done the right things to prevent the destruction of their house, and had not taken good care of them or of all those who had lost their homes. They used sound arguments, but their anger and aggression were tremendous. One of my colleagues talked to the whole family. The children's main concern was that they were starting their first year of college on September 1, and all their books and belongings had been destroyed. They were worried about their future.

My colleague and I pondered how to deal with the situation in a family setting. I suggested that he continue to see them all together, let each of them testify as to what had happened from his or her point of view, and have them listen to each other. The therapist told the children that it made sense for them to be worried about their future. They would be able to get everything they needed for school, but if they had lost their home and all their belongings, their parents had, too. We discussed how to transform the children's rage and hatred (which was apparently directed at the parents but was actually aimed toward the entire situation, including Hamas and Israel), how to rechannel this rage and the immense energy contained in it in the direction of cooperation and assistance. In our repeated conversations about this family we also considered how to encourage them to become part of what was happening in Gaza, how to motivate them to take to the streets along with the therapists and listen and talk to other people.

What is worth stressing here is that my colleague used all his time to talk to the family and help them think things through. He did not offer interpretations. What he did was simply to be with them and say something humane that was very valuable and helped them think and feel that their pain and suffering were being recognized by someone who knew how to listen. Afterwards, he conveyed all these situations to the team and they discussed them, and this discussion brought about an incredible transformation. One of the team members told me that these conversations were highly significant to him. Another one stated that he felt great support from the team and was able to think; there were times when thinking was not possible.

This account gives us an idea of what happens to a population that has suffered at multiple levels. Team members were learning about the state of mind of those around them: the mourning, the pain, the loss, the pain of the social. The pain …

Five

One of my colleagues receives a call from an important man in Gaza who asks him to see his daughter-in-law. His son's house was destroyed, so the man brought his son's family to live with him. His son's wife is not eating and is very sad. It seems that she is suffering from some kind of imbalance. They feel that something must be neurologically wrong with her. A neurologist saw her and said that all he could do at the time was conduct an EEG. Yet he told my colleague: "This is not a case for me. This woman is suffering from severe depression. There is nothing neurological." So the father-in-law brought her to see the psychologist.

We are in Gaza, which is a tribal culture. It is hard for tribe members to conceive of asking a person who works at a clinic to solve their problems. Problems are solved within the *hamula*, the clan. Several families form a *hamula*, which has its own chief, and several *hamulas* make up a tribe. When a family has a problem, the first one to be consulted is the father, then the chief of the *hamula*, and then the chief of the tribe. Advice is sought outside of the tribe.

A woman does not go to the doctor alone, much less to a psychologist. The father-in-law waits outside. She is pale and thin and looks very sad. She comes into the office and remains silent. The therapist says to her, "Your father-in-law talked to me and told me what he thinks is wrong with you." Silence. He continues talking: "Look, these are terrible times. Your home was destroyed, and you have to live with your father-in-law. Very bad, painful things have happened, not just to you, but to everyone. Many losses, many deaths, a lot of pain." The young woman, who is 23 years old, starts crying.

He lets her cry and says to her, "Do you want to tell me what happened to you personally that did not happen to anyone else?" She cannot open her mouth. Half an hour has gone by, and he is thinking about the father-in-law, who is sitting in the waiting room. My colleague has to go out and talk to him; it is not acceptable to spend so much time with the man's daughter-in-law without telling him what is going on. So he says to the patient, "I'll give you pen and paper. Please try to write everything you can't talk about, everything that happened to you."

In the waiting room, the father-in-law says to him, "She's in very bad shape. She doesn't eat. She can't. It's not depression. You have to give her a medicine right away." The therapist explains that they have to be patient with her, let her be sad and refuse to talk or eat. I'm not sure he knows quite what to tell this man. He returns to his office. The patient has not written a single word. He says to her, "Look, this is what I told your father-in-law." She starts crying, wailing ceaselessly for half an hour. "Here's my phone number," he tells her. "You can call me whenever you need to, and in two days I want to see you again." So much social pain! What to do about medication? I suggest a placebo, Omega 3.

I was invited to participate in this book, which serves as a frame to discuss a variety of points of view and clinical materials concerning the value, the necessity, the instability and/or the evolution of the frame or setting. Within the frame of this book, I was asked to write about the theory and practice of psychoanalysis in different sociocultural contexts and situations. I think that the invitation was issued with the idea that it is impossible to understand individual, family, or institutional crises without taking into account a culture that is also in crisis. In this sense, subjectivity is understood as developing in the space of intersubjectivity, within a culture. Singularity takes into account, bears in mind, realizes symbolizations that are historical and social. We understand individuality from the perspective of the plural. When we are born we are potentially singular, since we need a first other in order to meet with others.

Each culture has its own assumptions, rules, conventions, and traditions; it has its own fabric, constitution, and ways of processing. In psychotherapy, each technique bears its own assumptions (its frame), and hence its own "contents" or processes. In this sense, it is singularly important to situate the psychoanalytic frame as a particular instance of a more general phenomenon. The frame *is made up of constants within whose bounds the analysis takes place*: the couch, the closed door. Besides the patient's frame, these constants include analysts' training, their teachers, their affiliation with a certain psychoanalytic society, and their theoretical framework.

When working in a big shed for refugees, on Skype, at a coffee shop, in time of war or sociopolitical conflict I also try to establish a work frame. Yet outside the office we use different devices. For this reason, we have to acknowledge the existence of a context of social violence. Such acknowledgment implies welcoming the temporal dimension of the unforeseeable. It is as though analysts, through their acts, became agents of contingency. It is scary even to think about it. When I try to establish a relationship and a work frame as a response to a request for supervision, consultation, or intervention in such a setting, my invitation, as a point of departure, will not be, "Tell me whatever occurs to you." Instead, I will suggest having a conversation. In this context, I know I am practicing without knowing. In this way, I attempt to grasp the system of boundaries and exclusion and the cultural viewpoint.

I think that when I am working in my office with a patient four times a week, the frame is rooted in the specificities of a biography that unfolds within a specific sociohistorical setting. I am referring to a multi-layered phenomenon that includes the subtle, spoken but also unspoken transgenerational transmission and whose dimensions begin within the realm of the family. I would like to provide more elements to ponder the singularities of the frame outside the consulting room. I already discussed the notion of the event. Now I propose to create a dialogue between the event that occurs in the social context, on the one hand, and those aspects of the non-ego, those trans-subjective aspects that emerge in the analytic frame, on the other.

Such a dialogue does not point to the coexistence of these conceptualizations. Neither does it involve their comparison. Rather, it aims to bring together two concepts: the one that makes it possible to set the analytic process in motion and let it flow, and the one that enables us to see the social as a set of significant occurrences. The latter notion serves as a strategy to narrow down the field of research so as to encompass what "appears" in a situation – what was not already there in the individual or in the social realm. By setting the analytic frame in motion (it is stable and yet it is movement), something may also "appear" that was not already there.

Deleuze (1987) states that an event is a conjunction of converging series that tend toward a limit. Each, then, is characterized by a vibration, by an infinite series that enters into relationships with the whole and the parts. To go even further, I may add that the event is under the influence of something that acts as a screen in relation to an initial disjunctive diversity. I have already mentioned Badiou's distinction between event and situation, whereby the event is the entirely unexpected invasion of the out of the ordinary that constitutes subjects and demands loyalty (Badiou, 2005).

Bleger, for his part, claims that:

> until recently, we were comfortably working in the field of science, language, logic, etc., without realizing that all of these phenomena or behaviours (I am interested in all of them in so far as they are behaviours, that is to say, human phenomena) take place within a context of assumptions which we ignored or thought nonexistent or invariable; but we know now that communication contains a meta-communication, science a meta-science, theory a meta-theory, language a meta-language, logics a meta-logics, etc., etc. If the "meta-" varies the contents vary radically. Thus, the frame is constant, and is therefore decisive in the phenomena of the process of behaviour. In other words, the frame is a *meta-behaviour*, and the phenomena we are going to distinguish as behaviour depend on it. It is what remains implicit, but on which the explicit depends.
>
> (Bleger, 1967, p. 512)

If we see the event from this perspective, it is also a meta-event, and the phenomena we are going to distinguish as behavior depend on it. "It is what remains implicit, but on which the explicit depends" (Bleger, 1967, p. 512). With the event, the inconsistent multiplicity underlying every social order can emerge at the subjective level. An event is a representation in the act. It is violent, explosive, and represents those elements of social life that were being silenced and manipulated and can no longer be contained in the social space.

A psychoanalytic frame, in turn, makes it possible to bring back the repressed, what was marked in the body but has remained unrepresented, transgenerational radioactive residues, the non-ego; in other words, everything for which we have neither words nor images. Both in the social context and in the psychoanalytic frame, this unfolding of new representations stemming from an event produces truths, subjects, and new transformations that facilitate growth. In the social realm, the event gives rise to new social systems.

Bleger considers that institutions and the frame "*always* make up a 'phantom world,' that of the most primitive and undifferentiated organization."[4] Later he will add: "The non-ego is the background or the frame of the organized ego; the 'background' and 'figure' of a unique Gestalt. Between the ego and the non-ego, or between the neurotic and psychotic part of the personality, there is no dissociation but a cleavage" (Bleger, 1967, p. 514). Deleuze and Badiou, for their part, define the history of non-events (*le non-événementiel*), the history of territories, mentalities, madness, and the search for safety, as a historicization of which we are not aware, just as we are not aware of the non-ego that Bleger discusses in relation to individual development. We are thus going back and forth between the two realms, the social and the individual. This back-and-forth allows us to enter gaps, take hitherto untrodden paths, and sometimes to be surprised by our discoveries and keep moving on.

Notes

1   According to the dictionary, a device is "an object, machine, or piece of equipment that has been made for some special purpose" or "something that is done to achieve a particular effect" (*Merriam Webster* online). Available at: www.merriam-webster.com/dictionary/device). In this case, the effect has to do with the emergence of, or access to, certain phenomena that are tied to the content on which analyst and patient are working and to the types of

interventions made by the analyst. Each device allows us to see certain phenomena with greater or lesser clarity.

2   The next two paragraphs are taken from Gampel (1998, 2009).

3   In the second phase of our work with Gaza professionals, the Gaza clinic embarked on the creation of a training program in psychotherapy. Its goal was to offer a specialization in community mental health. It had formed partnerships with Tel Aviv University and with universities in other countries. In the context of this partnership, I traveled to Gaza regularly to teach psychopathology and to supervise.

4   I have modified the original translation, which rendered "*mundo fantasma*" as "ghost world," because in his comparison between the internal and the external realms, Bleger refers to the "*miembro fantasma*," the phantom limb, which was erroneously translated as "ghost member" (T.N.).

Works cited

Anzieu, D. (1987). Formal signifiers and the ego-skin. In Anzieu, D. and Houzel, D., *Psychic Envelopes*. Translated by Daphne Briggs. London: Karnac Books, 1990, pp. 1–58. [Les signifiants formels et le moi-peau, in Anzieu D. et Houzel D., *Les enveloppes psychiques*, (2nd ed. 1996). Paris: Dunod, pp. 1–22].

Badiou, A. (2005). *Being and Event*. Translated by Oliver Feltham. London, UK: Continuum.

Bleger, J. (1967). Psycho-analysis of the psycho-analytic frame. *International Journal of Psychoanalysis* 48: 511–519.

Das, V. (2007). *Life and Words: Violence and the Descent into the Ordinary*. Berkeley, CA: University of California Press.

Deleuze, G. (1987). Criba e infinito [Sieve and infinity]. Available at www.webdeleuze.com/php/texte.php?cle=143&groupe=Leibniz&langue=3

Deleuze, G. (1990). *The Logic of Sense*. Translated by Mark Lester. New York: Columbia University Press.

Freud, S. (1912). The dynamics of transference. *S.E.* 12: 97–108.

Freud, S. (1913). On beginning the treatment. *S.E.* 12: 121–144.

Gampel, Y. (1998). Liens inviolables et violation de liens [Invisible links and violation of links]. *Journal de la Psychanalyse de l'enfant* 25: 256–270.

Gampel, Y. (1999). Between the background of safety and the background of the uncanny in the context of social violence. In Bott Spillius, E., ed. in chief, *Psychoanalysis on the Move*. London: Routledge, pp. 59–74.

Gampel, Y. (2000). Reflections on the prevalence of the uncanny in social violence. In Robben, A. and Suarez-Orozco, O., eds. *Cultures under Siege: Collective Violence and Trauma in Interdisciplinary Perspectives*. Cambridge: Cambridge University Press, pp. 48–69.

Gampel, Y. (2002). Unavoidable links and violable links: Israelis and Palestinians in psychoanalytic psychotherapy training. In Bunzl, J. and Beit-Hallahmi, B., eds. *Psychoanalysis, Identity, and Ideology: Critical Essays on the*

Israel/Palestine Case. Boston-Dordrecht-London: Kluwer Academic Publishers, pp. 201–214.

Gampel, Y. (2005). *Ces parents qui vivent a travers moi: Les infants de guerres.* [These parents who live through me. Children of war]. Paris: Fayard.

Gampel, Y. (2009). Esplorazioni psicoanalitiche sulla crisi medio-orientale [Psychoanalytic explorations on the Middle-East crisis]. *Rivista di Psicoanalisi Applicata "Frenis Zero"* VI (12): 363–382.

Gampel, Y. (2013). The effects of social political violence in children, in the analyst, and in the psychoanalytic process. In Oelsner, R., ed. *Transference and Countertransference Today*. London: Routledge, pp. 150–176.

Green, A. (1972). Note sur le processus tertiaire [Note on the tertiary process]. *Revue Française de Psychanalyse* 36: 407–411.

Leguil, C. (2015). *L'être et le genre: Homme/Femme*. Paris: PUF.

Puget, J. (2013). Discontinuidades, superposición, articulación [Discontinuities, overlap, articulation]. *Revista Generaciones* 2(2): 385–399.

Puget, J. and Wender, L. (1982). Analista y paciente en mundos superpuestos [Analyst and patient in overlapping worlds]. *Psicoanalisis* 4: 502–503.

Winnicott, D. W. (1953). Transitional objects and transitional phenomena. In (1958) *Collected Papers*. New York: Basic Books, pp. 229–242.

Winnicott, D. W. (1955). Metapsychologic, clinical aspect regression psychoac. situation. *International Journal of Psychoanalysis* 36: 16–26.

Chapter 9

Revisiting the concept of frame[1]

Janine Puget

Introduction

Throughout the history of psychoanalysis, one of our tools, the frame,[2] has acquired different meanings due to the theoretical changes that take place in any evolving science as well as to the influence of social context, which is out of our control. In this paper, I focus on the contributions of Argentine psychoanalysts to the understanding of the analysand–analyst relationship both in the traditional setting of individual analysis and in family, couple, and group analysis.

The deconstruction of the notion of the frame led to the adoption of the concept of device, which incorporates the social field and takes into account the multiple elements at play in the analytic relationship. It became evident that there was a difference between interacting with oneself in the presence of the analyst, an interaction where the analyst is viewed as the object of the transference, and interacting with two or more others, which includes the analyst as a subject. This new awareness marked a break with the traditional psychoanalytic frame of reference. As a consequence, therapeutic practices that substituted the notion of device in place of the frame were placed outside of psychoanalysis.

The notion of link,[3] however, was gradually introduced into psychoanalytic vocabulary. This notion has received manifold definitions depending on the theoretical framework that supports it. As far as I am concerned, the link defines a relationship between two or more subjects that leads to the emergence of practices specific to the current situation. It favors the effects of interactions in the space *between* two people, of immanently doing together with an other or others. It is difficult or impossible to inscribe the events taking place within the link in the logic governing the dynamic of identification processes.

Two logics, then, overlap in this link. Therefore, besides conflicts pertaining to each individual, we must take into account the product of the overlap. In other words, we must make room for the alterity of each of the subjects inhabiting the relationship, an alterity that cannot be reduced to sameness. The singularity of each participant sets in motion a work that starts from difference. Following Derrida (1967), we understand difference as *différance*, that is, as deferred present. What emerges from *différance* cannot be symbolized; it exceeds representation and depends on presentation.

Presentation does not oppose representation. It belongs to the logic of the effects of the present, of a relationship between two subjects who do not lose their alterity in the encounter. In some Latin American analytic cultures the notions of link and *lo vincular* have acquired a unique slant. Greenberg (2012) stresses such uniqueness, and states that *lo vincular* cannot be translated into English or French because it is specific to the Rio de la Plata.[4] Why emphasize its specificity? Perhaps in order to distinguish among the contributions made by different cultures and acknowledge the cultural particularity of certain technical and theoretical innovations.

Interrelation with other sciences

We must be aware of the need to constantly redefine what it means *to psychoanalyze* and the need to reassess the validity criteria for our definitions. These needs open a wide range of possibilities that enable us to incorporate concepts originating in other sciences, which are supported by their own epistemologies and methodologies. In doing so, we try to show the advantages of the psychoanalytic method and its potential for verification and validation, or are led to accept that, like all human sciences, psychoanalysis oscillates between adopting contributions from other disciplines and building a solid base with the hypotheses that constitute the core of its theory. In the latter case, it will attempt to maintain Freudian postulates with few changes aside from the gradual broadening of these tenets over time.

An interesting exchange between a renowned Argentine epistemologist, Gregorio Klimovsky (1994),[5] and Adolf Grünbaum (1993) showed how easily we fluctuate between advancing formulations that claim that psychoanalysis is a science and advancing formulations that claim the exact opposite. These two philosophers reached the conclusion that psychoanalysis cannot be included among the so-called "hard" sciences. Rather, it belongs in the realm of the human, social, or "soft" sciences.

The frame and the rule of abstinence

How did a chance finding become a fact that spurred new inquiries? Freud discovered that when we establish an emotional relationship based on a modicum of trust and authority, while maintaining a certain degree of asymmetry between the suffering person and the person who is capable of granting new meaning to that suffering, transformations may be brought about in the mind of the suffering subject. Above all, a path may be opened toward a way of thinking that has been freed from certain obstacles, and we can penetrate the mystery of the functioning of the mind. Based on Freud's creative ability, a new therapeutic method was born to address mental illness.

At that time, finding causal relations between a current ailment and a past event constituted a novel idea that opened a path toward a boundless field of research. It was then that the psychoanalytic concept of representation emerged, giving rise to very fruitful theoretical developments. The analyst–analysand relationship, happening in the present, depended on the patient's past, which was stuck at the level of representation. A buried memory must be revealed; we must remember so as to work through and not repeat (Freud, 1914).

At the same time, Freud gradually discovered the power and dangers contained within intense emotional relationships between two people as well as the significant role played by the seduction that was taking place between him and his female patients. Consequently, he set up protective measures that would enable him to go deeper into the mysteries of the human mind while controlling the violence inherent to any relationship between two or more human beings. Freud established some ground rules that would safeguard both patient and analyst from acts of seduction and other enactments resulting from failures in symbolization, among other potential threats.

These rules facilitated intimate dialogue that enabled access to unconscious productions and repressed or split-drive expressions. They would shield both patient and analyst from the risks entailed by any link that has acquired a certain stability. In the same way, in everyday life there are conscious and unconscious rules of coexistence that shelter us from the violence typical of human beings, a violence that takes different guises depending on the context. In a session, for example, violence may arise in the form of sexual transgression as well as lack of commitment, the loss of the necessary distance between analysand and analyst that allows us to perceive the alterity of each member of the link, or the development of a fruitless relationship where the space between subjects has ceased to be respected.

The ways in which we protect ourselves and our analysands differ from country to country, from culture to culture, and probably also from link to link and from situation to situation. One such protective measure is the rule of abstinence, which allows for the maintenance and organization of the relationship. To this end, Freud switched from face-to-face dialogue[6] to the institution of the couch. This shift guaranteed the progress of the treatment by allowing analysands to let their thoughts wander without constraint, and analysts to feel free to observe and to form conjectures pertaining to the products of the relationship.

Gradually, the concept of the frame was defined; that is, a space-time framework was established in order to regulate what is and is not permitted in a relationship that evolves slowly over time and strongly engages the members of the link. In other words, it was clear that a relationship between two or more people constitutes a fertile ground for creativity as well as for different kinds of transgressions. These problems are typical of human relations in general.

Moreover, while the world has changed since the birth of psychoanalysis, at times we still wish to maintain in our daily practice some of the values that led Freud to formulate the notion of frame. How, then can we take into account new values that are being incorporated every day, and new modes of communication? In a way, we realize that some of the current problems faced by psychoanalysts stem from the obstacles to intergenerational coexistence posed by different ways of thinking and of interacting with technology. Younger generations around the world have become, in general, increasingly technophilic and favor connectivity, while the older generations continue to think in linear, causal, and hence associative terms. The overlap of these divergent logics generates new problems and challenges for psychoanalysts that extend to families and educational institutions. Younger people possess information unknown to older adults, a disparity that constitutes a real challenge.

In addition to these transformations we must add that in most countries, psychoanalysis has been affected by popularization, which has become an obstacle. Some concepts lose their signifying power or are used in such different contexts that they no longer account for the complexity of human relations. The trivialization of psychoanalytic thought resulting from the widespread but often superficial public knowledge of psychoanalytic ideas poses some threat to the field, but also offers some advantages; it forces us to set in motion an active, inquiring way of thinking. Thus the need to find new terms that can address what is taking place in the present.

The crisis of the notion of representation began a long time ago (Puget, 2003). In this context, to describe a production that depends only on the effects of the present, Berenstein and I (1997) introduced the notion of presentation. The social, a difficult concept insofar as it entails discovering what it means to inhabit and belong to groups (or to what I call collectives), has become increasingly relevant. Yet we should be wary of placing social subjectivity in a Procrustean bed. Herein lies the difficulty: how to grant independent status to subjectivation processes unrelated to the Oedipus complex, the unconscious, and the drives. In a way, doing so requires that we part with the Freud of *Group Psychology and the Analysis of the Ego* (1921).

Analysis today

Today an analysis requires that the analyst be capable of taking into account a variety of factors that affect the analyst–analysand relationship. We are leaving the field of binaries and entering into a field of multiplicity. This transformation has undermined the very fundaments of psychoanalysis, which have imperceptibly become increasingly open to change despite efforts to buttress them with ad-hoc hypotheses. When they multiply excessively, as Kuhn (1962) points out, hypotheses end up weakening the core of our theories. Regardless of attempts to preserve the original flavor of psychoanalysis, cultural and technological developments have made true orthodoxy impossible. For example, the ability of patients to "Google" their analysts has forever changed the nature of the privacy of the consulting room, and of the analyst.

Frame and device

Over the years, challenges posed to the definition of frame led either to attempts to render it invulnerable or to changes that responded to the demands of social life. We have gradually discovered this concept's

manifold meanings and learned that neither the frame nor its invulnera-
bility, even if we aim to ensure it by way of the rule of abstinence, grants
solidity to analytic relationships. The deconstruction of the notions of
frame and abstinence revealed the importance of analysts' active participation in the analyst–analysand relationship through their opinions, tastes,
values, politics, subjectivity, presence as subjects, and other factors.

Based on the ideas of present-day philosophers,[7] we revised the
concept of frame and were faced with the complexity of links. For this
reason, we incorporated the notion of device into link psychoanalysis, and
with it that of power relations, understanding power both as creative
potency and as appropriation. Power relations serve to describe a state of
tension between different forces that leads to the emergence of specific
practices. The device concerns a complex web of diverse, heterologous
elements tied to knowledge and power – a web made up of institutions and
our commitment to them, discursive practices, philosophical and philan-
thropic trends, scientific statements, and the social field.

The preceding description illustrates how for some modern philosophers and psychoanalytic theorists, coming into contact with the
unconscious and producing ideas and thoughts between two or more
people is not necessarily connected with temporality or causality. Rather,
these activities are tied to the things we do in the relationship and to the
way we do them. Consequently, we must ask whether the interaction
between analysts and patients is actually producing an analytic relationship, and whether or not the interaction goes beyond simply being an
interesting relationship between two or more subjects.

We must also ask what kinds of changes, what new obstacles or possibilities have emerged with the introduction of Skype and phone analysis.
It has become common practice for our patients to text or email us, and
we answer them in the same way.[8] In many countries present-day living
conditions make it very hard to see patients four or five times a week. It
is not only a financial issue; in big cities, for instance, people need time to
travel. Awareness of these changes has led many psychoanalytic institutions to modify their training standards, and forced us to find new
formulations to support analyses. The debate continues as to whether or
not psychoanalysis can adapt to these conditions without changing so
greatly that it can no longer be called "psychoanalysis."

A brief history of psychoanalysis in Argentina

I would now like to delve into the history of Argentine psychoanalysis, the progress of which was led by thinkers who dared to challenge entrenched hypotheses, especially in regards to the relationship between analysts and their analysands. I will start by highlighting contributions made by Pichon-Rivière (1977). By incorporating social reality into psychoanalysis, this author broke with established ideas and shattered traditional views of the frame. In order to introduce social subjectivity in the psychoanalytic theoretical corpus, he took into account a complex network of elements, an approach that was revolutionary at the time.

Pichon-Rivière suggested that social subjectivity is a component of the mind that communicates with the internal and the relational (and familial) worlds in the manner of a dialectical spiral. He developed a model called Conceptual, Referential, and Operational Framework (ECRO), which he defined as "an organized set of general, theoretical concepts referring to an area of reality, a certain universe of discourse from which emerges a practical approach to the particular – specific – object" (Zito Lema, 1985, p. 4).

Pichon-Rivière's developments gave rise to new therapeutic strategies that involved a profound transformation of the traditional frame. These strategies included working in psychiatric and social communities, as well as conducting group analysis with techniques that were adjusted to the context of the meetings. His formulations were made with a deep commitment to mental health and philosophy (and culture in general), including Gestalt theory, which he imbued with a psychoanalytic sensibility. At that time, his ideas shook the Argentine psychoanalytic world, which reacted ambivalently. Many analysts went as far as to consider him an iconoclast, while some accepted his ideas as long as they could place them in the realm of social psychology, outside psychoanalysis.

This sort of ambivalent acceptance tends to happen when a scientist challenges basic postulates and the scientific world realizes that it cannot ignore his or her ideas. Pichon-Rivière fostered the extraordinary development that group, family, and couple psychoanalysis underwent in Argentina, promoting the use of various techniques that are appropriate for a variety of communities. He went far beyond a simple modification of the established frame; his formulations already included the seed of what we would later call the analytic device. Still, the theoretical basis of his innovations did not contain hypotheses that would enable their incorporation into current psychoanalytic theory. Instead, his theories only laid the foundations for what would become the discipline of social psychology within the field of mental health.

Pichon-Rivière's work with communities and institutions brought about a kind of revolution in the psychiatric world. Yet despite the fact that he was probably the first psychoanalyst to address social and family subjectivities as heterologous entities, much had to happen before we would be able to incorporate his ideas into our theoretical corpus. Furthermore, a long time went by before these ideas became known abroad.[9] Some of his papers have been published in France, where his views have spread and his work is being cited. Nonetheless, it has gone unnoticed in other parts of the world, and his name rarely appears in the *International Journal of Psychoanalysis*.

Perhaps as a consequence of Pichon-Rivière's discoveries, other Argentine analysts attempted to outline more clearly the complexity of the analysand–analyst relationship and came up with important formulations. These analysts might be considered Pichon-Rivière's disciples, either because they were in analysis with or were supervised by him, or due to a cultural kinship. One was J. Bleger, a charismatic scientist with a solid Marxist and philosophical background who had a deep knowledge of Freud's work and incorporated Klein's ideas later in his career. His approach to psychoanalysis involved a clear political commitment as well as a dedication to engaging psychoanalysis in discourse with other fields of knowledge. His work focused on groups, institutions, psychosis, and addiction. He gradually shifted his inquiries toward social issues, though he never lost interest in the individual.

Bleger's findings regarding archaic mental functions and what he called the agglutinated nucleus of the mind allowed him to describe different modalities or behaviors related to social psychology. In his view, these mental functions play a role in the frame as mute aspects of the mind. The frame thus became a preferred space in which to understand the vicissitudes of the mechanisms of projective and introjective identification along with the workings of archaic mental aspects that had been overlooked until then. These were the once mute elements of the analyst–analysand relationship that had long remained unmodified.

Bleger discussed these ideas in his book *Symbiosis and Ambiguity* (Bleger, 1967). Different interpretive modalities emerged from these discussions, as well as a new definition of countertransference. In light of Bleger's theories, the frame does more than just protect us; it is also an invaluable tool that can be used to understand mental functioning and its repercussions on the analytic relationship. Bleger's work has gained recognition in recent years due to its translation into French and English, and thanks to Silvia Amati's work (Amati, 1992), which is based on his theoretical formulations. Amati has sought to uncover the ambiguous aspects of analysts' and analysands' social belonging, which sometimes lead to forced adaptations ("adapting to anything," in the author's words) and conformist behavior.

Other Argentine thinkers who suggested new vantage points from which the analytic relationship can be viewed were M. and W. Baranger (1961). The Barangers were also disciples of Pichon-Rivière and had a deep understanding of philosophy and culture, and their contributions left a mark in the Argentine analytic community. The philosophical pillars of their thought were phenomenology (Merleau Ponty, Sartre, and others) and Gestalt theory (Kurt Lewin), and their general approach was structuralist in nature.

W. and M. Baranger situate the analytic relationship within what they call the *dynamic analytical field*, where the analyst enters into a deep commitment to the patient. They do not conceive of this relationship as the result of the sum of two subjects but as something that is created between them. While they consider that this co-created relationship corresponds to a structure that does not originate in the analysand's or the analyst's impulses, they do not altogether dismiss such impulses.

The Barangers broadened the view of the analysand–analyst relationship by attaching particular significance to analysts' intense emotional commitment, which gives rise to transformations in their patients. This approach added increasing complexity to the notion of countertransference insofar as it granted greater relevance to analysts' subjectivity. The Barangers advanced their innovations simultaneously and sometimes in keeping with Paula Heimann's developments on the transference and countertransference. In the same way, they drew from Racker's (1968) postulates, which I will discuss later. Like Bleger, the Barangers are becoming better known in France due to a partial translation of their writings. Nonetheless, their ideas have not spread among the English-speaking psychoanalytic community despite the fact that some of their papers were published in the *International Journal of Psychoanalysis*.[10]

In the time since psychoanalysis first came to Chile, the concept of countertransference has gained more and more significance and has been further developed in a variety of ways. Most analysts no longer participated in the analytic relationship merely as the object of the transference. Rather, analysts have begun to accept that they are also subjects with their own feelings, which are activated by their analysands. As I mentioned above, Racker (1968) was intensely involved in developing this line of thought independently of, and simultaneously with, Paula Heimann, J. Lampl de Groot, and Margaret Little. He had studied anthropology, philosophy, aesthetics, history of religions, and music, and from this multifaceted perspective he made significant theoretical contributions to the understanding of countertransference.

Racker claimed that analysts must explore their countertransference in the context of their personal analysis. He defined various categories of this phenomenon, among them, concordant and supplementary countertransference. While he never stated it explicitly, he hinted that in the analytic relationship psychoanalysts might be more than just objects of the transference; they might also be fragile subjects, depending on a particular form of identification. Grinberg (1956, 1962) would later complete this idea by decidedly applying the notion of projective counter-identification.

Despite the innovations they advanced, Racker and the Barangers did not radically alter the pillars of the traditional psychoanalytic theoretical corpus. Their developments could be considered offshoots of conceptualizations on the transference. Used as a technical tool, countertransference offered access to the vicissitudes of the relationships of complementarity or sameness that develop between analyst and analysand. According to Kuhn (1962), the work of these authors corresponds to a period of normal science in the aftermath of the major break caused by Freud's findings. Before their contributions, it was still possible to define the analytic field in terms of the frame.

The changes that these theorists introduced implied the acknowledgment of the place occupied by the analyst in the analytic relationship in terms of his or her subjectivity. Furthermore, it was now possible to consider that the relationship between two people creates its own dynamic, which does not result from the sum of two subjectivities. Consequently, the concept of frame was already insufficient to address the new problems that were being considered.

Overlapping worlds

Some time later, in relation to an institutional crisis that led to the splitting of the Argentine Psychoanalytic Association (APA), Wender and I (Puget and Wender, 1982, 2007) started inquiring into changes occurring in analysts' minds when the frame, which was supposed to protect us from the so-called external world, became permeable. Our analysands spoke about the institutional crisis, about their doubts, and we were having some difficulties in responding to these concerns because we shared their questions and fears. We were torn between staying in the APA and founding a new institution. In the end, we did create a new association called APdeBA (Buenos Aires Psychoanalytic Association).

It was then that Wender and I suggested that when analysts and analysands live in overlapping worlds, the analytic function is altered. Analysts suffer a narcissistic wound and traverse a traumatic micro-situation due to their realization that they have momentarily left their neutral analytic position. We then found that we could extend the concept of overlapping worlds to our everyday practice whenever the reality of the external (social) world entered our consulting room through the window. This was a first step toward introducing our everyday experiences into the psychoanalytic theoretical corpus. Today I would no longer say that the social world enters through the window. Rather, it is one of the parameters of subjectivation.

At this stage my work with groups, families, and couples (Puget, 1986) led me to take into account the status of the other, who announces his alterity and cannot be reduced to an object. This is so insofar as the other is the subject of a link. Identification fails and gives rise to the dynamics of power relations. In this way, I attached increasing significance to those aspects of a relationship that are irreducible to the internal world and can only be understood as a singular space. Berenstein and I (1997) called this space *lo vincular*, or the space of links.

We thus defined a relationship between two subjects, each of which is an other who is irreducible to the self. The alterity of the other or others limits the possibilities offered by introjective and projective identification mechanisms. Therefore, we need to define the analytic relationship and the frame in a different way. The relationship between two people always exceeds what unitary subjects can envision. It is obvious that clinical psychoanalysis confronts us with methodological and epistemological problems that the authors discussed earlier had already begun to consider without, perhaps, assessing the import of broadening the frame of reference.

Lo vincular, or the space of links

One of the concepts on which my current investigations are based is that of the analytic relationship as a situation involving both the access to primitive, archaic experiences and the unfolding of unexpected and characteristic aspects of an encounter.[11] We thus witness the effects of two overlapping, discontinuous logics that undermine the illusion of harmony.[12] It becomes necessary to listen to all the effects of actions in the present (typical of relationships between two or more people), to gradually become part of groups, and to engage with the social, considering that each space has its own rules.

This complex web calls for a metapsychology that takes multiplicity into account. In the past, psychoanalysis ran the risk of leaving out of clinical practice the effects of what we call social reality, which also concerns politics and the political – the reality of everyday life. Resorting excessively to identification processes obscures the role of alterity. Today we need to dislodge the subject and his internal world from their favored place.[13] They have to coexist in both the theoretical and the technical realms and deal with the implications of being part of a broader world that lacks clearly defined boundaries. Our great challenge is to learn to understand the processes by which different modes of belonging are constructed within contexts that imbricate but do not coexist harmoniously. In addition, we must take into account the regulating principle of the new, that is, the Uncertainty Principle (Puget, 2010).

On cultural impositions

For quite a long time now I have been struck by the fact that in different countries, psychoanalytic practice can give rise to different types of interventions. At the same time, I have observed that on occasion, psychoanalysts tend to underestimate the effects of local culture, values, and behavioral patterns, which creates a resistance to adaptation. The assumption is that we must not shake the foundations of psychoanalysis despite the broadening of the web of meanings. How can we incorporate new topics to the theoretical edifice without causing its pillars to crack, as they were not built to withstand earthquakes, revolutions, politically complicated times, the effects of the local economy, and, in particular, the effects of technology? Moreover, how could Freud's Vienna have given birth to the same subjects as those who inhabit our century?

I have had the experience of not being the same person in the various countries where I speak about psychoanalysis as a participant in conferences and colloquia. In each place I focus on different aspects of our discipline and must accept that some notions are not universal. For instance, I wonder if the Oedipus complex is valid for every culture, if intimate relationships mean the same thing worldwide, if what individuals construct as unique subjects (emotions, affects, and so on) can be repeated in different contexts. Translating Freud's texts into every language and assuming that in doing so one does not alter the original meanings disrespects his writings. We should remain faithful to his major concern, namely, the discovery, invention, and encompassment of an increasingly complex world. Being faithful to this concern, then, entails questioning dogmas and somehow desecrating Freudian theory in order to maintain its vitality.

Today in the world: experience

The technological revolution, social relations ruled by the market (today's great totem [Puget, 2014]), fratricidal wars, the unavoidable effects of open and latent corruption, the institutionalization of more diverse devices, the realization of the effects of extreme ultra-objective and ultra-subjective violences (as Balibar [2010] has called them), and the emergence of new micro-wars worldwide have led some colleagues to wonder what makes a treatment a psychoanalysis. Is it the frequency of the sessions? Is it abstinence? And what do we understand by abstinence? Is it what we do when we are with our patients? Is it the means we use to achieve an analytic experience? And would the latter be defined by contact with the unconscious or by something else?

Is psychoanalysis defined by the set of practices that emerge in the space between two or more people, the space of irreducible difference? Does its specificity lie in the ability to accept that each device gives us access to something that might be called analytic experience, which is always incomplete? Does it consist in deciphering the manifold threads that make up everyday subjectivities? Today I would say that what defines psychoanalysis is no more than the ability to gain access to an analytic experience. Here the notion of experience acquires a more significant role. Furthermore, psychoanalysis involves the awareness that each experience is unique and does not totalize the world where we live.

By including corruption as one of the elements that forms our social subjectivity, I am taking for granted that in a way, and depending on a variety of circumstances, we are willingly or unwillingly in contact with some level of corruption. A European analyst said to me that he told new analysands that his fees varied depending on whether or not they needed an invoice. When I showed surprise, since to my mind he was announcing his own corruption, he seemed to disagree with me. This exchange made me wonder if corruption is so entrenched in our everyday lives that not even analysts are immune to it.

Furthermore, many of our analysands' narratives are likely to describe certain transgressions as benign or natural. In a way, this attitude is tied to that of modifying rules when they seem impossible to follow. While this topic would be worth an entire essay, my goal here is to focus on the difficulties posed by dealing with the implications of living in corrupt social worlds and on how we unwittingly adjust to these worlds.

Some specifications on the notion of device

In sum, thinking in terms of devices, as I have been suggesting, adds to the complexity of the dynamics of the analytic link. Moreover, it facilitates the production of psychoanalytic interventions that aim to discern various subjectivation contexts, challenge certainties concerning the centrality of the concept of identity, differentiate between becoming one and becoming the subject of a link, and acknowledge the implications of living in a changing world – in overlapping, discontinuous worlds (Puget, 2015). In other words, such interventions seek to distinguish between a circular, linear time, on the one hand, and a time of the present and the right now, on the other.

As analysts, we no longer confine ourselves exclusively to listening or to promoting associative processes. We also resort to interventions that take into account the vicissitudes of doing based on connective processes, interventions that increasingly expand the signs that indicate the existence of an irreducible difference. In this way, we gradually define and recognize the specificity of psychoanalyzing and, in my case, of psychoanalyzing families and couples.

In order to adapt to the use of these new techniques, we must establish some basic rules. These are a necessary condition for the development of any relationship, and that protect us from the natural emergence of chaotic situations and from the violence inherent in a relationship between two or more subjects. Let us see how these ideas play out in the consulting room.

This will never change

In a session with Victor and Maria, Victor says, "My name has been Victor since I was born, and this will never change … I can make an effort to adjust to a situation, but don't ask me to be someone else." I think to myself that he believes he had good primary experiences that will protect him for the rest of his life. Instead, I tell him I am struck by the fact that he is making this statement at a time when he senses that a shared routine has changed. Maria feels she needs Victor to take into account that he is married and that she is not the same person she was when they met. She does not know how to tell him that she exists. Victor thinks he does everything he needs to do for the household, the children, and the family but his efforts are not acknowledged. Maria needs something else but does not know how to convey her need.

They remain silent, and I wonder if they are perceiving other, unspecific signs. The quality of their silence suggests that they are reflecting. In my next intervention I observe that they thought that being in a relationship only required fulfilling their duties but maybe this is no longer enough for them. Victor says, "In my family I was used to …" I point out that he is confusing his current family with his family of origin. His life today is probably different from his life then.

It will take some time before Maria and Victor are able to have a link experience that will alter their relationship in such a way that it will cease to follow the logic of "one plus one equals two." In a later session, Victor seems to discover that if he breaks with his injunctions he might be able to do something he likes without necessarily producing a negative effect on Maria. Maria, in turn, mentions that they went out together and did not know what to talk about, and yet she had the feeling that they were together. Both had been through individual analysis and had become skillful at connecting their present difficulties to their childhood experiences and trauma, but their growth as individuals had not yet translated into greater closeness in their relationship.

Who is right?

Carlos and Anna argue constantly, sometimes subtly. Their conflict leads them to take turns pointing out mistakes in the other's narrative. If C. mentions a date, A. corrects him, and so on and so forth. This behavior creates an atmosphere of discomfort that prompts C. to ask A. why she is always contradicting him. A. says she is just trying to help. They think there is only one version of the story, I tell them. There must be a truth and an error, someone who is right and someone who is wrong, and they should be able to function as one.

They are annoyed and do not know how to move on. They recount several trips they took a few years ago, and their memories differ as well. They produce a material that could be analyzed perfectly well in terms of childhood memories: C.'s parents' disagreements, her relationship with her sister, his relationship with his brother. Each has a vision of what their life together should be like, but reality shows them that such visions are unattainable.

Traditional family versus present-day family

Julia tries vainly to get her husband, Pedro, whose obsessional functioning approaches delirium, to fulfill his paternal function as she sees right. She and the children wait for him to eat dinner, and he comes home late without letting them know in advance. Yet he is supportive and always willing to help in his own way. At some point, Julia stops doing things to see if he will do them instead. One day, however, she decides to get tickets for a trip and does not get one for him because she assumes he will not want to go. She thinks he will take offense when he finds out, but he seems to feel freed from the imperative of doing things together. He is glad he does not have to join the family in an outing he dislikes.

Julia becomes conscious of the fact that her mental family model differs from the model that unfolds in real life. She envisions a large, united family that gets together for harmonious family celebrations, and desperately tries to get her present-day family to follow this model. Pedro regularly fails to meet expectations, causing much discomfort in the family. At the same time, he says he does not have a place, and in order to find one criticizes everybody. Nobody can do what needs to be done better than he can.

The question remains as to what they can do together. One of their everyday tasks is to accept the limitations to their sharing of everyday activities. It is likely that what sustains them as a couple and a family is something indefinable, connected with love. Julia's relationship with her son is very good; they can share meaningful conversations even though they have different tastes. Yet while she expects to agree with her husband, she can value what she does with her son despite their differences. Gradually she realizes that if she stops demanding that Pedro measure up to her expectations, for example, if she invites friends without asking him, without his having to take responsibility for the gathering, he joins in and takes pleasure in the activity.

An obstacle to link dynamics: solidity

Some of the conflicts experienced by couples and families stem from their members' believing, wishing, and expecting that as time goes by, their coexistence will become a habit and their link will solidify based on the result of identity processes. In this way, they maintain the illusion that they know each other better and that their future is assured. Many couples seek help because they have discovered that their partner has become unknown to them. An analysand of mine once told me that after having lost his certainty about his love relationship, he felt it was impossible to "build on sand" and wanted to go back to what they had had before. In fact, erasing experience and returning to the past would be more than a pity – it would be an impossibility. The clock never moves back.

This search for security also becomes an obstacle for analysts when they expect to truly know their analysands. The ability to be surprised is lost. Furthermore, while some, following Bion (1967), claim that they enter the session without memory or desire, the material discussed shows that they assume they really know their patients. It is very important to refute the illusion of security created by knowledge. This type of knowledge prevents us from coming into contact with the effects of presence and with our process of becoming, which are always unpredictable. The effects of presence must necessarily surprise us and generate experiences. As I have been suggesting, these effects are among the components of the dynamics of power relations but are not part of the dynamics of identification processes.

The representational and presentational worlds have different logics. In the former, our experiences are incorporated as representations, granting new meanings to earlier experiences; while in the latter, effects result from the impossibility of reducing the other's alterity to what we already know. Thus my conclusion that confirming an identity, whether that of a subject, a group, a family, or a couple, provides a sense of solidity that may turn into a trap. This false sense of solidity impedes curiosity, the desire to know, surprise, bewilderment, and all other reactions that facilitate the emergence, from complexity, of alternatives that will enrich link life.

Moreover, while confirming identifying traits that enable us to differentiate a subject or group from other subjects or groups may be necessary and reassuring, this does not mean that having such identifying traits grants the intimate partner, the family, or the link a quality of "forever," something that will protect it from becoming. It is certainly necessary to incorporate bewilderment, complexity, the present-day world, and fleetingness into our theory and practice.

Notes

1   Translated by Judith Filc.
2   In Spanish the word *encuadre* may be translated as *frame* or *setting*. Since the author differentiates between traditional and innovating forms of the frame, I have chosen to use always the same word to render *encuadre* (T.N.).
3   Bion, Winnicott, and Kaës, among others, have used this concept in different ways in keeping with their theoretical developments.
4   In this way, we can identify a region that includes Argentina and Uruguay and is slowly expanding to some Brazilian psychoanalytic centers.
5   Klimovsky was guest of honor at the 39th IPA Congress, held in San Francisco in 1995.
6   Years later we were able to return to working face to face. This modality ceased to be problematic because new hypotheses enabled us to understand the vicissitudes of the analytic relationship.
7   Among them, Foucault, Badiou, Agamben, Deleuze, and Guatari.
8   Agamben, Deleuze, and other thinkers further developed the notion of device, making it more complex. An in-depth discussion of these developments exceeds the purpose of this paper.
9   The *International Journal of Psychoanalysis* did publish some articles that reference this thinker's ideas, among them, Arbiser (2014), M. Baranger and W. Baranger (1961 [2008]), and Beceiro (2005).

10 Beatriz de León de Bernardi (1999) thoroughly analyzes the ideas of the Barangers in an excellent article.
11 Berenstein and I introduced a new definition of the concept of link.
12 To some extent, these ideas may be the result of a further development of Pichon-Rivière's conceptualization regarding the ECRO.
13 A kind of Copernican revolution.

Works cited

Amati, S. (1992). Ambiguity as the route to shame. *International Journal of Psychoanalysis*, 73: 329–334.

Arbiser, S. (2014). David Liberman's legacy. *International Journal of Psycho-analysis*, 95: 719–738.

Balibar, E. (2010). *Violence and Civility: On the Limits of Political Philosophy*. Translated by G.M. Goshgarian. New York: Columbia University Press, 2015 [*Violence et civilité*. Paris: Galilée].

Baranger, M. and Baranger, W. (1961). The analytic situation as dynamic field. *International Journal of Psychoanalysis*, 89: 795–826, ["La situación analítica como campo dinámico". *Revista Uruguaya de Psicoanálisis*, 2008, 4(1): 3–54].

Beceiro, A.M. (2005). Identifying marks of Latin American psychoanalysis: Towards the definition of a River Plate model. *International Journal of Psychoanalysis*, 86: 1559–1572.

Berenstein, I. and Puget, J. (1997). *Lo vincular. Teoría y clínica psicoanalítica* [*The Space of Links: Psychoanalytic Theory and Clinical Practice*]. Buenos Aires: Paidós.

Bion, W.R. (1967). Notes on memory and desire. *Psycho-analytic Forum*, II(3): 271–280.

Bleger, J. (1967). *Symbiosis and Ambiguity: A Psychoanalytic Study*. Translated by John Churcher, Leopoldo Bleger, and Susan Rogers. Hove, UK, New York: Routledge [*Simbiosis y ambigüedad*. Buenos Aires: Paidós].

De León de Bernardi, B. (1999). Un modo de pensar la clínica: Vigencia y perspectivas del enfoque de W. y M. Baranger [A way of thinking of clinical practice: Current perspectives on W. and M. Baranger's approach]. In: Kancyper L. ed. *Volviendo a pensar con Willy y Madeleine Baranger. Nuevos Desarrollos* [*Revisiting Willy and Madeleine Baranger's Ideas. New developments*]. Buenos Aires: Lumen, pp. 47–72.

Derrida, J. (1967). *Writing and Difference*. Translated by Alan Bass. London: Routledge and Kegan Paul, 1978 [*La escritura y la diferencia*. Barcelona: Anthropos, 1989].

Freud, S. (1914). Remembering, repeating and working-through. *S.E.* 12, pp. 145–156 [Recordar, repetir y reelaborar. *O.C. T. XII.*, pp. 145–157].

Freud, S. (1921). Group psychology and the analysis of the ego. *S.E.* 18, pp. 67–143.

Greenberg, J. (2012). Editor's introduction. *The Psychoanalytic Quarterly*, 81(3): 527–530.

Grinberg, L. (1956). Sobre algunos problemas de técnica psicoanalítica determinados por la identificación y contraidentificación proyectivas [On some problems of psychoanalytic technique caused by projective identification and counter-identification]. *Revista de Psicoanálisis*, 13: 501–511.

Grinberg, L. (1962). On a specific aspect of countertransference due to the patient's projective identification. *International Journal of Psychoanalysis*, 43: 436–440.

Grünbaum, A. (1993). *Validation in the Clinical Theory of Psychoanalysis*. New York: International Universities Press.

Klimovsky, G. (1994). *Las desventuras del conocimiento científico. Una introducción a la epistemología* [*The Misfortunes of Scientific Knowledge: An Introduction to Epistemology*]. Buenos Aires: A-Z.

Kuhn, T. (1962). *The Structure of Scientific Revolutions*. Chicago: University of Chicago Press [*La estructura de las revoluciones científicas*. Translated by Agustín Contín. México: Fondo de Cultura Económica, 1971].

Pichon-Rivière, E. (1977). Clase N° 2 de 1° año, dictada el 29/4/1970 en la Primera Escuela Privada de Psicología Social [Second class of the first year, taught on April 29, 1970 at the First Private School of Social Psychology]. www.psicologiasocial.esc.edu.ar/psicologiasocial/la-escuela-3/publicaciones/   ecroesquema-conceptual-referencial-y-operativo/ Retrieved November 19, 2015.

Puget, J. (1986). Identidad del psicoterapeuta de grupo y coordinador de grupo desde su marco referencial teórico-clínico en su contexto social [Identity of group psychotherapists and group coordinators from their theoretical-clinical frame of reference in their social context]. *Rev. de Psicología y Psicoterapia de Grupo*, 9(2): 125–133.

Puget, J. (2003). Intersubjetividad. Crisis de la representación [Intersubjectivity: Crisis of representation]. *Psicoanálisis APdeBA*, 25(1): 175–189.

Puget, J. (2010). The subjectivity of certainty and the subjectivity of uncertainty. *Psychoanalytic Dialogues. The International Journal of Relational Perspectives*, 20(1): 4–20.

Puget, J. (2014). *Comment penser après Freud le lien social* [*How to think social ties after Freud*]. Colloque International Centre de Recherches Psychanalyse Médecine et Société. Université Paris Diderot. Centenaire de Totem & Tabou, Paris, January.

Puget, J. (2015). *Subjetivación discontinua y psicoanálisis. Incertidumbre y certezas* [*Discontinued Subjectivation and Psychoanalysis: Uncertainty and Certainties*]. Buenos Aires: Lugar.

Puget, J. and Wender, L. (1982). Analista y paciente en mundos superpuestos [Analyst and patient in overlapping worlds]. *Psicoanálisis*, 4(3): 502–532.

Puget, J. and Wender, L. (2007). El Mundo Superpuesto entre paciente y analista revisitado al cabo de los años. *Revista Asociación Escuela Argentina de Psicoterapia para Graduados*. 30: 69–90.

Racker, H. (1968). *Transference and Countertransference*. New York: International Universities Press.

Zito Lema, V. (1985). *Conversaciones con Enrique Pichon-Rivière. Sobre el arte y la locura* [*Conversations with Enrique Pichon-Rivière: On Art and Madness*]. Buenos Aires: Ediciones Cinco.

Part III

Variations in the frame

Chapter 10

Contemporary developments and challenges of analytic training and practice

Cláudio Laks Eizirik

The present chapter starts by highlighting certain characteristics of contemporary analytic practice, since the ultimate goal of our educational institutions is to provide trainees experience with analytic practice in order to prepare them to work as analysts. Next, I examine specific aspects of personal analysis, supervision and psychoanalytic institutions, as well as the challenges I consider most relevant in this endless process of developing and striving to maintain an analytic identity.

Have the patients we treat changed?

From about the 1980s, references began to appear in the literature concerning changes in analytic patients (Gaddini, 1987; Ahumada, 1997) and new descriptions gradually emerged that contrasted with Freud's classic depictions of neurotic patients. Kernberg's research on borderline patients is well known, as are the studies by Marty on psychosomatic patients (Aisenstein, 2014), new maladies of the soul (Kristeva, 2002) and perversions (McDougall, 1983), a set of clinical conditions in which difficulties with verbal expression and symbolization present specific barriers to analytic work. André Green's psychoanalytic work, in which he described, understood and suggested possible approaches for non-neurotic structures (Green, 2002, 2010; Urribarri, 2013), is based on French theoretical and clinical observations and the contributions of Bion and Winnicott.

All these contributions indicate that contemporary practice includes new types of patients, while simultaneously raising more questions than answers: are all of these in fact new pathologies or are some merely new versions of the structures described by Freud and his contemporaries? To what extent do cultural changes, which increasingly encourage what has been described as liquid modernity or hypermodernity, contribute to these new versions of pathologies? To what extent has a new vision of the psychoanalytic approach made it necessary to attempt to access more regressive patients, and has the further development of our ability for analytical listening made us more capable of penetrating areas previously considered inaccessible or invulnerable to analytic methods?

Regardless, a number of possible approaches have identified changes in clinical practice and the types of patients now seeking treatment (e.g. Eizirik et al., 1999). In observing my own practice and considering it along with my colleagues' practices, I have found that neurotics or those with personality disorders continue to predominate, with a relatively small number of patients such as those described by the aforementioned authors. The major difference between our practices and those of the past seems to be that we may not previously have accepted these "new" patients for analysis or would not have had the resources available now to pursue emotional contact with them. Additionally, the presence of elderly patients appears to be a growing trend, both in the literature (Junkers, 2006) and current practice. As I described recently (Eizirik, 2014), with the notable exception of Little Hans, in the first decades of the last century all analysts and patients were adults.

Over the last two decades, it seems we have made a new discovery: old age exists, and the mind and psychological distress of the elderly are a new area of psychoanalytic study and treatment. Here, it is important to consider another variable which seems to have been largely disregarded: the life cycle of patients and analysts, and the extent to which each moment in the analyst's life is likely to attract certain types of patients, in relation to whom we are either more or less open to a proper analytic listening. It has been reported that elderly analysts experience greater difficulty (including physical) conducting systematic analysis with children, and that analysts with more experience or who have learned more from their therapeutic failures than successes may be more emotionally available to listen to regressive situations (Baranger, 1993).

Has the setting changed?

Although I am aware that the setting is far more akin to a mental framework within which we work with the patient, it is important to point out that the method and structure developed by Freud as ideal for analysis have invariably undergone changes, adaptations and modernization.

In and of themselves, formal elements of the setting such as the contract, payments for sessions, frequency, vacations, using a couch or not, etc., are not the most important aspects of the setting. They are safeguards, beacons, in short, a framework within which we seek to combine the ideal conditions for psychoanalytic treatment aimed at profound and intimate emotional contact with the inner world of both the patient and the analyst. These details are part of the scenario in which we establish specific psychoanalytic fields with each patient. Just as every analyst's office is unique in a variety of ways, although they are likely to share some common features such as the presence of an armchair and couch, each analysis is also unique, though all of them involve the search for the unconscious (even though we know there are different versions of this search).

In my view, the field of psychoanalysis is at risk of transforming some of these elements into a type of fetish and, unfortunately, there is much controversy surrounding the selection of a single element as the focus of dispute and bitter disagreements. There has been extensive discussion and approval of three analytic training models (Eizirik, 2011) aimed at recognizing the diversity of possible training formats. Across formats, frequency of sessions has consistently been highlighted as one of the few elements that is relatively consistent among recognized models of psychoanalytic training and treatment. However, with respect to current analytic practice, analysts are less frequently seeing patients four or five times a week, as was once common, with most cases now involving one to two weekly sessions. Several reasons have been put forward for this decline in session frequency, including financial problems, resistance, the large distances in urban centers, analysts' difficulty protecting and defending a setting suited to the method, competition with other methods requiring fewer sessions, the current trend favoring less contact and faster treatment, etc.

Thus, a major current question is the following: can treatment consisting of less than three weekly sessions be considered analysis? It seems insufficient to define a treatment as "psychoanalytic" or not based on this factor alone. It is important to consider whether an analytic process is underway, if there is an established transference neurosis, dream analysis, or an analytic field established, whether countertransference is being addressed or psychic changes have been observed and if the analyst has a developed and established analytic identity and sufficient experience with the usual method to deal with less frequent sessions. If the answers to these questions are yes, I see no reason not to use the term analysis, regardless of session frequency. After all, this is one of the many themes talked about in the hallways at conferences: we have all heard of patients who came (or come) four times a week yet make little headway, while others attend analysis less frequently but make significant progress. That said, extensive clinical experience has taught me that analytical methods tend to benefit from more frequent sessions, though some patients who cannot commit to frequent sessions can still be accepted and successfully analyzed.

In regards to other elements of the setting, some patients are unable to use the couch for a period of time (sometimes indefinitely), for a number of reasons (control, paranoid anxiety, etc.); others have such a rigid mental structure that they collapse on the couch in the first session and cannot move beyond this for some time, or the entire time; and there are those who follow a predictable course of spending some time face to face, and then moving on to the couch, satisfactorily completing their analytic treatment.

In relation to establishing a mandatory regime of paying fees for sessions, the time in which patients were solely responsible for maintaining this arrangement seems to be long past; today, individual situations are examined to determine resistance and real need so as to pursue a course that is neither too rigid nor laissez faire, but as analytical as possible. The same is true for vacation time, both on the part of analysts and patients.

There is also the interesting and challenging issue of distance psychoanalysis conducted via phone, Skype, or using other forms of virtual communication. In fact, patients are increasingly communicating with analysts (and vice-versa) via text message or WhatsApp, rather than by the almost obsolete answering machine, and more and more images, videos, iPhone or iPad recordings etc. are being brought into sessions, forming part of the modern-day setting. The literature demonstrates the effectiveness of these approaches (Scharf, 2012), but it is important to continue studying the advantages and limitations. In my opinion, it is important and even indispensable that analysis involves a period or periods of in-person treatment, as this is the manner in which the method was developed and continues to provide the conditions for an optimal setting.

What about the mind of the analyst?

On the one hand, it is increasingly easy to be an analyst in modern times, and on the other, increasingly difficult. It is easier because we have the work of Freud, Ferenczi, Abraham, Klein, Bion, Winnicott, Lacan, Erikson, Kohut, Mahler, Laplanche, Green, Betty Joseph and others in our wake, alongside our own experience with analysts and supervisors. All of this vast experience allows us to navigate paths, depths and shortcuts with a contemporary clarity unavailable to our predecessors; however, our successors will be even more successful for the same reasons. There have also been a series of innovations in the psychoanalytic community, such as those provided by programs like CAPSA (Analytic Practice and Scientific Activities Committee), which emerged from the pioneering and passionate work of Haydée Faimberg and her "listening to listening" groups, which multiplied into working parties that are perhaps the most stimulating part of every psychoanalytic conference.

However, analysts' work has also become more difficult, partly because of the same reasons previously stated: the problems inherent to adjusting to so many new developments, contributions, forms of listening and proposals, as well as the ongoing struggle of institutional rivalries, nitpicking, competition and professional envy, alongside undeniable moments of cooperation and creative work. How does one keep abreast of a world that is constantly changing and challenging us with its complexity and almost endless supply of ideas, books, movies and expressions of popular and classic culture which we are required to have at least minimal knowledge of, since they are also part of the world of our patients and their associations?

The mind of the analyst is increasingly considered a vital element of the analytic relationship. In an interesting summary of psychoanalytic work, Levine (2010) suggests the existence of two models. The first is the so-called "archaeological" model, which is best suited to situations in which psychic elements have achieved representation and are more or less symbolically invested and associatively linked to one another. This model works well in the treatment of neurotics, but is problematic for other analytic patients, for whom Levine suggests the "transformational" model. He argues that this second model is more appropriate for some patients, since it centers on the functioning of the mind of the analyst as part of the analytic dyad in the creation and reinforcement of psychic elements, rather than, or in addition to, their discovery. He emphasizes that psychoanalysis is a two-person activity that involves the creation of symbols, thoughts, feelings and unconscious material as opposed to the analysis of defenses or the uncovering hidden meanings. In short, the analytic process is a double operation that gives a container to the patient's content and content to his or her container. This conceptualization echoes the ideas of Green, Ferro, Ogden and the Barangers.

The contemporary challenge for psychoanalysis is that of switching between the archaeological and transformational models, between states of understanding and not understanding. It is also a challenge in which we must of tolerate the inevitable fluctuations in our own mental state, the mental state of the patient and the shared psychic setting that we build together. It is here perhaps, in addition to all the aspects cited above, that the incomparable fascination of psychoanalysis lies (Eizirik, 2014).

Construction of the analyst

Are analysts constructed or do they construct themselves? Are they constructed or under construction? As I wrote this chapter, I was reminded of a poem: "Construction Worker," by Brazilian poet Vinicius de Moraes (1960), in which he describes a construction worker's growing realization of his particular circumstances, acquiring in the process the notion that he constructs himself as a person.

I reference this poem as a means of saying that I am not a great believer in the idea of a constructed analyst, but rather in a dynamic, continuous and always incomplete process of an analyst under construction. Contrary to the poet's sorrowful conclusion, I feel that our case is not one of a constructed analyst, but rather that we experience a fluctuation between mental sates in which we feel more or less constructed or under permanent construction (Eizirik, 2012).

Since 1920 and the onset of formal analytical training at the Berlin Polyclinic and the developments that followed, it is undeniable that the tripartite system of personal analysis, theoretical and clinical studies and supervision, have been maintained, and that since the International Psychoanalytical Association (IPA) finally acknowledged reality and approved the three training models, we are now more easily able to recognize that these aspects have countless variations and nuances that vary from one institution to another. Committees in charge of studying what goes on at different institutes have carefully examined the situation and found, for example, that despite following the famous tripartite system, the more traditional and prevalent Eitington model exhibited countless variations. Successive modifications within the IPA under different management have observed and described with increasing realism the multiplicity of formats used in different institutions to organize psychoanalytic training (Eizirik, 2011; Kernberg and Tyson, 2011; Widlocher, 2011). Freud likened psychoanalytic technique to the game of chess, in that while opening and closing moves can be specified, there are an endless number of possible variations that occur throughout the game. Similarly, after visiting countless analysts' offices in recent years, I have found that while all of them had a couch and an armchair, as well as other furniture, each had a feature that distinguished it from the rest. For example, the relationship between the armchair and the couch varies significantly from office to office, with positions ranging from the analyst being completely outside the patient's field of view to being almost beside them, so the patient need only shift his or her head to see the analyst. In short, institutions provide the conditions for analysts to construct, but whether this occurs or not is outside of institutional control.

Personal analysis

I feel there is a consensus among the analytic community that we must maintain strict training procedures and strive to ensure the internal consistency of the model we adopt. Nonetheless, analysts will develop or not for reasons that go beyond our best intentions. I have read and heard that, to some degree, the key element of training is the personal analysis of future analysts and, in general terms, I agree with this statement, but is this always the case? At this point it is important to underscore the complex web of unconscious fantasies, projections and disassociations that are established between patients and their analysts, supervisors, teachers, colleagues, institutional authority figures and culture, as well as the traditions of each society and their countless family dramas. All of this combines with the experiences of each future analyst with their family, background, tradition and fantasies about the future they are building in their mind. Bolognini (2013) carefully examined a series of situations that analysts in training experience, illustrating what he calls their institutional and imaginary family throughout the training process.

In the best cases, personal analysis is a space in which these elements can be examined within the possibilities of each analyst, who also participate in this drama either in fantasy or reality. Often, even when analysis is successful and the analyst is humble enough to recognize his transitional role in the patient's life, without expecting the patient's eternal gratitude, mention of the analyst in training's future papers, referral of patients, or idealization etc., this development will occur a posteriori through self-analysis, by observing the facts of institutional life, analytic experience and shared experiences with colleagues and friends. Several authors emphasize that this type of analysis is necessarily contaminated by all of the external factors involved.

In my own experience, and I have had the opportunity to hear of similar experiences from colleagues, there are roughly two major groups of analytic patients who undergo training. The first consists of patients seeking treatment for their personal needs and emotional suffering, who, at a certain time during treatment or following years of psychoanalysis, perceive a desire or motivation for analytic training. In general, or in most cases, training is only one period in their analysis, which continues on after institutional procedures until formal completion of the analytic process. For these people, training was something incidental that occurred during analysis. The second group is comprised of people who seek out analysis first and foremost for the purpose of training, despite recognizing the existence of emotional difficulties. There is often an element of urgency or pressure in this type of analysis, and the patient frequently ends it as soon as they achieve the institutional requirements. There are many apparent reasons for this: cost, distances, family demands, etc. It would not be fair to generalize, but my observation demonstrates that the first group contains those analysts who identify more closely with analytic function and identity.

This is where a question emerges that I feel deserves greater attention: why did Freud have the curious idea of recommending reanalysis every five years? Was it because analysis at that time was insufficient or too quick, or because his usual astuteness allowed him to perceive the self-limited nature of all analysis, and the powerful presence of resistance to the unconscious that leads to our tiresome tendency to repress, reject or deny the unpleasant aspects of our selves and our realities that our analyst(s) spend years trying to show us. Perhaps I am being unfair or misinformed, but I have the impression that reanalysis is not very common among analysts; as a working hypothesis, I suggest that it is difficult to remain sharp and up to date in our field if we do not have the humility to undergo what Freud refers to as periodic psychoanalytic purification.

The psychoanalytic institution

One element that can either stimulate or fail to stimulate the construction of an analytic identity is the institutional climate that predominates in each society or institute, as well as how the trajectory of each future analyst is viewed within each psychoanalytic culture.

To what extent is critical and independent thinking welcomed? To what degree do procedures and rules become a type of fetish that must be obeyed "just because"? To what extent are analysts in training encouraged to establish and administrate their own candidates' groups and associations? How often are theoretical differences welcome and listened to with respect and interest? To what extent are curricula flexible and do they include optional seminars, allowing each student to follow his or her own interests? To what extent does the institutional climate stimulate future analysts to participate in its activities and offer opinions at meetings or to conversely to remain in shy and fearful silence which will only be broken many years and countless meetings later? To what degree are topics related to analytic training discussed with those who are undergoing the experience? Do institutions revise and modify their curricula, procedures and manner of understanding analytic training over time, as new national and international ideas on the subject and the learning process itself emerge?

All of these questions as well as detailed discussion on many of them have been the subject of a number of papers by Otto Kernberg. One of the aspects most highlighted by Kernberg (2000) is the so-called training analysis and the concentration of power to a limited number of training analysts, an imbalance that often results in an oppressive and paranoid institutional climate. Personally, I have observed situations in which this does in fact occur, and others in which the existence of a growing number of analysts who analyze future analysts offers a form of dilution of power, facilitating dialogue and open, free discussion. Even institutions that adopt the Eitington model have undergone changes in terms of allowing all full members to analyze candidates. But what is the justification for keeping the analysis of future analysts solely in the hands of those who are training analysts or full members? Aside from the obvious argument that it is easier to distribute power among fewer hands, I feel the justification that a select few training analysts should be invested with greater power because they have greater psychoanalytic experience is an insufficient excuse. I have observed and experienced situations where an analysis with an associate member progresses satisfactorily until the patient decides to undergo analytic training and must then switch to a training analyst. In many cases this change may ruthlessly interrupt an analytic relationship that was developing well, while in others it might be beneficial. Perhaps we should put more emphasis on the fact that an adequately trained analyst, recognized as such by his society, may be capable of carrying out analyses, regardless of who is being analyzed. After all, a training analysis does not actually exist, since it is not a pedagogical or educational procedure, but rather simply an analysis of a person that might one day become an analyst.

In a recent study, Garcia (2014) discusses several aspects of the institutionalized transmission of psychoanalysis. His central thesis is that of the singularity of each analyst's training. He argues that the role of institutes should be to offer the best possible conditions for every future analyst to carry out their own training, including the values learned from previous generations with current cultural characteristics, as well as protecting future analysts from institutional resistance to essential freedom and individuality.

About analytic supervision

There is also extensive literature on analytic supervision and it is well known that its relevance varies according to the model adopted. In any event, it is undeniably an area that significantly affects the training of analysts since it is a more open relationship than personal analysis. Supervision can be a source of stimulation as well as mutually enriching work, or a space for transmitting a way of thinking or analyzing centered on the figure and authority of the supervisor. It is a delicate relationship in which maintaining a certain distance and asymmetry alongside natural and spontaneous interaction requires constant attention on the part of the supervisor. As with the analytic relationship, the supervisory relationship is naturally ambivalent, but has the potential to stimulate creativity and foster the independence of analysts in training. In my opinion, the most noteworthy among many significant contributions to our thinking about analytic supervision is the recent special issue of *Psychoanalytic Inquiry* (2014), edited by Imre Szecsody and Melvin Bornstein and entitled "Never Ever Stop Learning More About Supervision."

"Never Ever Stop Learning More About Supervision" is a very adequate title for this gathering of excellent papers on supervision, as well as a very proper motto for Imre Szecsody's extraordinary and tireless contributions to our current understanding of this complex process at the very core of analytic training.

In my view, the papers presented in this issue show the many dilemmas, complexities and controversies that exist in relation to analytic supervision. On one side, we see nowadays a consistent search for objectivity and of measurable learning objectives, as the papers from Moga and Cabaniss (2014), and Watkins and Scaturo (2014) clearly suggest. For instance Watkins and Scaturo describe how to use the Learning Alliance Building and Maintenance and state that psychoanalytic supervision is a formative, developmental learning experience and intervention; that it is educational in its mission, process and product and should be guided by a vision that is founded upon and grounded in educational psychology and theories of learning; Moga and Cabaniss present a plea for clearly delineated measurable learning objectives and show how this can be used and its relevance for analytic training.

From another perspective, we can see a qualitative research on two cases of supervision of analytic psychotherapy and follow Stromme's (2014) exploration of what characterizes a good and a bad supervision process. One of her findings was that the expression of negative views of the supervisee regarding the supervisor might have a negative impact on the supervisory process. Kahl-Popp (2014) criticizes the use of transmitting and learning goals from one generation to the next, stressing the importance of freedom in the learning process. Kahl-Popp also illustrates the usefulness of analyzing dreams both from the supervisee and the supervisor to understand what is going on in the supervisory process. The relational experience in supervision and its influence on the psychoanalyst's identity are studied by Nagell et al. (2014) in a study conducted with different psychoanalytic institutes in Germany. The authors were able to identify four working styles in the supervisors (defensive-controlling; pragmatic; experiential and relationship oriented; facilitating-holding) and in the supervisees ("phobic"-avoidance; open-interested; authentic-researching; reserved-adaptive); these and other findings of this study seem to be extremely useful when one thinks on his/her experience with supervising younger colleagues.

Taking advantage of his long experience in several settings of analytic training, Gabor Szonyii (2014) offers us a stimulating discussion on the Budapest model of supervision, wonders why it is not more well known or widely discussed, and shows the possible strong and weak points of it. While reading this paper, what came to my mind was the fact that from time to time even the most conservative analyst cannot avoid playing the Budapest model during a session with a supervisee who is having trouble with a difficult case.

So, in my perspective, there is certain tension here between two sets of papers: one group of them stresses the relevance of clear learning objectives, and sees supervision as part of a training in which skills and abilities can be clearly established, pursued and monitored. The other group relies more on a process of building inner abilities and expanding the mind, or suggests a sort of emotional learning, following Bion. Here, the emotional relationship between supervisor and supervisee takes the main role.

These two views seem to be related to cultural factors, economic pressures to demonstrate effectiveness, the presence of competing therapies with supposed greater effectiveness, and the greater current trend to idealize so-called "competence." While I understand and acknowledge the relevance of establishing and trying to use more objective tools for researching and monitoring analytic skills, at the same time I am concerned about the risk of failing to adequately consider the unique and idiosyncratic nature of each analytic relationship and the process by which each analyst acquires some kind of analytic identity. Furthermore, this identity, as Kahl-Popp also stresses, is not something that is simply obtained after a certain number of hours of analysis, supervision and seminars, but an ongoing process of working through one's own inner world and navigating the continuous fluctuations among different mental states. This process is called *"Bildung"* in German, "training" or "education" in English, *"formation"* in French, *"formación"* in Spanish and *"formação"* in Portuguese. Perhaps we may learn from these apparent minor linguistic differences two basic differences in understanding that are clearly reflected in the volume of *Psychoanalytic Inquiry* under discussion.

I see all of these papers as extremely well grounded, following a clear and well-designed methodology, and each one of them as capable of stimulating the reader to never ever stop learning more about supervision. I also think that they show the state of the art at this particular moment. As is the case with so many other aspects of analytic activity, diversity is the trademark of our international community, and while reading each of these papers, I was reminded of several situations from my own experience as a supervisor, supervisee, researcher and teacher. This might be one of the richest contributions of this collective effort, compiled under the inspiring leadership of Imre Szecsody: the volume will certainly stimulate further research along these and other lines, it will increase the interest in seeing supervision as an area full of life and possibilities and, last but not least, it will help both supervisors and supervisees, as well as analytic institutes in the long and never-ending process of guiding new analysts towards becoming part of our shared work in progress.

Becoming and remaining an analyst

And what of this person who will one day be able to call him or herself an analyst?

Again, there is relevant literature on the complex process of becoming an analyst. Particularly useful are texts in which analysts reflect on their own motivations and personal journeys in the complex process of acquiring an analytic identity. At the same time, I feel that the very notion of an analytic identity may contain a threat, in that it prioritizes the idea that analytic identity is obtained or established and is not a work in progress or an ongoing process. To cite three examples, a good illustration of the vicissitudes of this process can be found in "A committed psychoanalyst" (Green, 1986), about the professional and personal life of André Green; in a special issue of *Psychoanalytic Inquiry* (2005) in which several Latin American analysts reflect on their individual careers; and in the more recent *Comment on Devient Psychanalyste ... et Comment on le Reste* (2010) by Daniel Widlocher. These accounts and countless others attest to the fact that each analyst develops based on a series of cultural, conscious and unconscious motivations, identifications, life experiences, traumatic situations, a wide range of neurotic aspects, the search for reparation, ideals and so on.

I believe that a central element in becoming an analyst and remaining one in subsequent years is linked to clinical experience and the accumulation of psychoanalytic hours, as well as the accumulation of successes and failures with the patients treated. The ability to share in a patient's psychological changes, to aid the expansion of their mind and ability to love, feel and work helps strengthen belief (according to Bion) in our method. Tolerating failures teaches us humility in regard to the scope and limitations of this method.

Meltzer (1967) highlights the combination of athletic and artistic activity present in psychoanalytic work, and the importance of simplicity and stability in clinical activity, ideas I have also heard from Bela Grumberger (Grumberger, personal communication).

It is perhaps even more difficult to remain an analyst than to train to be one, given the countless temptations to relax in the difficult work of addressing the unconscious within an analytic field that requires constant maintenance and protection. Once the formal steps within an institution are complete, each analyst follows his own path and the inevitable vicissitudes of his personal and professional life cycle, facing not only the difficulties of demanding clinical work, but the circumstances of a culture that challenges the relevance and validity of psychoanalysis. Remaining an analyst means being able to tolerate attacks and challenges that emerge naturally from the work itself through emotional suffering, as well as an often ambivalent external reality. Remaining an analyst means being able to move between tradition and innovation without denying the inevitable fluctuations of mental states or the losses and gains of each stage of the life cycle. Since analysts potentially work for longer than other professionals, the aging process deserves special attention, not only because of the limitations it can bring, but because analysts, as they age, may gain greater clinical acuity and courage in dealing with close analytic contact and working with more primitive levels of the mind. Analytic institutions can play an important role in this process in that they maintain programs that could be referred to as continuous, stimulating psychoanalytic training. Despite the inevitable disappointment of many analysts with their local, national and international institutions, I still observe that a feeling of "us," a certain sense of belonging and pride in the achievements that can be obtained through joint work, are elements that may have a containing function that diminishes the different types of anxiety faced by analysts.

Is there a way to characterize how analysts feel about their work, their fluctuations between tradition and invention, and their successive mental states? Between their moments of understanding and non-understanding, as Betty Joseph would say? Between feeling constructed and in construction?

As I wrote this paper I remembered a long-forgotten time when, in the voice of Brazilian actor Paulo Autran, I heard the words of Louis Javet and Jean Louis Barrault, collected by Millôr Fernandes and Flávio Rangel (1997) for the play *Liberdade liberdade* (Liberty, Liberty), staged as a demonstration against the dictatorship that had taken political power in Brazil at the time. For me, this voice reflected more astutely than any analytic descriptions what it means to identify with a profession: "I am simply a man of the theater. I always was and always will be a man of the theater. Anyone capable of dedicating their entire life to the humanity and passion on these few meters of stage is a man of the theater."

References

Ahumada, J. Crise da cultura e crise da psicanálise. *Revista de Psicanálise da SPPA*, 4(3): 243–257, 1997.

Aisenstein, M. Abordagem psicodinâmica do paciente psicossomático. In: Eizirik, C.L., Aguiar, R.W. and Schestatsky, S.S. (eds) *Psicoterapia de orientação analítica: fundamentos teóricos e clínicos*. Porto Alegre, Artmed, 3rd ed., 2014.

Baranger, M. The mind of the analyst: From listening to interpretation. *International Journal of Psychoanalysis*, 74: 15–24, 1993.

Bolognini, S. The institutional and fantasy family of the analyst. *Psychoanalyse*, 29(3): 357–372, 2013.

Eizirik, C.L. The IPA administration from 2005 to 2009. In: Loewenberg, P. and Thompson, N. (eds) *100 Years of the IPA*. London, Karnac, 2011.

Eizirik, C.L. O analista em construção. *FEBRAPSI Notícias*, ano XIV, no. 46, Rio de Janeiro, 2012.

Eizirik, C.L. Algumas questões sobre a clínica psicanalítica contemporânea. *Psicanalitica*, XIV(1): 9–16, 2014.

Eizirik, C.L., Blaya Luz, A., Keidann, C., Iankilevich, E. and Dal Zot, J. Algumas modificações na prática psicanalítica da SPPA: um estudo retrospectivo. *Revista de Psicanálise da SPPA*, VI(2), agosto: 205–219, 1999.

Fernandes, M. and Rangel, F. *Liberdade, liberdade*, Porto Alegre, L & PM, 1997.

Gaddini, E. Cambios en los pacientes psicoanaliticos hasta nuestros dias. *Monografía número IV*. Associación Psicoanalitica Internacional, 1987.

Garcia, J. La transmisión institucionalizada del psicoanálisis en los comienzos del siglo XXI. *Revista Uruguaya de Psicoanálisis*, 118: 139–155, 2014.

Green, A. *On Private Madness*. Madison, Connecticut, International University Press, 1986.

Green, A. *Idées directrices pour une psychanalyse contemporaine*. Paris, Puf, 2002.

Green, A. *Illusions et disillusions du travail psychanalytique*. Paris, Odile Jacob, 2010.

Junkers, G. (ed.) *Is it too late? Key papers on psychoanalysis and ageing*. London, Karnac, 2006.

Kahl-Popp, J. Evaluation of learning in psychoanalytic clinical practice. *Psychoanalytic Inquiry*, 34: 538–553, 2014.

Kernberg, O. A concerned critique of psychoanalytic education. *The International Journal of Psychoanalysis*, 81(1): 97–120, 2000.

Kernberg, O. and Tyson, R. The IPA administration from 1997 to 2001. In: Loewenberg, P. and Thompson, N. (eds) *100 Years of the IPA*. London, Karnac, 2011.

Kristeva, J. *As novas doenças da alma*. Rio de Janeiro, Rocco, 2002.

Levine, H.B. Creating analysts, creating analytic patients. *International Journal of Psycho-Analysis*, 91: 1385–1404, 2010.

McDougall, J. *Em defesa de uma certa anormalidade: teoria e clínica psicanalítica*. Porto Alegre, Artes Médicas, 1983.

Meltzer, D. *The psychoanalytical process*. London, Heinemann, 1967.

Moga, D. and Cabaniss, D. Learning objectives for supervision: Benefits for candidates and beyond. *Psychoanalytic Inquiry*, 34: 528–537, 2014.

Moraes, V. *Antologia poética*. Rio de Janeiro, Editora do Autor, 1960.

Nagell, W. et al. Research into the relationship experience in supervision and its influence on the psychoanalytical identity formation of candidate trainees. *Psychoanalytic Inquiry*, 34: 554–558, 2014.

Scharf, J.S. Clinical issues in analysis over the telephone and the internet. *The International Journal of Psycoanalysis*, 93: 81–95, 2012.

Stromme, H. A bad and a better supervision process. *Psychoanalytic Inquiry*, 34: 584–605, 2014.

Szonyii, G. The vicissitudes of the Budapest psychoanalytic model of supervision: Can we learn from it today? *Psychoanalytic Inquiry*, 34: 606–618, 2014.

Urribarri, F. *Dialoguer avec André Green*. Paris, Itaque, 2013.

Watkins, C. and Scaturo, D. Proposal for a common language, educationally-informed model of psychoanalytic supervision. *Psychoanalytic Inquiry*, 34: 619–633, 2014.

Widlocher, D. *Comment on devient psychanalyste ... et comment on le reste*. Paris, Odile Jacob, 2010.

Widlocher, D. The IPA administration from 2001 to 2005. In Loewenberg, P. and Thompson, N. *100 Years of the IPA*. London, Karnac, 2011.

Chapter 11

A tale of two cities

Harvey L. Rich

The frame of psychoanalytic therapy is not a rigid structure like a picture frame. It does not enclose a static tableau. There might have been a time in the early days when the method was in its inception and analysands were largely neurotic. At that time a more fixed sense of the frame was reasonable. However, today our patients largely suffer from mixed neuroses, character neuroses, or high-level borderline and narcissistic character disorders. Our field has matured and expanded to include everything from intersubjectivity to micro-ego analysis and many other modifications into the "classical" methods.

The other major change that has occurred since the beginning of psychoanalysis at the turn of the 20th century and since its heyday in the 1950s and 1960s is the continued development of technology and telecommunications. So many colleagues now take advantage of these changes in both technique and technology, but not as many speak about the use of telecommunications. It is these advances that have enabled me to work in two cities.

So let's get a few things on the table from the beginning. I live and work in two cities – Washington, D.C. and Paris, France. I have been in Washington for the past 40 odd years and in Paris for the past 14 years. I do work on the telephone with patients living in whichever city I am not present. My patients have the same session times; it is I who shifts my schedule six hours back and forth. I do both psychoanalytic psychotherapy and psychoanalysis on the telephone. And, yes, working on the telephone is quite different from being in the same space with a patient. Given the rising popularity of conducting therapy by phone or via other forms of remote communication, I feel it is necessary to contribute to the scant literature on the subject of telephone psychoanalysis or therapy. Specifically, I hope to describe how to maintain a rigorous stance while using new modes of communication.

Having said all of that let me now start from the beginning. Fifteen years ago I decided to give myself a small sabbatical. I had received an advance on a book and decided to put it to that purpose. While living in Paris, I met with several colleagues socially and contrary to the general American opinion of the French, I received a very warm welcome. We quickly discovered a mutual interest in learning more about the similarities and differences of one another's work.

At the same time, my wife and I toyed with the idea of having a small place to stay in Paris for future visits – a second home. At about that time a colleague in Paris called and offered to refer an American ex-pat who needed therapy. "But I don't live there full time," I said. "Yes, you will have to do something about that," my colleague responded in a most French manner. My own French was quite rudimentary at the time.

And so, this adventure – this new phase of my life – began. I decided to divide my time between the two cities. At first mostly in Washington and less so in Paris, but that has reversed over time. I spoke to my patients and told them that I would continue to work via telephone, should they wish to continue, or I would refer them to a local analyst with whom they could continue their work in the traditional fashion. No patient chose to take a referral, though one or two were somewhat skeptical and reserved the right to change their minds after a trial period.

Mechanics

I learned much from this new technique, as well as from my French colleagues. However, this paper is about the technique of working on the telephone, so I will stick to that subject. It did not take a long time for the lessons to commence. The first thing that I discovered was the fatigue involved in being on the telephone listening to patients for hours a day. I had been in practice for many years and had forgotten that in the early days just listening in the office was exhausting. It had become less so over the years, but now that same fatigue was resurrected.

I chose not to use Skype, because I did not want to sit fixed before a camera all day. Also, in traditional psychoanalysis the patient does not face you, or you the patient, so I chose to use a VoIP (Voice over Internet Protocol) product called Vonage. It had a low, flat monthly fee for an endless number of hours on the telephone. My patients would dial a local number and it would ring in Paris at no charge to either of us. The sound quality was excellent. I chose to wear a very lightweight, wireless earpiece with a microphone attached so that I did not have to hold a telephone handset. My patients came to do the same to ease their relaxed posture during the session.

Using an internet telephone system had one drawback. If the internet went down for any reason, the telephone connection would not work or the call would be dropped. Therefore, I had a backup fixed line telephone number that patients could use to reach me through regular telephone systems. Again, it was a local number for my patient, which was automatically forwarded to my France Telecom home landline system.

While using the telephone, I found it essential to ask my patients to try as much as possible to recreate the undisturbed privacy of my office setting. I also cautioned against engaging in distractions like reading email or using the computer during the session. That instruction was for me too. I had to avoid the temptation of distraction and use it as an opportunity to examine the implied counter-transference when distraction preoccupied me.

Technique

I will say it from the outset: working on the telephone is different from working in person. I truly disagree with colleagues who say, "It is not really analysis." It is as different as going from three sessions per week to five. It is as different as switching from seeing a patient sitting up face to face to having them recline on a couch. It is as different as shuttle analysis, where analyst and analysand meet for several consecutive sessions over a short period each month, is from traditional analysis. It is simply different. So let's examine some of the differences.

The frame is both different and the same. If you think about it, the traditional posture of the psychoanalytic session is recreated in telephone work. The patient does not look at the analyst (of course this does not apply to face-to-face psychotherapy) and the analyst is free to participate with free-floating attention. The frame is expanded to allow the two parties to sit in vastly different places and spaces. There is a need for the two parties to include that fact in their sense of the space in which they collaborate. This obviously requires some higher level of psychological development. I have found that borderline patients and those with hysterical character structures or other forms of severe psychopathology do not do well in such a setting. However, those individuals with higher psychological developmental structures do well.

There is also a difference particular to French patients. In France patients are greeted with a handshake, which is repeated upon departing. Of course that is not possible on the telephone, which in fact brings it closer to the American tradition of not touching the patient. On the telephone the patient is greeted with a simple "hello." On occasion, the patient might repeat the greeting or ask if I were actually there. This must be examined as an element of uncertainty upon "entering" the session that mirrors some earlier experience. I am reminded of Hannah Segal who spoke of such a moment as a replica of the birth experience and the reception that the infant (now patient) encountered.

In evaluating patients for either psychoanalysis or psychotherapy with the use of the telephone one must humbly admit that not everyone is well suited to this modality. (Of course, over time we all become humble enough to admit that even the most traditional methods are not suited to everyone who seeks treatment.) In the case of the telephone, it is of the utmost importance to evaluate the patient's psychic structure to assure his or her capacity to hold the image or sense of the analyst in their mind's eye even if the analyst is not visible in real time. This is an evaluation of the capacity for object constancy in each patient.

That means that patients with elements of core psychotic, borderline or deeply narcissistic character structures will not do well on the telephone. Also, deeply depressed patients do not fare well. However, higher-level character structures and neurotics fare quite well. Another group that does well are very busy business people who spend a good part of their day on the telephone. The earpiece has become part of their body ego (many report going home with it still in their ear) and for some, the combination of distance (safety) on the telephone and intimacy (in their ear) works very well to provide an ideal environment for free association.

Getting started is a subject in and of itself. Because the word is out that I work on the telephone, I have received referrals from distant lands, places where obtaining quality therapy or therapy in one's native language is often difficult or impossible. "Can we start on the telephone?" they ask. In these cases I am left with little choice other than to say "yes." However, I add that at some time in the near future, it is important to spend time together in person to solidify an alliance.

This brings up the question of creating or solidifying an alliance over the telephone. Is it possible? Yes, but with a few reservations. Some patients can do it from the outset, but they are few. In fact, I believe that it is best to start in person and then carry the treatment to the telephone. You may say, "Ah! Then you admit that speaking over the telephone is not the same as being in the same space." I would remind you that I had already said that, but there is more detail to it. If you recall, I spoke of the image that the patient must carry in his or her mind's eye. For many (maybe most) that means a real image at first. An image does not only comprise the real person, but the emotive facial and body sense that are conveyed during the opening interviews. In our universal experience, not all patients come prepared and capable of immediately starting their analysis on the couch. It is sometimes necessary to start out face to face, sometimes with less frequency, until the patient can use the couch. It is not so different with the telephone.

I recall an analysand many years ago who was asked by a curious friend seeking a referral to me, "Is he tall?" My analysand, after some thought, replied, "Not until you get to know him." There is more to image or presence than just the physical. Have some managed to do the work without meeting me? Yes, but they are the exceptions. The same is true for me. I gain some knowledge during the consultation interviews from the patient's physical presence that is much harder to gain without it.

And that brings up the hardest part: gaining a sense of the subtleties of the patient's psyche and building an alliance over the telephone. This demands a very focused attention to the voice, intonation, and cadence of the patient's speech patterns while maintaining a capacity for free-floating attention. The voice carries many subtle variations to which one can attune oneself over time on the telephone. This is part of what fatigues the listener. I remember on one occasion telling a patient that I had an image of him sitting in the fetal position as he described a very difficult issue of his childhood. "You must have a camera!" he exclaimed. "I am sitting in a reclining chair with my knees to my chest." What I had heard was slightly labored speech with a slight shortness of breath.

I have colleagues, particularly here in France, who are very attuned to words but not so much to the verbal nuances that accompany those words. I think of music education. There are courses on "ear training" meant to develop the capacity to hear not just the notes, but also the nuances of tempo, timbre, etc. The same is true in listening to a voice over the telephone. Listening over the phone is a skill that comes with both time and focus. This is part of a larger issue of psychoanalytic listening, as focusing too much on words and associated phrases reduces the focus on other nuances of communication.

I recall an art teacher I had in university. I was sitting at my table carefully (a bit obsessively) sketching a still life that the teacher had arranged in the center of the table. I worked in very careful short strokes of the pencil. My teacher approached me and said, "Harvey I want you to stand." I did so, and she removed my stool. "From now on I want you never to sit. I also want you to not bend your elbow. You are getting the details but missing the action of the object." As I stood and moved my straightened arm, the lines I drew and the lines I came to see were large and sweeping. I began to see that still life objects are not really "still." The same is true of the human voice.

Building an alliance requires the "presence" of both parties. Despite some of my colleagues' best efforts to be blank screens (something that I feel is a contamination in itself), they nonetheless communicate (hopefully) a sense of their own humanity. Over the telephone this requires some real technique and attentiveness of its own. I have always subscribed to the use of gentle humor to judge the level of a person's psychic development. The use of, and reaction to, humor over the telephone becomes very revealing of both parties. Humor is a very high-level character trait that reveals important aspects of the patient *and* the analyst/therapist.

On the telephone, a patient must be aware of your presence, and that requires that the therapist make an occasional sound. How and when one makes his or her presence known depends on the flow of free associations coming from the patient. The famous "ah ha" or "mmm" works well. If a patient is going along at a good and free-flowing pace nothing is required, but at some point one has to make one's presence known and felt. Most of the time this is not difficult, but on occasion it requires some activity on the part of the analyst/therapist. I am probably slightly more active on the telephone at times than I would be if the patient were in my physical presence. However, I have discovered that as the patient becomes more comfortable and confident with this modality, my activity returns to its usual state.

Working over the phone is hardest when the patient is not used to speaking freely. Verbal encouragement is needed. Without that, the patient is likely to feel abandoned, which, in and of itself is analyzable once the patient learns to speak freely. I doubt this is much different over the phone than it is in the consulting room, but on the telephone it takes on greater importance. I think of one of Winnicott's comments about play in therapy. He said that the action of therapy takes place in the shared arena of play between the patient and analyst. He went on to say that if the patient did not know how to play, the first order of business was to teach the patient how to do so. He also said that if the therapist did not know how to play, he or she should get out of the business. I fear some analogue of this statement is applicable to working on the telephone.

Case example

Anna, a patient with whom I met for analysis four times a week, always said that the telephone was "not as good" as seeing me in person. I often inquired into her thoughts about that. Usually, she said little other than it was "not as personal." Despite her complaint, she moved on in the same animated manner as when she was in my office.

Anna had taken the trouble to create a space that was quiet, private, and comfortable for her telephone sessions. Frankly, I could not discern a difference between the free associations she made in person versus those she made on the telephone.

One day, during our first session on the telephone after a four-week stay in my office in her city, she again said, "It is simply not the same," referring to the telephone session. "Tell me how you experience the difference," I asked yet again.

This time she gave a new response. Anna was silent for a few long moments. "I have an image of my father on the telephone," she said. "An image?" I inquired. "Yes, an image of him speaking to me on the telephone," she responded. "Describe the image of your father speaking to you on the telephone," I suggested. "He is multitasking, as we say now. However, I felt he was distracted. He really was not interested in my call. He usually had people in the office with him, and if he was alone he was busy with committee reports or legislative papers. He did not bother to come to the hospital when I was born. I was his fourth child and a girl to boot."

Anna had come from a political family. Her father was the second generation of his family to be in Congress. His father, Anna's grandfather, had been quite a potent force politically. Her father felt great pressure to meet or surpass his father's fame and power. To that end, he was seldom home except for what Anna called his "photo op appearances."

As a young girl, Anna would only call when absolutely necessary, because she could feel his irritation at the interruption. It simply was not worth the call, and often she simply let the issue drop. Once she did not attend a class outing because her mother was away and she wouldn't call her father to get his signature on the permission form.

"I hated calling his office!" she exclaimed. "In fact I feel a momentary indescribable feeling when I am about to call you. Now I realize that it is not about calling you but about calling him. Even now, all these years later, I still don't call him. I call mom and let her convey the message."

This became a significant turning point in Anna's analysis. She had been holding back her free associations from me – particularly the angry or ugly ones. She also began to understand that I was different and wanted to hear her. She spoke of the fact that I was always there, whether in person or on the phone, and greeted her with pleasure in my voice.

It turned out that I was not the only one from whom Anna withheld thoughts that contained bad feelings or images. She did so with her husband, her daughter, and her friends. One day not long afterwards, Anna confronted her father by describing her experience of his absence and her feelings about it. She spoke carefully and even lovingly to her father, but was clear about the painful nature of her experience and feelings. After a short pause, her father said, "I couldn't care less" and walked away.

At first Anna was very sad. She then got angry and realized that this confirmation of our reconstruction was really liberating. She, too, walked away from her longing to have more from her father. She would have to settle for her husband "and you" she said, over the phone.

Further thoughts

I wish to comment further on the issue of "ear training." Without the view of physical body language, ear training is of the utmost importance. I was astonished by the nuances I learned to pick up on from just verbal cues. I used to teach "ear training" to newly licensed mental health practitioners. To do so, I used the 11-hour BBC production of *Brideshead Revisited* as an instructive tool. Each lesson consisted of viewing one hour of the series followed by a discussion of "what did you hear?" The idea was to listen on many different levels at the same time. The hardest aspect for students to learn was listening for the nuanced verbal cues uttered by the actors. When was a voice tight, and for what reason? Was the tightness indicative of suppressed anger, fear, jealousy, or desire? This is exactly what I mean by the ear training one can develop on the telephone.

Throughout more than a century of psychoanalytic thought and practice, we have seen much evolution and innovation in technique. There have been gains, compromises, and loses. The use of the now universal technology of the telephone and internet, tools that shrink great distances in time and space, is part of this evolution. Yes, there are elements lost, but there are also elements which are gained. Our job as clinicians is to apply our tried and true techniques to these new parameters.

Patients have often shared with me their fantasies of my living abroad and of my daily life in Paris. These became the oft-mentioned "grist for the mill." The telephone has become its own form of screen upon which the patient projects his or her thoughts, fantasies, and transferences. For example, one day, as I answered the telephone, my patient heard the sirens of passing police cars outside. "They are coming to get you," he joked. "And what would be my crime?" I asked. The patient protested that he was just kidding, but I pointed out that while I knew that he wasn't serious, we could learn from what might be associated with his joke. It became necessary to kindly nudge the patient to see this as a useful opportunity and not just a social way of starting a telephone conversation. In fact that exchange brought forth some very important negative transference that the patient was avoiding.

In my opinion, the frame of the analytic setting is not a fixed frame. As with all bonds of attachment, it is the oscillations between libidinal pull and the repulsive forces of Thanatos that create the unique texture of that attachment. This dynamic does not disappear over the telephone. The frame of the analytic setting is a dynamic frame, the texture of which is determined by the same forces, be they in the same room or on the same telephone call. What really determines the character of the analytic frame is the emotional, instinctual, and cognitive commitment to the alliance.

In the end, the use of the telephone is a personal choice. Some can do it, while some cannot or choose not to do so. However, it should not be ruled out without real clinical observation and critique. As with so much of our methodology, a rigorous attitude on the part of the analyst is imperative. When I was a candidate in psychoanalytic training, I was introduced to the phrase that we must "tie ourselves to the mast" as we listen to the patient and contemplate our interventions. This holds true when working on the telephone. The phone is just another instrument of communication, the *art* of using the phone is the way in which we use this instrument as a form of contact and influence.

Chapter 12

Psychoanalysis and cyberspace
Shifting frames and floating bodies

Luca Caldironi

Psychoanalysis has undergone continuous changes both in theory and practice since the very beginning. This is true for what concerns its founder's methods and procedures, but also for the following contributions given by his most influential successors.

We feel it's important to underline this characteristic in order to stress how 'shifting frames' and 'floating bodies' were always a part of psychoanalytical clinic and research. In fact, we could say they are true trademarks of this profession which can only be understood by approaching our work according to Freud's own teachings, that is by having the courage to look at things, including our failures, and to 'blind ourselves' in order to be able to see deep inside the darkest corners (Freud, 1992). To do this, even within the confines of this brief contribution of ours, we ourselves need to recover some theoretical references to guide us along the way we're undertaking. Let's start by giving a closer look at the distinction made by the analysts of the Association Psychoanalitique de France regarding the two terms of psychoanalytic 'doctrine' and 'theory'.

> For 'doctrine' we mean the whole set of radical experiences, and elaborations thereof, that we all need to go through to become and to be called psychoanalysts ... This includes, therefore, the unconscious experience ... the possibility of treading along ancient paths again, but also the experience of the limits opposing this. Not just our own resistances, but also those limitations that can typically be perceived with matters such as those tied to bisexuality; to the adventures we encounter from the moment object relationships are born, to the feeling of seduction (active and passive) and of trauma, up to their culmination into the Oedipal issue and into its resolution ... Theory

instead, is at the opposite end, it is the field where the discussion takes place and includes all possible theoretical constructs. As much as doctrine – after the initial radical separation between who has the 'knowledge' and who doesn't – unites those who share the experience, so does theory divide, separate, complicate, ultimately identify.

(Semi, 1988, pp. 476–477, author's translation)

These clarifications allow us to better evaluate without prejudice what is happening in the current psychoanalytical reality. Much has already been said and written on how certain rules characterizing the patient–analyst encounter have changed during the years, but we feel that there is more. We believe another important distinction must be addressed and that is what it means to stay true to a certain cultural legacy. As in the Parable of the Talents, one may think that burying the Talents is the right thing to do to faithfully preserve what was consigned to him, and another will instead believe that using the Talents is the right way, with all the related risks that may come with either hypothesis. As for us, we believe, and in this we are comforted by the parable's moral, that the right way to be faithful lies within the variable of 'creativity' and that this variable should be investigated and pursued. What we mean by this is trying to be true to a kind of implicit intentionality present in Freud, the intentionality to explore and study, with every available tool, the comprehension of the deepest aspects of human nature. This applies to the psychoanalytic frame as well with all the new variations brought upon it by today's cultural changes especially in the communications field. You can think that being 'faithful' to the frame means freezing it, or you can believe that these variations are the expression of an initial creative urge and that, save for that share of experiences that we defined as 'doctrine', we can embrace them with the same open mind and dialogue that any theory deserves. We find this to be useful in considering other variables of the analytic relationship as well. For example it gives us a way to observe what has been called since the beginning of the history of psychoanalysis the 'setting'. As Di Chiara (1971, p. 49) observes, "the setting is what allows the patient to actualize a range of experiences related to his/her unconscious, childhood, personal conflicts, and where actualizing certain experiences means experiencing transference".

This definition helps us understand that the setting is not defined (only) by other, just as important, moments of the therapeutic relationship such as: preliminary meetings, the analytic contract (in all its possible variations), schedule and frequency of sessions and puts the setting much closer to the psychoanalytic process itself; the setting thus becomes a valid environment in which this process can take place. Following this way of thinking, the above-mentioned concept can also be compared to what Bion defines as 'Container–Contained Interaction' (Bion, 1959). Now the setting becomes the 'container' in which, through the analytic relationship, the process can evolve. Looking at Bion's concept side by side with that of setting, according to Di Chiara's (1971) definition of the latter, the actual architectural location where it takes place is not very relevant anymore. This opens to the possibility that even methods apparently very distant from the relationship of patient–therapist, like those that make use of technological means of communication such as smartphones, texting, chat and video chat, become more acceptable or at least are perceived as representative of a reality within the context of the analytic relationship. This applies not only to the new communications techniques, but also to the possibility of using clinical material deriving from these as an integral part of the analytic work. Today, in fact, it is not uncommon for patients to show us things like images or text messages during a session. Clearly we realize the differences and the risk of falling into some form of dangerous eclecticism, but we also know that in our profession, something Freud taught us from the very start, the object of the research is one and the same with the tool used for such research. Therefore, if on one hand we believe in the importance of being faithful to a certain method of analytic work, on the other we must consider how our 'container' must necessarily adapt to the profound cultural changes that are taking place today.

The fact is, we're going through a moment of transition that I would describe as a real anthropologic mutation, in which not only our thoughts or our way of thinking are apparently being transformed, perhaps even our 'neuronal' system is being rewired. I believe that the subject of how 'inner' and 'external' scenarios in psychoanalysis are changing cannot be approached without first examining in which way or ways we actually access knowledge and information.

We are in a period of changes so radical that it reminds us of another moment of profound transformation of the ancient past, described by Plato in his *Phaedrus* when he speaks about the passage from oral communication to writing. In Plato's *Phaedrus* (274d–275c) we find the Egyptian King Thamus worried about the change that is being presented to him and it's easy to draw a parallel with our current concerns about the use of new and different media. When the inventor of writing claims to the king that this will soon become a great aid for individuals and society alike, the sovereign expresses words of caution on the matter, as recalled here in an interesting interview by Stefano Moriggi:

> when writing will be spread among the population, our way of remembering will not be the same as before: instead of recalling/retrieving memories from the inside, we will do it from the outside … for Moriggi this observation is not as simple as it appears, especially considering how important memory dynamics are in the processing of concepts, and not only in the realm of Platonic Gnoseology. Externalizing knowledge, therefore, means changing our way of thinking forever, and our way of living and interacting with others in space and time.
>
> (Moriggi, 2014, p. 184)

But isn't this externalization process exactly what characterizes on a massive scale today's methods of acquiring and sharing knowledge through the so-called new technologies? We believe that our considerations may contribute to the debate on the problem of 'cyberspace'. We also feel that this kind of procedure/approach will help us avoid simplistic enthusiasm and/or hasty judgments and condemnations. For us the subject of memory and the different ways of using it are very fascinating, particularly from a psychoanalytical viewpoint. Regarding this aspect, we find it useful to mention a basic method used in analysis, commonly known as the 'rule' of free association. This is an actual technique that uses memory in a specific way. In this case we are talking about the associative memory, which, as opposed to the 'written' trace/code follows a fabric of links/threads that are an inherent part of the analysand's psychic apparatus and that intertwine with those of the analyst in the here and now of the analytic session. It is a form of knowledge that derives from within and is brought out through the association technique. But things aren't always as simple as they appear, that's why Plato, in his reflections on the 'new technology' of his time, introduces the suggestive term *'pharmakon'*. We know how this term paradoxically contains the two opposite and contrasting meanings of 'remedy/cure' and at the same time 'poison'. Ambiguous meanings that bring us back to our days in which it is difficult to live this intense moment of transition without feeling the need to remain kind of suspended above the complexity of what we try to embrace. The question now is: can psychoanalysis with its theoretical-experiential 'corpus'/body be of help with this (transition)?

Marzi writes:

> Virtuality, in all its different meanings, revamps and complicates certain controversial themes of the psychoanalytic world of these last decades. The fact that it's not an actual space in a physical and material sense, which cannot be seen or concretely perceived in any way and is therefore impossible for humans to detect with any of their physiological senses, makes the virtual space strikingly similar to the Kant-Bion concept for which it is impossible to know the thing in itself, meaning that it is something that can be conceived but not perceived.
>
> (Marzi, 2013, p. 164)

Can the analytic instrument, which inevitably also inhabits our 'changing world', become a critical observer of the changes it is part of itself? We believe this challenge can be accepted. With this, we don't mean to over simplify the possibility, but rather, we wish to maintain ourselves within that margin of paradox, ambiguity and indefiniteness that always characterizes the work with the unconscious.

What's certain is that we're going through an irreversible process and, as with the passage from speech to writing in the past, today, our means of learning and communicating will have to necessarily deal with the new tools that come with it. As Moriggi says quoting Heidegger:

> the way we 'inhabit the world', that is, how we relate to others and how we perceive our own body in space and time, as well as our 'body' of knowledge and learning, is necessarily dependent on the equipment with which we inter-act and connect every day.
>
> (Moriggi, 2014, p. 197)

In these last observations, we are indirectly introduced to the concept of '*corpus*', or body, in its broader meaning. A body can be 'theoretical', 'technological', 'experiential', of 'text' and the body finds itself at center stage in all its possible diverse expressions. As psychoanalysts, we're well aware of the importance of this concept from the very beginning of psychoanalysis. But what (exactly) is this body that we're dealing with? We're not talking about the anatomical-biological body, but rather a body clad with pulsions, a 'driving body' where the word 'Trieb' is used to describe that leap from the 'body' to 'mind-body'. The leap that made Freud (1937) describe that irreducible aspect he calls 'biological bedrock', '*Gewachsener Fels*'. Where, in between the paradox of these two terms, one belonging to the organic world and the other to the inorganic, we find once again, something set on the border between a dialectical proposal and a state of impossibility. Is all this somehow related to the analytic request? Is this, in a way, the actual limit of analysis and even more so in today's context? Obviously these questions cannot but remain open-ended and, precisely because they are undetermined, they become an integral part of that thought apparatus that can help us better comprehend what is happening around us in general and in our analytic work in particular.

By this process, I mean the establishment of a differentiated psychic space. Indeed I underline that a sort of 'caesura' or 'limit' comes to be between what we could call the intra-psychic and the inter-subjective. Such a limit becomes a privileged place for processing, thus, a limit that has its own 'thickness' within the boundary of the analytic work. It becomes a limit and a container at the same time, because it has a space inside that is established in the patient–analyst dyad and it finds in the setting, in particular meant as the analyst's internal setting, the champion of the process itself. The concept of internal setting becomes particularly important when talking about virtual reality and new technologies. With this, I don't mean to diminish the value of the acquired set of rules that constitutes the physical framework of the setting as we know it now, but only to underline how we have to confront ourselves with a changing reality and with a process of progressive 'dematerialization' of relationships. But exactly how is all this evolving? And how can we identify the limits/boundaries of it all? We know that knowledge has become more and more fragmentized, both in regard to the information and to the means to retrieve it. Through cyberspace we can access an incredible variety of information, on any subject, and we can interrupt the flow rapidly shifting at any moment, from web pages to videos and all sorts of social networks. So the question now is, is this procedure changing our analytic scenario as well and if so, in which way or ways? The world that we are getting a glimpse of and seeing in our analysis rooms today is spinning fast. Everything is accelerated and, as we will further examine, the 'objects' that have become part of our session are becoming more and more tangible.

We already mentioned, for instance, the intrusion of technological objects (patients may occasionally take out their phone to show us a text or something or they'll have background sounds of ringtones and beeps and blinking lights coming from their devices) creates a constant over-stimulation of the senses that doesn't necessarily help symbolization, in fact, it often inhibits it. This should definitely make us reflect on how 'connection' is not the same thing as 'contact', and of how, as analysts, it is fundamental to maintain our listening ability integrated within the space and time of the session.

As Bjòrklind writes:

> The idea of the ego as being first and foremost a bodily ego (Freud, 1923), a theory of the emergence of the mind as being a necessary consequence of our existing within in a body, could be described as the main foundation for psychoanalysis as a whole. How we repre-sent, fantasize, and structure our experience of living from within a body, will largely determine the workings of our inner lives, as well as our existence in external reality.
>
> (Bjòrklind, 2014, p. 5)

And furthermore:

> A fundamental question for our discussion today, is whether these new technologies can be thought of as interfering with and possibly changing the structural relation between the human body and the human mind, and this in a qualitatively different way than all earlier tools. If we conclude that all psychoanalytic discourse is deeply rooted in this relation between body and mind, then the main issue is whether recent technological development is changing the world and the human mind in such a way that psychoanalysis is losing its relevance. Or less polemically, how can psychoanalysis evolve to still be of relevance to future generations.
>
> (Bjòrklind, 2014, p. 5)

But the 'web' can also become an observation point through which to observe a situation and rethink it through new, different filters. After all, as psychoanalysts we are used to working with a 'psychic reality' brought to us by our patients that we know can hardly ever be reduced to or match with the objective reality.

In fact, we know from the history of psychoanalysis, how provocatively important and bemusing Freud's statement was, when he defined the 'ego' as "not being master in his own home" and what a true anthropologic revolution this was as a consequence of the shifting of 'vertex' it brought about.

The psychoanalytic thought is permeated from the (very) start by an 'estranging/-unsettling' function ('*Unheimliche*'!). Even further attempts to 'map' mental processes, through the 'first and second topics', left us somewhere difficult to locate/in an undefined location. This fundamental aspect of the psychoanalytic thought can be further radicalized within a theoretic model that expects "for the unconscious to always come to the surface in conversation as well as behavior. Conscious and unconscious experiences are constantly tossing and turning one inside the other" (Civitarese, 2013, p. 147).

And even today, when cell phones, GPS and an internet connection allow us to know our exact position at any given moment, where we are located in the world, and though we can access a myriad of information, we continue to engage in matters such as the different types of memory and/or different forms of reality. These subjects inevitably bring about questions on concepts such as 'internal reality', 'psychic reality', 'external reality', 'Reality' with a capital 'R', as in Bion's 'O', 'imaginary reality' and consequently lead us to addressing the so called 'virtual reality' as another polysemous aspect of reality. In fact, this is located an intermediate area, a space in between reality and fantasy, which results in a reduced transitional area, that also becomes itself an actual 'transitional cyberspace' that allows us to confront ourselves with several paradoxes and possibilities.

In agreement with Antinucci (2013) we see "the creative virtual space as an oneiric space", stressing Khan's concept (1972 [1974] and following elaborations) that consists in an application of the scribble technique used by Winnicott (1953) in pediatric consultations. "Khan suggests important distinctions between the capacity to dream, the oneiric process and the space in which the dream takes place, as a structured place of the ego's functions capable of accessing and using symbolic discourse" (Antinucci, 2013, p. 142).

This distinction makes the 'virtual space' even more problematic by emphasizing the possibility of evolutionary aspects but also defensive ones within it. Evolutionary aspects will be those that bring this space closer to the transitional space with consequent transformative effects; while defensive aspects will be those in which "this contracted/limited space brings to avoiding the recognition of oneself and the other" (Antinucci, 2013, p. 142).

Another characteristic of cyberspace is the over-accumulation of data. The overload of information is so overflowing that we are literally bombarded by it, making our capability to discern much more difficult. We often hear that: "the web is always on, and it's always there even when we're not". Day and night, twenty-four/seven, the internet is being accessed and all sorts of data and information gets uploaded and down-loaded from the web. If on one hand this phenomenon is very exciting, as it awakens in us a certain feeling of omnipotence, on the other, the risk is that it is saturating the interlocutory and potentially transformative impulse that is implicit in the frustration we experience when we have to wait for satisfaction.

If I may borrow a quote from Blanchot, previously used by Bion as well, "La réponse est le malheur de la question" (the answer is the question's sickness). What Bion draws from Blanchot is a challenging invitation that becomes harder and harder to meet. We live in a time that allows us to get answers to our queries in real-time (virtually!), with search engines, online encyclopedias and other sources at our full disposal competing to make us wait the least time possible for an answer – digital logic characterized by a great big indistinct mass of answers.

This is why, when dealing with the flow of information coming from the web, we need to approach it with the same regard that Freud recommends when talking about Michelangelo's work, suggesting to proceed "not by putting, but rather by taking away/chipping off". It's a form of knowledge that isn't based on adding more and more elements to the construction, but rather on taking parts off, in order to let the most incredibly diverse, unpredictable shapes and forms emerge. But this brings about another dilemma. Who is the creator? Who creates whom? Here we are indeed closely related to the analytic work. Does this mean that we are seeing the birth of a pervasive form of implicit memory, which totally transcends us and whose limits are increasingly fleeting? Are we experiencing a new evolutionary phase that makes us question the notion of subject itself.

Psychoanalysis has always followed and been involved in the historical, cultural and social relationships of its time and now it inevitably questions itself, using everything in its power and all the possible tools available, in the attempt to 'photograph' these passages.

On this subject a good example of such a passage is what happened with the introduction of the analytical technique with children. At the time, the concept of setting had to undergo an important transformation and found a valid solution in the use of 'play'. About this, we like to think of play, not just for its playfulness and associative components, but also as an actual potential 'space in between things' ('a kind of wiggle space' is also one of the meanings of '*gioco*', play in Italian).

And it seems even more relevant to put concepts such as cyberspace at use in our work with adolescents, not only because they represent the actual physical passage and consequently a link between generations as well, but also because: "Adolescents give analysts the chance to see how overwhelming and 'ungraspable' changes are in ways of thinking, of representing inner and external reality ... (highlighting) the discontent of contemporary culture" (Bonaminio, 2013, p. 100).

The environment is changing all around us and it's becoming hard to distinguish how this affects the new network of relationships. In fact, things become even more complex when taking into consideration concepts such as Winnicott's 'maternal holding' and Bion's '*reverie*', and more specifically when the latter introduces the theorization of the 'alpha function'.

Ogden reminds us that:

> for Bion, the 'alpha function' (a formerly unknown and perhaps unknowable, new set of mental functions) transforms raw 'sensory impressions tied to the emotional experience' into alpha elements that can be connected (together) to form affect-laden dream-thoughts. A dream-thought presents an emotional problem that the individual needs to cope with (Bion, 1962; Meltzer, 1983), thus providing the stimulus/impetus for the development of the capacity to dream (which is synonymous with the unconscious thinking) ... Without an alpha function (either one's own or that provided by another person), an individual/one cannot dream and therefore cannot make use of (do unconscious psychological work with) one's lived emotional experience, past and present. Consequently, a

person unable to dream is trapped in an unchanging and endless world of what is.

(Ogden, 2009, p. 16)

But fantasies and dreams are also part of (the) virtual reality and ultimately part of that potential space which allows for:

> virtual reality and psychoanalysis to share, metaphorically speaking, the presence within these two dimensions, not of real, definitive and 'final' (or original) objects, that could escape perception and acquisition on behalf of the subject, even if they are both present, but rather those 'narrative derivatives' that theoreticians in the analytic field, following in Bion's and others' steps, have always considered a fundamental/basic presence within the analyst-patient intersubjectivity.

(Marzi, 2013, p. 163)

In the 'virtual' (realm) one can configure infinite possibilities that can have an endless number of representations within the mental space, from highly evolved ones, down to the collapse or the psychopathologic implosion of the 'concrete thought' consequent to the failure of the alpha function.

Ferro says, drawing upon Bion's thought, that the mental (realm):

> derives from the transformation of sensory experiences into alpha elements, in the newborn through the passage of this sensory experience through the mother's alpha function, and then later through the passage of the sensory experience through one's own alpha function, once this has been introjected and is sufficiently functioning.

(Ferro, 2009, p. 9)

First of all, this means that, in order to acquire this function, the passage through another person's mind and the subsequent introjection of the thinking capacity are both necessary. Acknowledging and recognizing the presence of the Other, both in the transitive and intransitive forms, come to be essential experiences.

But how is this changing today and which and how many minds are we talking about?

Civitarese, in his review of the movie *Nightmare Detective* (2006), tells us:

the cyborg is imagined as a being which is self-reproducing and there-fore has no need for the other; it is not born and does not die. Cyborgs therefore do not dream, because to dream – that is, to construct the dream space – it takes two. For this reason, the cyborg becomes a modern symbol of the incapacity to dream, of the non-living areas of the mind and of the falseness of existence.

(Civitarese, 2010, pp. 1012–1013)

We're not dealing with a three-dimensional space here anymore, since the referring coordinates have been shattered and the relationship with the external reality could turn into something dramatically immaterial. But, at the same time, we may ask ourselves if all this could, also, provide, in the same way, endless possibilities of ever-newer forms of symbolization.

Marzi says:

we do not know if the psychic space is actually disappearing, as Kristeva sustained (1993); (but) ... we can think of the virtual space, immense and undefined, as something that can be imagined or used as a form of 'acting' by subjects who, not having the possibility to use their own interior mental space, may attempt (playing the card of) exporting to the outside, into virtual reality or simply cyberspace, in order to use it as an extroflexion of oneself and from oneself, but also as an attempt, (to see if it is possible) to try and see one's psychic space in this way, to touch it with one's hand, opening up to possibly disastrous results, or, perhaps embryonically evolutionary/develop-mental ones.

(Marzi, 2013, p. 169)

In conclusion, we feel that as psychoanalysts it is fundamental for us to maintain our critical function. A function that can help define, or at least attempt to do so, what is happening in today's society. Indeed, we believe that in the analytical room, it's not only the complex emotional history of the patient that is actualized, but it's also a good representation of the complexity of the human mind itself and of how this works in general. This last assertion must not deceive however into thinking that the repre-sentation is the same as the object of the representation, but it can be useful as a sort of mapping system of the ongoing changes, including the ones related to the risks that the use of the new technologies entails. Risks such as the loss of a 'physical' individual encounter, the confusion between internal and external worlds, the addicted relationship with 'separation' that has been eliminated by 'constant connection' etc. However, we cannot help considering all the opportunities that these new 'worlds' offer as well, and also how they are impossible to stop anyway. The best we can do is try to 'contain' them and containing also means exploring and embracing them as any other experience.

We realize that this is only the beginning of a process in which we human beings are deeply immersed and that, at the same time, it is a process that has always belonged to us. Once again we find ourselves proceeding by sight like Odysseus sailing in between Scylla and Charybdis and if, on the one hand, we cannot avoid falling victims of such seductive techniques offering easy cognitive shortcuts, on the other, we must always be aware of how important they are, especially considering their pervasiveness. This must awake our sense of responsibility (Caldironi, 2014), and as Bion (1991, p. ix) says, "we have also to consider the urgency of this commitment and that there are changes which can be picked up only by those who can effort what is needed".

References

Antinucci G. "Lavoro dell'identità nello spazio del tempo cibernetico", in A. Marzi (ed.) *Psicoanalisi, identità e internet. Esplorazioni nel cyberspace*, pp. 119–143, Angeli Editore, Milan, 2013

Bion W.R. "Attacks on linking", in W.R. Bion *Second Thought*, Karnak Books, London, [1959] 1993

Bion W.R. *Learning from experience*, Karnak Books, London, 1962

Bion W.R. *A memoir of the future*, Karnak Books, London, 1991

Bjòrklind C. "Psychoanalysis and the new technologies. The future of talking cure and the bodily ego in the digital era. Psychoanalysis in 2025", Pre-puplished papers, FEP meeting, 2014

Bonaminio V. "A perfect world", in A. Lemma and L. Caparrotta (eds) *Psychoanalysis in the technoculture era*, pp. 97–113, New Library of Psychoanalysis, Routledge, London and New York, 2013

Caldironi L. "Di-orinta-menti, tra Mito, Arte e Pensiero: una via sghemba per il futuro a partire da W.R. Bion", in S. Beggiora, M. Giampà, A. Lombardozzi, A. Molino (eds) *Sconfinamenti* (Escursioni psico-antropologiche), S Mimesis editore, Milan, 2014

Civitarese G. "Do cyborgs dream? Post-human landscapes in Shinya Tsukamoto's nightmare detective – 2006", *International Journal of Psychoanalysis*, number 4, pp. 1012–1013, August, 2010

Civitarese G. "Cyberspazio e il luogo dove avviene l'analisi", in A. Marzi (ed.) *Psicoanalisi, identità e internet. Esplorazioni nel cyberspace*, Angeli Editore, Milan, 2013

Di Chiara G. "Il setting analitico", *Psiche*, 8, p. 47, 1971

Ferro A. "Transformations in dreaming and characters in the psychoanalytic field", *Int. J. Psychoanalysis*, 90, pp. 209–230, 2009

Freud S. *Breve compendio di psicoanalisi*, Volume 9, 1917–1923, Opere, Boringhieri, Milan, 1923

Freud S. *Analisi terminabile e interminabile*, Opere, Boringhieri, Milan, Volume 11, 1937

Freud S. "Letter to Lou Andreas-Salomé of May 25, 1916", in *Letters from S. Freud to Lou Andreas-Salomé*, Dover Publications, New York, 1992 (originally published Basic Books, Inc., New York, 1960)

Khan M.R. "The use and the abuse of dream in psychic experience", in M.R. Khan, *The privacy of the self*, Hogarth Press, London, [1972] 1974

Kristeva J. *Le nuove malattie dell'anima*, Borla editore, Roma, [1993] 1998

Marzi A. (ed.) *Psicoanalisi, identità e internet. Esplorazioni nel cyberspace*, Angeli Editore, Milan, 2013

Meltzer D. *Dream life a re-examination of the psychoanalytical theory and technique*, Clunie Press, Perthshire, 1983

Moriggi S. "La condizione postumana", *Aut/Aut*, 361, pp. 181–194, 2014

Ogden T.W. *Rediscovering psychoanalysis: thinking and dreaming, learning and forgetting*, Routledge, London, 2009

Semi A.A. (ed) *Trattato di psicoanalisi*, vol. 1, Raffaello Cortina Ed., Milano, 1988

Winnicott D.W. *Collected papers: through paediatrics to psychoanalysis*, Tavistock, London, 1953

Chapter 13

Spiral process as place

The ineffable architecture of analytic space

Kim Rosenfield

> One of the great beauties of architecture is that each time, it is like life starting all over again.
>
> (Renzo Piano, *Piano: Complete Works 1966–2014*)

Our consulting rooms, the actual spaces where we ply our trade, in addition to technique, training, and affiliation, identify us and, more importantly, become the musculoskeletature for how we work and think. All molecularity within this particular architecture is geared toward creation and absorption, where psychic material can be heard and held in mind and body. These built spaces hold us within a particular and necessary envelope, one of container/contained, while simultaneously providing the sensation that within our office walls, we are set to journey, along with our patients, on the royal road to Bion's "limitless infinite" or at least some approximation thereof.

Both analyst and patient rely on the brick-and-mortar frame of the office in order for self and mutual regulation, a sense of order and structure, thinking, and refuge, as well as a sense of venturing into the unknown to be permissible. Think of the unease that occurs when patient and analyst cross unexpected paths outside the office walls. This "in real-life" encounter breaks down, even if for a fleeting moment, the aforementioned constructs that occur naturally within the analytic dyad when housed in its prescribed built space.

Yet when we're inside the materiality of our offices, being caught off guard is an unexpected aspect of an expected and desirable part of the work. When both patient and analyst enter the physical space of the analytic setting, they are opening up to the potentiality of feeling intruded upon, unprepared, understood, unsafe, loved, confused, supported, held, or many of the myriad dynamical phenomenon that constitute venturing into the analytic field. Our offices become a silent third, providing a concrete form of tacit permission for both analyst and patient to enter into an encounter with the unknown. Can we then think of our built space as part of the intrapsychic forces that form a part of the treatment, infusing how time and analytic space impact each other?

Madeleine and Willy Baranger, influential French-born Latin-American-trained psychoanalysts, were pivotal in originating ideas on the analytic setting and how analytic time and space function in the analytic field. Their work encompasses, among many other far-reaching ideas, an articulation of analytic time as wrapped into what Enrique Pichon-Rivière (1958) has termed the "spiral process." To simplify, the spiral process is a way to conceptualize analytic temporality or the ways in which space and time work on the unconscious, undulating between past, present, and future, for both analyst and patient and for the dyad together.

What would happen, then, if we link the setting/built space to the spiral process as well? What if our actual physical offices act as embedded structures with their own linking functions? Functions that can hold psychic time and space for, in absence of, and alongside of the analytic couple.

When we meet outside our offices in chance encounters with patients, we lose this framework of "the dialectic of the spiral" (Baranger and Baranger, 2009). Time exists at the moment of surprise encounter only in the present. The "movement of deepening into the past and construction of the future" (Baranger and Baranger, 2009, p. 49) must wait until we bring the material of the encounter back into the office, into the built structure that provides a shelter for the instantiation of the spiral process to occur. Then the byproducts of the spontaneous encounter can become an integrated part of the "meat" of the analytic treatment.

Additionally, many of our patients loathe the idea of knowing/seeing us outside the bulwark of our office. It is imperative to them that we stay lodged in the known constancy of our consulting room, lest we become "too real" and individual within our own right as separate from the dyad. Others long to break open the frame and be with us outside what feels like restrictive boundaries to the intimacy between us. Yet it is only within our brick and mortar settings that these fantasies and longings can safely take flight. There are always exceptions to going outside the architectural frame – Skyping, phone contact, etc. when neither patient or analyst might be in the office; attending patient events, performances, weddings, hospitalizations, etc. but these encounters are beyond the focus of this paper. In other words, the actual structure housing the analytic dyad has significant impact, known and unknown, on both patient and analyst's functioning.

To torque an idea of Descartes, the idea that knowing defines us as a subject, lends itself to the idea that perhaps our offices can act like another form of knowing. Our material space can function as an additional interpretive instrument that facilitates unconscious psychic work in both analyst and patient. When there is failure of containment or unlinking within the analytic dyad, our offices hold time as continuous, even when we or when our patients can't. Space and structure (barring any changes to the office setting) function like the Winnicottian idea of "no baby without the mother" (Winnicott, 1960). The analytic dyad as baby and the space as mother creates the holding environment necessary for all intrapsychic experience of the dyadic couple – destructive, loving, and everything in between.

In his seminal paper *Hate in the Countertransference*, Winnicott (1994) asks a colleague if he works with his neurotic patients in the dark, and his surprised colleague replies that it would be "too out of the ordinary." Here, Winnicott is equating the function of the space and setting as a kind of third in the analytic process: "this provision and maintenance of an ordinary environment can be in itself a vitally important thing in the analysis … in fact it can be, at times, even more important than the verbal interpretations that also have to be given" (Winnicott, 1994, p. 353). We can then begin to think of the Barangers' idea of a "progressive construction of an interpretation in the bi-personal field" (Baranger and Baranger, 2009, p. 804) as manifest through the actual interiority and architecture of the physical space in which we work. Not merely how the objects or re-arrangements of objects in a room affect our patients, but how our spaces form an external structural third, a stimulus barrier that functions as an additional alive filament inside the analytic undulations of containment and seepage. Working as an additional agent of change within the therapeutic space, and between the dyad at work within the space, the material space itself serves as interlocutor. I hope to show, through the following descriptions of my office space, ways in which the analytic field can expand to encompass built space.

My office is a sub-ground basement space. In order to reach the front door one must descend through a wrought iron gate off a noisy New York City street, down steep granite steps, to enter. This descent to the basement is akin to Bachelard's idea of the cellar, or underground force of the unconscious: "it is first and foremost the dark entity of the house, the one that partakes of subterranean forces. When we dream there, we are in harmony with the irrationality of the depths" (Winnicott, 1994, p. 352).

The street door has a small indentation, "a hole of the shadow of the hollow of the day" (Pontalis, 1974, p. 133), or what I imagine was a bullet hole rendered during its past incarnation when the neighborhood was under siege from drugs and racial violence. "Doors stop and separate. The door breaks space in two, splits it, prevents osmosis" (Perec, 1977, p. 37) or does it? The door serves as a threshold to the oneirics of analytic space, signaling entry into a change in interiority of the physical and psychic environment. As Winnicott notes, hate can be expressed by "the existence of the end of the 'hour'" (Winnicott, 1994, p. 352). The end of the hour means the patient must leave the setting, walking through the door that partitions the "world out there" into chronicity different from interior analytic time.

When I first encountered it, the shell of my office space was battle-wrecked, boarded up, neglected, grafitti'd, dank, dirty, and completely forsaken. I fell instantly in love with it and had a vision of its future as a protective bastion of psychic firings. The rent was low (unheard of in this trendy part of Manhattan) and would be lowered if I asked nothing of the landlady. I signed my first long-term office lease to include the clause: "the premises will not be used for the making of pornography." A vestige of its former life perhaps? As I readied the space to work in, I grew to know intimately every crack in the walls and ceilings, every exposed pipe, boarded up window, makeshift ventilation system, broken faucet, and gauged floor of its four rooms. I began to have my own experience with the space itself as having moved "from a constructed to a dreamed world" (Bachelard, 1969). This new working environment was opening up a space in my unconscious, was already working as an implementation of spiral process within my own psychic functioning.

Sure enough, the night before my first day there, I had an intense dream. In the dream I was going to the office (getting lost, naturally) but finding that it was already fully inhabited by a colony of elderly ex-vaude-villians (the bulk of my practice is working with performers, writers, and visual artists) who had camped out in the consulting room. They were lavishly adorned with heavy costumes and face paint and told me that this used to be one of their homes. The room was thick and unctuous with layers of stuff – baskets, chests, antiques, containers, curtain atop curtain covering windows and doors, dogs and cats curled up in closets full of old papers and bric-a-brac. My office was fully inhabited, an encampment of performers already invading my dreaming life. The dream was epic, and I don't set it out here to decode its contents, but to underscore how the interior sonority of this new space was already at work inside me – had already slipped strange psychic portents to (through?) my door.

Within a week or so of my move, a patient who had originally entered treatment six years ago with an unbearably "dark and ugly" secret that could never be revealed nor vaguely enunciated, poured the actual secret out into the space. Something had loosened in him, unbidden. Something he responded to in the modification of the actual material setting enabled a structural change in our conscious and unconscious communication. The change was something in him, and something in me, and something in how our dyadic structure was changing within the confines of a new architecture. This emergence was as close to the depths of a dark space as we had ever gone, and it had tumbled out unbidden, crystal clear, without fanfare or the fraught adieu of its coming into being. The space seemed to me to working along a Bionion register as well, allowing for more beta to alpha transformations.

Within the same week, another long-term patient reported proposing to her partner of 30 years after spending 10 years with me in an ambivalent, fraught relationship to her decision to make this long-wished for experience of her partner happen. Another patient surprisingly began IVF treatment after years of debate and hesitancy about having a child. Yet another patient ended a long and protracted abusive relationship rather definitively and suddenly. So, are all these sudden structural shifts coincidental? I tend to think not, although of course, there's no way to prove otherwise. But something about the deeply protracted nature of each situation, and the velocity with which the material sprang forth in the new office, led me to believe that the space itself was working on the inner life of me and my patients in a newly constructed way.

How this could be happening is difficult to articulate, indeed, but I began to think of the space functioning like Pichon-Rivière's "urgency point" in the turning of the spiral – the point in the present that holds open a portal to new dialectics between past, present, and future. My office is the urgency point that not only opens the treatment to further exploration, but remains a constitutive element within the analytic situation and the "various sides of a person's destiny that change within each turn in the spiral" (Baranger and Baranger, 2009, p. 50). If this sounds mystical, well, it is. What could be less rational than the notion that my subterranean office is unleashing powerful intrapsychic forces? Can the dreaming experience manifest, as Masud Khan believes, as a *space*, not an object? The "dreaming experience is any entirety that actualizes the self in an unknowable way" (Baranger and Baranger, 2009, p. 328). My office had become part of the dreaming subject, a vital entity that also served to actualize the self of both analyst and patient in new and unknown ways.

Rather than a theory of dream space, the concrete structure of my office is the actual material reckoning of dream space that serves as a powerful agent in how fantasy shapes reality and the inverse. The Barangers' idea of "modification in the field" was thrown into stark relief for me by moving my office to this underground world. My patient's material has become richer, deeper, more saturated, and more rapidly surfacing. We are both responding to an understanding *by* the setting, the progressive construction of an interpretation that includes the actual architecture of place. My office has unlocked and become, for me and for my patients, a profound "space of elsewhere" (Khan, 1976), a space of imagination, and reverie, infused with materiality, an experience I hope I've had some success in conveying to you here.

References

Bachelard, G. (1969) *The Poetics of Space*. Boston: Beacon Press.

Baranger, W. and Baranger M. (2009) *The Work of Confluence: Listening and Interpreting in the Dynamic Field*, ed. L.G. Fiorini. London: Karnac.

Khan, M. (1976) The changing use of dreams in psychoanalytic practice: In search of the dreaming experience. *International Journal of Psychoanalysis*, 57: 325–330.

Perec, G. (1997) *Species of Spaces*. New York: Penguin.

Piano, R. (2017) *Complete Works 1966–2014*, ed. P. Jodidio, Cologne, Germany: Taschen.

Pichon-Riviére, E. (1958) Referential schema and dialectic spiral process as basis to a problem of the past. *International Journal of Psychoanalysis*, 57: 325–330.

Pontalis, J.B. (1974) Dream as an object. *International Journal of Psychoanalysis*, 1: 125–133.

Winnicott, D.W. (1960) The theory of the parent–infant relationship. *International Journal of Psychoanalysis*, 41: 585–595.

Winnicott, D.W. (1994) Hate in the counter-transference. *International Journal of Psychoanalysis*, 30: 69–74.

Chapter 14

Psychoanalytical turmoil in cyberspace

Monica Horovitz

> *Le silence eternel des ces espaces infinis m'effraie* [The eternal
> silence of these infinite spaces frightens me.]
>
> (Pascal, 1669, author's translation)

How do we cope with change when it threatens to overwhelm us and
lead us towards the unknown? How do we overcome the fear that it
produces? By avoiding the question? That was my first impulse when I
was asked to participate on this panel, but I quickly became aware of a
defensive withdrawal in my analytic superego, where morality is indis-
tinguishable from absolute knowledge which would also like to be
constituted once and for all.

I was tempted to reassure myself by withdrawing into a bastion
(Baranger and Baranger, 1961–1962) closed to curiosity about change so
as not to have to study the contemporary forms of subjectivity nor their
cortege of symptoms and sufferings that new technologies have brought to
light. Thus we deny our difficulty in maintaining a psychoanalytic
attitude, that is to say our internal frame, open to dreams and to thoughts
still without a thinker, and we project it onto those we think do not know
about the specificity of the psychoanalytic method.

How does one preserve the necessary discipline, that which is needed
to conceptualize intuition, when the question is to observe these changes
while, at the same time, promoting reflection on the generational differences we are witnessing? Should we put ourselves "off-side", so to speak?
My inclination is always to be willing to go on playing so as to be able to
continue to feel and maintain my links with what is new.

Bion (1965) says that all change is a catastrophic experience, in the
sense of the Greek etymology of *katastrophè*, which means "reversal".
Thus, accepting the crisis and collapse of earlier concretions of identity,

the reversal of meaning, of the vision of meaning, of the vision of things and of the world requires us to face up to pain, solitude and fear. These feelings arise from the disorientation produced by the earthquake that the ego then undergoes. The only path towards psychic growth is not to deny catastrophic change that destroys the pre-existing state of mind and opens out onto thoughts that are in the shadows of the future.

In 1990, Didier Anzieu wrote that it was no longer sexuality that was repressed but the sensual body, the body that comes to life through the presence of the Other. Nowadays, new technologies lead us to think that we can achieve the virtuality of bodies.

How should we define the change of our bodily experience, that is, of the limits of reality, if the encounter of bodies becomes superfluous in a virtual world that annihilates the constraints imposed by psychosomatic unity? In cyberspace, what becomes of the destiny of the body in the mind as an experience of true intimacy? This felt experience of the body is a fundamental aspect of emotion, since the latter connects the psychic to the somatic. Emotional truth brings us face to face with the speaking being that we try to be and the wild instinctual body we never cease to inhabit. It is a global psychosomatic emotion that does not deceive because it concerns my own bodily experience. For me there are two essential moments here: the emotion of the impact with the object and then its elaboration.

What I am trying to say is that emotional experiences occur more in the body than in the depths of psychic states.

While new technologies reduce spatial distances and the difference between time zones, in some cases they also sometimes prevent contact with primitive states of the mind, the very states that we can only be open to in a fleeting way during the analytic encounter.

The question I am raising has its source in the model of the bipersonal field and its intense investment of the psychoanalytic relationship through the caesurae of the transference/countertransference. I would like to say that in my view, the way of establishing and inhabiting the *setting* is part of the function and identity of the psychoanalyst, for it preserves and delimits his engagement, that is to say, his frame, while helping him to get things back on an even keel when the non-process becomes a threatening obstacle: the setting, where the non-ego deposits itself (Bleger, 1966), then functions like a fog horn.

Our subject takes us back to Descartes (1637), whose method of radical doubt led him to a single certainty: "I think, therefore I am", thereby inferring that thinking is at the basis of certainty and that the body depends on the laws of matter. We know Descartes was tempted by a historical compromise that sought to avoid the question of knowing how thoughts affect on the body and cause actions, and how bodily sensations can give rise to thoughts – that is to say, how body and mind interact.

Dangers of linking. Dangerous links

I am thinking of a patient whose case illustrates both the need for bodily presence and absence in the *setting* in order to pick up on primitive states of the mind, but also what I want to say about certain pathologies that cannot be treated outside the *setting* in situ.

Following a delirious episode, the family of Emmanuel, aged 18, brought him to me for a consultation. I proposed we meet for analysis five times a week, with each session right at the end of the day. Three times out of five, he would vomit in the tiled entrance but stop vomiting right in front of the door of my consulting room. This symptom created in me feelings of helplessness, disarray and sometimes disgust. But I also felt the desire to help this likeable young man with tousled blond hair. After a few sessions, I nicknamed him my "chick".

In his delusion, Emmanuel doesn't know whether he is the Count of Valmont or the Marquise de Merteuil, a free thinker or a victim. One sees that, as in the work of Pierre Choderlos de Laclos, author of *Les liaisons dangereuses* (1782), what matters is not so much the act itself but its telling and its consequences. The epistolary novel describes perversion to the letter. Dangers of linking, I said to myself. In view of his state, and to avoid a hospitalization during the summer break, I suggested an appointment by telephone every other day for six weeks. These communications only lasted a few minutes but sufficed to maintain a thin thread that, in spite of distance, made me present for him. However, these telephone calls prevented me from having a restful holiday and I sometimes found myself feeling resentful towards him-myself because of this constraint. Upon my return, even though he had been so present during these weeks, I now completely forgot about him and decided to have a carpet laid in the entrance to my office to make it warmer.

On the first Monday after the summer break, I consulted my diary and saw his name written in for the last session. I was shocked, recalling immediately his vomiting. My anxiety increased during the coming hours to the point that, at moments, I thought: "Oh, no, if he vomits on my carpet, I'll throw him out". At the time of his session, he rang the doorbell. Trembling, I opened it; he looked at the ground with great surprise and muttered: "*Madame*, you have put your bra on". After that he never vomited again. Here the unconscious bi-personal fantasy shows the specific object of analysis and its flow. Its purpose: to mobilize the field and to allow the projection and introjection processes to reactivate themselves through transformations of sensorial and emotional experiences into thoughts and meanings.

Could this analysis, which is now finished, have been conducted by Skype or email? Would the impact of the external object have been the same? I very much doubt it.

Furthermore, although I have no personal experience of treatments by telephone, SMS, email or Skype, I supervise colleagues who acquire it when their patients are away but want to continue their sessions in this manner, and will venture to formulate a few hypotheses. The impression I have had is that, in the dynamic of these virtual exchanges, the immediateness of the communication and the physical absence and presence of the other accentuate a fictitious intimacy and lend themselves to a lack of inhibition, favoring remarks on sexuality of unusual crudeness. I have asked myself, and am asking you, if, for the patient, it is the fact of being alone, safe in his "fish bowl", that allows him to escape from his inhibitions and to let fantasized idealizations (or demonizations) emerge easily. From the point of view of the countertransference, I have noticed that these analysts have a tendency to over-evaluate the session *in absentia*, to fear the resumption of sessions in the consulting room owing to the risk of the reappearance of attacks on the *setting*, the doubts the patient may have about continuing the treatment and the impoverishment of their free associations.

Moreover, the facility of these modes of communication and the fact that they are free of charge reinforce certain aspects of the relationship. Specifically, split or schizoid personalities, in whom the emotional sphere is dissociated from intellectual and imaginary aspects, may find that the absence of a gaze and voice modulations suit them. For other patients, schizoid or not, these modes of communication may encourage the construction of castles in the air, without limits and without any fear of the intrusion of concrete reality in one form or another.

We are faced today with the still scarcely apprehended problems linked to the new *settings*. Between megalomania and claustrophobia, between agoraphobia and soft transitional objects, a whole world is opening up for psychoanalytic research to originate new germs of thought in the corpus of our works to come.

As Bion (1997, p. 44) puts it in *Taming Wild Thoughts*: "Although we tend to have shifted our observations away from the body to the sphere of the mind, the body has not ceased to exist".

References

Anzieu, D. (1990). *L'épiderme nomade et la peau psychique*. Editeur College Psychanalyse Groupale, Paris.

Baranger, M. and Baranger, W. (1961–1962 [2009]). The analytic situation as a dynamic field. *International Journal of Psychoanalysis*, 89: 795–826.

Bion, W.R. (1965 [1984]). *Transformations*. Karnac, London.

Bion, W.R. (1997 [1984]). *Taming Wild Thoughts*. Karnac, London.

Bleger, J. (1966). Psychoanalysis of the psychoanalytical frame. *International Journal of Psychoanalysis*, 48: 511–519.

Choderlos de Laclos, P. (1782 [1975]). *Les liaisons dangereuses*. LGF, Paris.

Descartes, R. (1637 [2001]). *Discourse on the Method, Optics, Geometry and Meteorology*. Hackett, London.

Pascal, B. (1669 [2004]). *Pensées*, Edition de Michel Le Guern, Folio Classique, Paris.

Chapter 15

Shifting the container

Psychoanalysis and cyberspace culture[1]

Velleda C. Ceccoli

The psychoanalytic frame has been a concept that is understood and used across all schools of psychoanalysis regardless of individual allegiances or particular theoretical orientations. For those of us who work psychodynamically, the frame delineates and contains the terrain of the psychoanalytic encounter, shaping itself to the individual configuration of each analytic dyad while retaining the boundaries that help analytic work to progress. Traditionally, the frame was established in the first encounter with the patient, even prior to the first session, when the analyst began to gather information about the patient, and the patient began to gather information about the analyst, each filling in a blank canvas with personal and transferential material. The factors that outline the configuration of the analytic relationship are usually established within this initial exchange, which includes determining the frequency of meetings, the duration of sessions, deciding for or against the use of the couch, setting the fee, communicating cancellation and vacation policies, and establishing a therapeutic approach. For some, these factors delineate the analytic workspace, constructing boundaries that are solidly adhered to because they are believed to help create the necessary safety – for both the patient and the analyst – required to promote changed change.

However, modern advances in communication systems, including but not limited to the invention and use of the telephone, internet, Skype, FaceTime, and social media have introduced new possibilities for connection and impacted the way in which analytic treatment takes place.

Until recently, it was widely accepted that the initial phone contact and referral information began to sketch out the analytic frame. Yet all of this has changed a great deal since the advent of the internet, Google, Wikipedia, and all manner of social media applications (Balick, 2012). Such technology has opened up and made available information that used to be private and discretionary. As psychoanalysts we are no longer a "blank canvas" for the patient. Instead, patients can now look at photographs of us, read professional and even personal communications, follow us on Twitter, and find out the kinds of things we buy and consume, all without ever having met us. With the advent of the internet, patients are potentially informed about their analysts *a priori* – so that important dynamic aspects of the treatment begin *intrapsychically*, rather than coming about interactively within the actual first encounter (whether on the phone or in person) between patient and analyst.

Our current culture of virtual interconnectivity and instant information has upended the concept of the psychoanalytic frame, forcing us to rethink what it is that our patients know about us, how much they know, and how that knowledge might influence the analytic relationship and the principles it is based on. Furthermore, there have been significant changes in the way that the current generation approaches communication, relationships, and the creation of personal meaning, and this directly influences the way they think about and approach therapy. Cyberspace culture has already changed the way many people seek out help: many prefer to log onto therapy chat rooms or attend sessions via Skype or FaceTime, or even via text and email. Thus, the space where treatment is conducted has shifted from the privacy of the analyst's office to the individual computer or phone screen. In the advent of these technological advances, psychoanalysis must begin to question conceptual issues regarding the "frame" of the treatment. In considering these ideas, I look to include current cultural and generational trends as both interweave and shape perception, experience, and brain structure. I will also address cyberspace along with other new technologies as potential areas of play that provide opportunities to rehearse identity and selfhood. I argue for a psychoanalytic frame that is fluid and assembled interactively within a "transitional space" which may take many shapes and configurations while still providing containment and safety.

Psychoanalysis meets technoculture

Cultural ideology impacts each generation anew and propels an evolution from the previous one, creating an actual neurobiological adaptation to the evolving cultural and social context. In todays' generation, technology has become the predominant cultural force. The internet and social media in particular are changing the way that people think, feel, and act. With more information than ever at our fingertips, our ability to look something or someone up is a Google search away. Often our patients already know a great deal about us before they appear in our offices, and this impacts the psychoanalytic frame, not only concretely, but also dynamically: intrapsychically and intersubjectively. Furthermore, today, information is assimilated quickly and multitasked into meaning as it is commonplace to interact with multiple screens, texts, and people at once. Social media has blurred many boundaries in the name of increased connectivity, so that the personal and the public have become fused. This adds yet another layer of meaning to the use of information and its sharing, since it moves the user across boundaries, doors, and walls at the touch of a send command. Such techno-connectivity demands that as psychoanalysts we both become involved in and integrate the use of technology into a working frame. The collision between the culture of psychoanalysis, which was built around the classical Freudian "blank screen" model, and the techno-culture of today strongly effects the way that we think and conduct treatment and demands a re-evaluation of some basic psychoanalytic premises, the frame is first among them.

Generations X, Y, Z, and P

What constitutes and shapes the worldview of a "generation"? In particular, we must consider how each generation looks and thinks about internal experience. Each generation has been influenced by cultural, historical, and technological events, and has been encouraged to believe certain ideas, consume specific products, and make particular choices. Thus, each generation has to deal with a particular host of *necessary* adaptations that require the individual brain to rewire itself in order to absorb and *survive* the cultural and societal onslaught of information and change. Our brains respond and adapt to the shifts and changes in our cultural context by rewiring themselves in order to process and deal with current contexts and situations (Doidge, 2007). It is the sort of adaptation that is necessary in a Darwinian, "survival of the fittest" kind of way. Such an adaptation happens first at the neurological level and then generates important changes in learning and communication patterns that effect behavior (Damasio, 2010). While this occurs outside of immediate awareness, it has deep personal and societal implications. As a *necessary* adaptation to the shifting nature of the world and the way it is perceived, experienced, and communicated, it is of particular relevance for psychoanalysis.

The culture of psychoanalysis was borne within a scientific revolution that inquired into the nature of human motivation and looked to the nervous system to understand it. Despite the success of its search for meaning and the discovery of the unconscious, the talking cure came about within the context of Victorian culture, which emphasized social deference, conformity, and discretion. These values also applied to the psychoanalytic space, where the doctor was to remain "objective" and "uninvolved" so as to be able to create a working environment where the patient was able to free associate. The personal privacy of both patient and doctor helped to create the treatment space. The climate of the culture of psychoanalysis and our current culture could not be more at odds.

Our current culture of virtual interconnectivity and instant information has changed the way most of us read information, reducing our ability to focus on communications that are unassisted by media applications: Email beats *snail* mail, texts beat phone calls, videos beat photos, etc. For some, this extends to an ongoing *stream* of information that condenses meaning to the clicking of a *"like"* button. Technology is shaping the way that we communicate, interact with and think about others as well as ourselves. None of us can deny that the way we communicate and relate to others has been reconfigured and continues to pattern itself according to the technological possibilities offered to us by our various devices and our use of them. Social media blended the personal and the public to the point where they have fused themselves in tweets; real friendships and virtual ones have joined through Facebook, and online personae (known as *avatars*) act as symbolic selves for their creators, perhaps merging true and idealized selves. Reciprocal and direct communication has been conflated into an ongoing gabfest, and language itself has been abridged to accommodate it. And all of this occurs in the NOW, without pauses and as a constant flow, so that time itself is blurred. Realtime (no gap in between real and time) is nonstop, it *streams*. According to Nick Carr (2012) this also blurs the boundaries of space, dimension, and depth: moving us from the three-dimensional world to two-dimensional screen spaces and "intimate portable worlds that increasingly enclose us" (Carr, 2009). Can psychoanalysis survive a new type of embodiment, a shift from the actual carnality of the doctor and patient to the virtual, two-dimensional image? For those of us who work within a relational model, the nature of relationship and intimacy within virtual worlds that can be manufactured and undone at the touch of a button is a very real one.

The self in (virtual) relation

Perhaps one answer to the question of how all this social media and technology impacts the fate of the relational self is that this new way of being is central to how today's generation navigates relationships and information, and this includes the therapeutic relationship and its frame. For those that need to be *streaming* in order to feel connected, to be part of a community, to establish an identity and have a life, such a life is not real until it is documented and aired, until it is reported and received – thus the advent of TV shows such as *Web Therapy*. With *streaming* all interpersonal communications are broadcasted continuously to an active network of "friends." Often, therapists are among those "friends." Broadcasting has become a way of living for some – a means of validating their actions and existence, as well as a means of staying connected. Previous generations have struggled to obtain validation about the same things, through relationship and connection to others, and technology (although not today's kind) helped to advance this for them as well.

We are relational beings, and as such we need to connect with others to get to know ourselves, to see ourselves through the eyes of another, or in this case, through their *streamed* commentary. We need other people, individually and collectively. Social media has the ability to connect us instantly, virtually, to the one and to the many, and the current generation has cut its teeth on it. As psychoanalysts we can question the impact of such connectivity on the ability to communicate and understand one another and remain curious about its potential for self-elaboration. While it is possible that some mistake *streaming* and broadcasting for living, it is also possible to think of social media and cyberspace as potential play spaces in which to test out one's identity, transitional spaces *ala* Winnicott (1971), that can afford people the opportunity of experimenting with relationships – virtual *and* real. Indeed, the virtual does not necessarily have to disrupt one's ability to interact and be, it may provide a chance to *begin to be*. So if we consider the internet and the new technologies as a playground, then we can see them as potentially providing opportunities for play.

Consider the concept of adult play (Bollas, 2002; Ceccoli, 2007) with regard to the opportunities that cyberspace providing for the elaboration and integration of self-states, particularly within the psychoanalytic situation. The consulting room, and the person of the analyst has traditionally provided a demarcated area of potential play space, a safe container that holds the patient in interaction with the analyst through numerous narratives and enactments, as well as shifts in perception, time, and self-states. Winnicott (1971) was the first to speak of analytic space as potential play space, where the patients' various self-states are at play with one another and with those of the person of the analyst. When we consider cyberspace as a similar kind of playground it becomes a potential space to hold, articulate, and rehearse unelaborated parts of the psyche, with an important caveat: it is done without the "actual" presence of an other. Within this context social sites become potential arenas in which to test out omnipotence as well as areas to free up the transgressive nature of desire without injury to another, and perhaps, to oneself. Thus, virtual sites can become a place where one can be and not be at the same time: one can be anonymous, can embody another identity, be at a distance, and play at and consider closeness. In this sense, the internet and social media can be seen as providing a laboratory-like environment (Bollas, 1987) in which to experiment with identity and sexuality, to push personal limits, and to truly play in a suspension of reality *with all the toys.* Yet perhaps this is the trouble with cyberspace and its fluidity: it blows up all frames, permeates boundaries and ignores limits, so that there is just you and everything you want and want to be and do. The web has as many hyperlinks, portals, chat rooms, services, and games as your desire can spawn. In this virtual realm one can configure infinite possibilities with an endless number of intrapsychic representations that live within the virtual and allow rehearsals of interpersonal situations without having to deal with a real object and the limitations imposed by its configural and/or corporeal frame.

The implications for psychoanalysis are ripe with meaning, particularly as it applies to treatment that takes place in virtual reality. Cyberspace has opened up a limitless space for the exploration of personal fantasies, and where there is no physical container, no embodied "other" who interacts with or demarcates the play space, there may appear to be no analytic frame. As analysts we must adapt and assimilate the demands that technology imposes through a consideration of its potential as a transitional space between the intrapsychic experience of our patients and the intersubjective dynamics that come alive within the analytic *relationship* – virtual or embodied.

We have arrived at a moment in our history where the mode of our communication has begun to dictate the terms of how we should communicate. The use of technology and the instant stream of information it allows us has changed our alphabet and shortened our words and sentences, so that we have "LOLspeak," and so that some have dropped the "niceties" of inquiring after the weather, thanking one another, beginning emails and texts with Dear, etc., in short, changing the way that we relate to each other. Perhaps this is one of the inherent differences between text and pictures on a screen (the portable intimacy that Carr (2010) talks about) and sitting in front of a flesh-and-blood human being. It may well be that our technology and social media has just made it more difficult to be "really" connected by providing too many ways and options of being virtually connected. Yet virtual connectivity is very real, and does not have to be at odds with psychoanalysis if the frame can be reconfigured to include virtual space as an important transitional working space. This would involve being able to filter through the use of technological devices and information, so that the treatment relationship could remain privileged regardless of the context it works within. Thus it would be the relationship that established the boundaries that would determine the rules around using technological objects in particular ways. After all, "if we are to survive psychically, desire has to be brought to bear on a real object" (Phillips, 2007, p. 125), and it is all about *how we use our objects* technologically or otherwise.

There is no question that the analytic frame in the age of cybertechnology is in need of expansion in order to allow for the limitless possibilities that are contained via the analytic relationship. For me, it is helpful to conceptualize the virtual reality that technology has introduced as located in an intermediate space: cyberspace itself becoming the transitional space; an area for many potential elaborations of the self and the self-in-relation, whether they be embodied, imagined, virtual, and/or "real." This requires a radical revamping of our psychoanalytic "frame" and of what constitutes a holding environment, as well as the various possibilities that can be at play within it and around it. We have necessarily arrived at a deconstructed notion of the analytic frame that is fluid; assembled, disassembled, and reassembled on an ongoing basis, following the cultural pull of each generation while respecting the dynamic interplay of intrapsychic and interpersonal dynamics. I submit that such revisions in psychoanalytic ideas and clinical technique are not only necessary in order for psychoanalytic treatment to retain its relevance across generations, but are also critical in order to address the complexity of human experience and interaction.

Note

1   Sections of this chapter stem from ideas elaborated in the blog *Out of my Mind* by Velleda C. Ceccoli (www.drceccoli.com).

References

Balick, A. (2012) TMI in the transference LOL: Psychoanalytic reflections on Google, social networking, and 'virtual impingement'. *Psychoanalysis, Culture & Society*, 17(2): 120–136.

Bollas, C. (1987) *The Shadow of the Object*. New York: Columbia University Press.

Bollas, C. (2002) *Free Association*. Sussex: Routledge.

Carr, N. (2009) Realtime Kills Real Space. Online: www.roughtype.com/?p=1233

Carr, N. (2010) *The Shallows: How the Internet Is Changing the Way We Think, Read and Remember*. New York: W.W. Norton.

Carr, N. (2012) Realtime kills Real Space. Online: www.roughtype.com/?p=1233

Ceccoli, V. (2007) The Play is the Thing: Rediscovering Wonderland. Paper presented at Division 39, Toronto.

Damasio, A. (2010) *Self Comes To Mind: Constructing the Conscious Brain*. New York: Pantheon Books.

Doidge, N. (2007) *The Brain That Changes Itself*. New York: Penguin Books.

Phillips, A. (2007) *Side Effects*. London: Harper Perennial.

Winnicott, D.W. (1971) *Playing and Reality*. New York: Basic Books.

Index

absence 60
abstinence, rule of 186–8, 189, 196
abstinent non-gratification, atmosphere of 75
active technique 105
adapted ego 31
adaption to meet, concept 79
adaptive need 97
adolescents 242
adult play 262–3
agglutinated nucleus 17, 19, 20, 191
alpha function 242, 243
alterity 8, 185, 187, 194, 195
Amati, Silvia 192
ambiguity 19–20
ambiguous personality 19
anachronism 44–5
analysands *see* patients
analysis: absences in 60; accommodating surprises 125–6; Bion 81; constant recalibration of the frame 92–3; contemporary 188; enactments 126; frames 60, 116; ground rules 128–9; here and now 61, 62, 66–70; impasses in 124; rules and frames of 121; syncretic activity 106; variable arrangements of 127
analyst–analysand relationship 186, 188; Barangers' view of 192; complexities of 191
analysts: acts of freedom 117; analytic intentions 122; attention and interpretation 60–2; becoming and remaining 219–21; changes during therapeutic relationships 136–7; as co-authors of a dramatic art 118; comings and goings 60; construction of

212–13; difficulty of work 211; elderly 208; fees 111, 112–16, 128, 131–3, 210; functional role of 146; functioning as surgeons 75; inductive dimension 105–6; Klein on 77; life cycle of 208; maternal reverie 80; minds of 211–12; office availability 64; offices 209; overlapping worlds with patients 194–5; presence 105–6; psycho-physical presence 105–7; psycho-physical responsiveness 104; reverie 76; rules/policies 116, 117; self-disclosure 120; unconscious minds 74–5; unconscious openness and neutrality 76; working by telephone 224
analytic asymmetry 150
analytic attention 60
analytic couple 125
analytic device 190
analytic dyad 211, 247, 249, 258
analytic frame, model of 92; as an active ongoing dimension of analytic technique 104–5; always-evolving configuration 92–3, 96, 104; animated structure 103; anti-contact barrier 97, 103; Bleger on 99–101; clinical process 96–7; and clinical technique 104–7; dual tendency towards boundary deterioration and bureaucratization 97–8; dysfunctions 102; fixed and mutative characteristics of 96–7; flexibility 96; frame-as-contact-barrier 94, 97; heterogeneous demands on 93; heterogeneous functions of 94–5; inductive dimension of the analyst's presence and its framing function